The Grays
2 Lake Village Drive
Durham, NC 27713

BEST SEAT IN THE HOUSE

BY

The Honorable John H. Hager
With Nancy P. Wheeler

John Hager

Published by The Dietz Press
Petersburg, Virginia
www.dietzpress.com

Library of Congress Control Number: 2017950425

Hard Cover
ISBN: 978-0-87517-150-0
Soft Cover
ISBN: 978-0-87517-151-7

Dedication

To Maggie, Jack and Henry – without them,
none of this could have been possible.

Table of Contents

Introduction

Across more than four decades, from my post at Richmond's daily newspapers I watched John Hager's life unfold.

When in the form of an unnecessary freak polio a freight train roared through his living room just as he stood on the cusp of a private career headed skyward, John soldiered on relentlessly to overcome.

One searches his vocabulary almost in vain for the phrase why me? His story provides compelling testimony to the virtue of press on. He cleared each of the multitudinous, seemingly mountainous obstacles in his path to fashion perhaps the most affecting and consequential Virginia public/private/political career of his generation.

John recounts here his astounding can-do saga. His has been a life of grit, gallantry, and grace. It's one for the books — this book. Readers cannot help but come away from it shaking their head in awe-struck wonderment.

Ross MacKenzie, Editor of the Editorial Pages,
The Richmond News Leader (1969-1992)
and the *Richmond Times-Dispatch* (1992-2007).

Chapter 1

Early Years

My childhood was a fortunate one, shaped by a loving family in comfortable circumstances among genteel, Southern neighbors. Born on August 28, 1936, in Durham, North Carolina, I was named John Henry after my father's two brothers: John, who was always called Jack and was the uncle I knew, and Henry, who long before I was born had been killed in a car accident as he and my father were driving home from college. My parents, Virgil Duke Hager and Ruth Rabbe Hager, welcomed me home from Watts Hospital to 910 Dacian Avenue, where I joined my sister, Nancy Ann, who was almost seven years old by the time I arrived on the scene, an age difference that through our childhood kept her one or two stages ahead of me in interests and experiences.

My mother, who was from Hamilton, Ohio, and my father, from Louisville, Kentucky, had met as students at Purdue University. They married on October 6, 1928, and began their married life in Louisville, Kentucky, where my sister Nancy was born on January 16, 1930. My father worked first for Colgate Palmolive, then for the American Cigar Company, and by June 1931, he had begun what would be his lifetime career with The American Tobacco Company. Initially, Dad worked in Richmond, Virginia, at American Tobacco's cigarette factory and in the Research Department. In July 1933, he was transferred to Durham, where he rose through the ranks to become factory manager in 1941.

Dad was "American Tobacco" through and through, devoted to the company and unflinching in his work ethic. Meanwhile, his brother Jack was also flourishing at American Tobacco's Louisville site. Both sons were following the footsteps of their father, whose successful career culminated with his position in Louisville as manager of

Nancy and John, 1939

1

J. Finzer and Brothers Company, one of the many manufacturers that were amalgamated to form The American Tobacco Company. From my earliest days, I was immersed in a strong set of values that extolled hard work, honesty, public service and respect for others. It has been only in the last few years that I have fully come to realize that my parents' strong value system was shaped to a great degree by their Midwestern ancestors, whom I recently chronicled in *The Hager Family History*. These values, passed through the generations, have served me well as I navigate through life.

By the time I have clear childhood memories, World War II was in full swing, and my hometown Durham, like the rest of the country, was caught up in a flurry of wartime activity. True to the war effort, we raised chickens in the back yard and planted a victory garden. My dad had been in ROTC, but because his job as manager of The American Tobacco Company factory was certified as essential to the war effort, he spent the war years in Durham. Under his watch, the huge operation there, covering more than a million square feet, ran two ten-hour shifts every day for twenty full hours, and the total output of tobacco products, including billions of Lucky Strikes, went to the military. Machinery and shift workers were pressed to the hilt, and Dad put in long hours keeping production running smoothly.

It wasn't unusual for him to come home for dinner with the family and then return to work, and on Wednesday or Thursday nights, he took me with him for the evening shift. My mother must have had some other obligation on those nights, and my dad would drive us downtown to the factory, where I walked around the bustling machinery and belts while he tended to business.

Mother, who was loving and attentive, volunteered in civic and community activities and tended to household affairs. In a time when many women let the help handle kitchen duties, Mother was a great cook and loved her recipes. Her passion was Kappa Alpha Theta Sorority, and she served as advisor to the chapter at Duke University. Among her many interests was collecting china snuff boxes, half of which Maggie and I now display in our home – a reminder of my mother's diverse pursuits.

My parents' good friend, Bus Yeager, was an important ranking officer at Camp Butner, the Army training facility located north of Durham. During the war years, First Lieutenant Yeager had an Army uniform made for me that was identical to his, only in miniature. As a six-year-old, I was immensely proud to wear my Army khakis.

I distinctly remember when Japan surrendered at the end of the war. My family, like most everyone else in Durham, went downtown on August 15, 1945, for the huge celebration — a spirited, joyous occasion. I still have a copy of the next day's local newspaper that documented the long anticipated victory.

With my family's move from Dacian Avenue to Hermitage Court in Forest Hills, I attended public kindergarten and first grade at George Watts School in Durham. For the most part, life moved at a comfortable, predictable pace, peppered with the usual assortment of unanticipated events, like the passing of my paternal grandmother, Matilda Coldewey "Bunny" Hager. We quickly left Durham during the Christmas season of 1947 to join the rest of the family for her service. The American Tobacco Company's driver steered us through snow-covered mountains to Louisville, where the funeral was held. We stayed with Uncle Jack at The Anchorage, their home in the country.

During second through sixth grades, I attended Calvert Method School, a small, private institution that touted a rigorous academic schedule, emphasis on character development, daily outside play, and — particularly attractive to a young boy — early afternoon release. One unique aspect of Calvert was that each student's accumulated schoolwork was compiled annually and bound in a black books, detailing my progress and proving that my grades were pretty good. In 1948 at the end of sixth grade, there was a graduation ceremony that was impressive enough to be remembered in detail, even after all these years.

Calvert Method School became the precursor to today's Durham Academy, which formed in 1959 and began an expansion that now includes 1,100 students in pre-kindergarten through grade twelve. As an alumnus, my relationship with this re-named *alma mater* includes two particularly special events. In October 1992, the school awarded me the Distinguished Alumnus Award from Durham Academy, a presentation that was made during a grand reunion weekend, attended by some of my classmates as well as my mother, father and sister. When my great-nephew Jay graduated from Durham Academy in 2004, they asked me to deliver the graduation address to his class.

Shortly before I finished Calvert Method School, my family moved to a modern house on Dover Road in Hope Valley, a development about six miles from downtown Durham. By this time both of my parents enjoyed strong social connections, and my father was active in civic affairs. He, Hollis Eden, who was president of Duke, and Asa Spaulding, president of North Carolina Mutual Life Insurance Company, were "movers and shakers" in the city. They shared many lunches together and strongly influenced key issues in Durham. As a family we were loyal attendees of First Presbyterian Church on Sundays. It was there that I was confirmed by The Reverend Kelsey Regen, who later moved to my church in Richmond.

In the spring of 1947, at only eleven years old, I started my own newspaper which was dubbed the *Hope Valley Times*. Technology was very rudimentary compared to today's high-tech possibilities, but with an old portable typewriter and thin typing paper layered with carbon paper, I managed to eke out about five copies at a time – with those on the bottom progressively lighter than the top copies. I stapled the pages together and sold the "newspaper" to our Hope Valley neighbors for a nickel apiece. Advertising was also available for a nickel per ad, though ad space was a tough sell. It wasn't a grand publication, but it did require work, and it is indicative that early on, a business sense was developing. Some copies of my fledgling rag are still in the files at home.

My family was fond of dogs, and when he had time, my father loved quail hunting, for which dogs play an integral role. We never saddled our puppies with names that were pet-like. Ours were dubbed with names fit for people. Our setter Fannie was our first family dog. Then there were Ike and Mamie, and later, we acquired Mike, Ike's replacement, a pointer to whom I was especially close.

My friends were schoolmates as well as kids in our neighborhood. During the war years and into the post-war years, adults didn't concern themselves with entertaining

Four members of the golf team are shown above with Coach Brewbaker. The team has had a successful season, so far. Left to right, they are: Coach Brewbaker, Tate Lanning, Johnny Hager, Freddy Lloyd,
and Fred Dula.

Photo by Harold Moore

High school golf team, John – third from left, 1954

young people or orchestrating their activities, an indulgence that seems to have developed in recent years. We kids made our own fun. Ball games would pop up on an empty
lot in the neighborhood when someone happened to show up with a ball, and we sponta-
neously joined the action, while organized sports were generally confined to school teams
or church leagues. For better or worse, we faced fewer distractions than young people
today and consequently, fewer temptations to misbehave. I was always very close to my
parents, and ours was a tightly-knit family, so we often did things together, particularly
during holidays and vacations. I enjoyed sharing activities with them, and since I was
used to interacting with their friends, I was comfortable in adult company.

With the community of Hope Valley built around a golf course and country club, it
was easy to indulge a growing passion for the game of golf. My father, who loved playing, when he had time, introduced me to the sport as a young boy, and throughout my
middle and high school years, I hit the links at every opportunity. By ninth grade – still
in middle school – I was asked to join the high school golf team.

Hope Valley Country Club played a significant role in my family's social life. Dad
served on the club's board, eventually as president, and even after Nancy and I had left
home, it continued to be the site of many special occasions. After Dad retired, my sister
and I hosted several large birthday and anniversary parties at the club. One especially
memorable gathering on October 3, 1998, celebrated our parents' seventieth wedding
anniversary, their Platinum Anniversary. Numerous toasts to "Mo" and "Po," as my sister's children had named their grandparents, included one I wrote to highlight the long

marriage and to wish them and our guests well.

For a time after Calvert Method School, my parents seriously considered sending me to prep school, and I remember actually being accepted at Woodberry Forest School, but I convinced them that it was better for me to stay home for my middle and high school years. I was intensely focused on golf, and I'm sure they hesitated to take away that pursuit, but I suspect some other factors played into their decision as well. My parents were not ready to be empty-nesters, and with Nancy already graduated from Durham High in 1947 and enrolled in Purdue University, too far away to afford frequent visits, they were enjoying my school years. Also, they knew that my father was likely to be transferred to American Tobacco's New York office – a move that would be disruptive enough to the family without adding boarding school for their son.

With prep school discussions behind us, I attended Carr Junior High School for three years. My sister Nancy, meanwhile, returned to Durham after her junior year at Purdue, and on October 6, 1950, she married William Kenan Rand, Jr., an up-and-coming businessman in the city. Their wedding was a big occasion, and I was the rambunctious little brother, chasing the cameraman and scheming with the groomsmen.

In 1951, I entered Durham High School, which I attended for tenth, eleventh and twelfth grades. Early on, I had been nicknamed Mickey, but by high school, everyone called me Johnny, and everyone knew that Johnny's passion was golf. I took my studies fairly seriously and participated in activities at school. One recollection involves my being co-chair of the post-graduation, senior dance, a position shared with Nancy McLain, whose father was the company doctor for American Tobacco.

The Dean of Men at Durham High was also the golf coach, and with a nod from him, I had little difficulty leaving school in the middle of the day whenever Duke, the University of North Carolina or Wake Forest held a match at Hope Valley. In those days, universities did not have their own courses, and when they came to our club, I had the opportunity to caddy for their players, many of whom went on to successful careers in golf. Some of golf's big names – Art Wall, Mike Souchak, Buddy Worsham, Arnold Palmer, Harvie Ward – were among these college players during my high school years, and it was a real treat to caddy for them and their teammates.

Summers included swimming and golf at the Hope Valley Country Club, but once I turned nine, I began attending Camp Morehead in Morehead City, North Carolina. The continuing war effort and especially the associated gas rationing made camp an ideal summer venue since it could provide a variety of experiences in one location. There was also a widespread polio scare during this period, and a closed environment like camp, with limited exposure to the public at large, minimized the possibilities of exposure to the disease.

I loved Camp Morehead, and during twelve years of attendance, I moved through the ranks from camper to junior counselor, assistant counselor, senior counselor and finally, the summer after college graduation, to head counselor. The only summer missed from age nine to twenty-two was after my junior year of college, when I was obliged to attend ROTC camp in Fort Riley, Kansas.

Camp Morehead, 1950 John – second from left

Camp Morehead's primary focus was on sailing, which I enjoyed, and I became proficient enough to win the Lightning Class sailboat race one year. Returning summer after summer produced strong bonds with special friends at camp, and over the years we shared adventures, especially when hurricanes came and we pitched in to tie down boats and secure camp property. There was one girl who caught my eye, though I remained too focused on the activities to be really serious, and we all lost contact once summer was over. My faithful dog Mike suffered when camp took me from home, and during one session at Morehead my dad wrote that Mike had died of a broken heart.

Even at an early age, I was goal-oriented and took my preparation seriously. With my eye on a future in business, I began to consider colleges and decided to go into engineering. At first my plan was to check out *all* the engineering schools, and with Duke so close to home, it was the first candidate. Tempting as it was to stay in Durham, it wasn't realistic to plan on making a living at golf. It was time for me to grow up, leave home and focus on academics and the future.

Not that my family's devotion to Duke basketball and football ever waivered. My parents held season tickets there, and we were all staunch fans. I attended many a game with my mother when my father's business travel took him away from home. Bob Gantt was my favorite football player, especially after he gave me a prized Number 45 jersey.

This was the era of the old Southern Conference, but Duke was as good as it is today – particularly in basketball.

As my college search intensified, we toured Georgia Tech in Atlanta, which did not strike my fancy and North Carolina State, which was a strong contender. Numerous other possibilities came under the radar.

In the fall of 1953, my senior year of high school, Purdue University's football team played Duke in Durham, an event that set in motion my final college decision. During a brunch prior to the game, my parents and I met the president of Purdue, Frederick L. Hovde, who asked about my plans for college. My honest response was that while various schools were under consideration, no decision had been made. My preference was to attend an engineering school and then work in industry, possibly with one of the big companies of the day.

When he returned to Purdue, President Hovde basically recruited me. He shipped a package that included a sweatshirt, information about the university and an invitation to visit the campus. Both of my parents and my sister had attended Purdue, so I had grown up knowing about the university, and though I realized that going to Purdue, a large, Big Ten school, would be quite a step for a boy who hadn't traveled much farther from Durham than Camp Morehead, I recognized the value of attending college outside my home state. Once I submitted my application the realization set in that Purdue was the best choice for me. With that decision, the era of my life in Durham, at least for the most part, came to an end.

Chapter 2

College Years

In September 1954, I ventured off to Purdue University. My parents drove me to Lynchburg, Virginia, where we said goodbye, and I caught the train to Indianapolis. Longstanding family friends, the Combs, met my train and drove me to the university town of West Lafayette, Indiana. In those days, people didn't travel extensively, and the trip to West Lafayette on my own was a challenge in itself. It seemed very far away from Durham, and I didn't know a soul, but immediately, I began to meet people and learn my way around. Despite my respectable high school preparation, the first semester was tough enough to require serious work and determined concentration on two things: academics and survival.

Soon after arrival, I was one of four new students who appeared on the cover of the Purdue alumni magazine as "legacies." Like my father, I was determined to accom-

The Purdue Alumus Magazine, November, 1955

plish the goals before me and to throw my body and soul into my college experience. Majoring in mechanical engineering was not the easiest route but it was the one that interested me, and so even after I learned the ropes and settled into the routine of college, my class load remained challenging. Requirements were stringent, and almost every semester in addition to ROTC, I took over twenty credit hours, one semester topping out at a whopping twenty-three, far more than the standard schedule but necessary to graduate on time.

By the time I entered college, I had come to be called John, the name that stuck from then forward. I went through rush and considered several fraternities. My dad had been a Phi Gam, so Phi Gamma Delta was a strong contender, but I settled on Sigma Alpha Epsilon. Once I moved into the fraternity house, where I lived my last three years on campus, SAE became the center of my social life.

We had a close group in the fraternity and shared many good times. Some of the best fraternity experiences came when we matched up with a sorority and tried out for the campus-wide Varsity Varieties. Our group usually qualified, and we had untold numbers of practices before the big event in the gigantic Purdue Hall of Music. We also had other singing sessions at the fraternity, though my abilities never qualified me for the fraternity choir.

One fall, Sigma Alpha Epsilon won a campus lottery drawing that earned a super prize. Louis Armstrong and his group performed professionally for a Saturday night, post-game victory program at the Music Hall, and then, thanks to our lottery win, they made their way to our fraternity house and played for a really memorable party there. Free alcohol with a good time apparently went a long way in keeping Louis Armstrong's group in performance mode because the fun continued nearly all night. I am not sure where their schedule took them when the bus finally pulled out in the early morning, but hopefully it was far enough away to allow the group some snooze time.

In those days the draft was in effect, and if a young man didn't volunteer for some form of military service, he faced the possibility of being called up for duty. I joined Army ROTC, a time-consuming commitment. I also was very enterprise-focused and stumbled into a few business ventures on campus. When learning of a graduating senior who owned Coca-Cola and cigarette machines in several frat houses, I decided to buy out his business for the duration of my Purdue days. I also worked part-time as a representative for the Student Marketing Institute, a group on campus that represented The American Tobacco Company and some other businesses. I figured I could gain some worthwhile experience as the campus point person who gave out samples, ran promotions, set up displays and did audits. In addition, through the Student Marketing Institute, I was able to visit the local tobacco wholesale houses and watch sales trends. The compensation for my work was the princely sum of one dollar per hour! As these responsibilities unfolded, it became obvious that the professor who was supposed to be in charge of the campus program was neglecting his job and defrauding the institute. My intervention cost him his position, and though my pay didn't increase, I did receive a certificate of commendation for my efforts.

As a sophomore, I bought a used car in West Lafayette with money saved from counseling at Camp Morehead and from my enterprises on campus. I enjoyed the freedom that owning my own car allowed, especially when it came time to leave campus for vacations. During a memorable, lengthy drive back home from college, I slid off the road on ice while driving through Ohio, a mishap that could have been a serious accident. Winters were long and cold in the Midwest, and I gained a healthy respect for the hazardous conditions.

My four years at Purdue were exciting ones, though my chosen field of mechanical engineering involved stringent requirements beyond the usual academic calendar. For instance, in the summer before my junior year, there was a month-long Mechanical Engineering Laboratory, an eight-hour per day program in August. It was demanding, but the curriculum was right up my alley.

Students at Purdue, while serious about their academic studies, still managed to have a good time. Even in those days, when the world seemed far larger than it does today, about ten percent of the student body was international, a factor that added an interesting layer of diversity to the campus. With its strong football program, game days were particularly exciting for this Big Ten school.

As a state university with a private endowment, Purdue is a rare institution, and over the years I have continued to appreciate the level of excellence fostered there. Returning to campus as an alumnus, I marvel anew with each visit at how fine a place it is.

By the time I left for college, my sister Nancy and her husband Kenan had two children, Bill, born in 1952, and Ruthie, born in 1953. The Rands were living in Durham, so whenever I returned for vacations or visits, I always made a point of seeing them. Nancy and Kenan eventually had four children, with Ginny born in 1956 and Hager, the last, in 1960. There is still a close bonding with all of my nieces and nephews and now their spouses and children. They like to remember the stories I used to tell them during get-aways to their cabin on Buggs Island Lake.

Dr. William Kenan "Bill" Rand III and his wife Kristine live in Norfolk, Virginia, where he practices as an obstetrician/gynecologist. Ruth Rand Waldrop and her husband Allister, a retired lawyer, live in Houston, Texas. Ginny Rand married John Bowman from Richmond, and they now live in Durham, where John is a lawyer and Ginny manages Northgate Mall, which her father owned. Marshall Hager Rand and his wife Stephanie, who is a pediatrician, also live in Durham, and he has assumed management of the Coca-Cola Bottling Company, which my brother-in-law also owned. Together, Nancy's offspring have eleven children of their own, and presently, that generation is beginning to marry.

In 1957, the move that my parents had anticipated took them from Durham to Ardsley, New York, in Westchester County, a relocation necessitated by my father's promotion to Vice President of American Tobacco. The new position was a tribute to Dad's importance within the company, but his farewell from Durham was bittersweet, especially because he had enjoyed the proximity to Nancy and her family and because he had formed such strong business and civic ties. It is indicative of the esteem in which my father was held that the city of Durham feted him with a rousing farewell banquet and presented him with a huge, engraved, sterling silver punch bowl, an impressive gift which we still use on occasion.

The summer after my parents' move, I drove from Purdue to Kansas for ROTC camp. The long drive was an experience in itself but only the beginning of my journeys that summer. When my ROTC obligation was fulfilled, I drove from Kansas to Dallas, Texas, to see my first cousin, Ginny Lee Woods. Ginny, who still lives in Dallas, showed her college-aged cousin a great time in her city. Undaunted by distances, I drove back to Durham and then to New York before leaving for West Lafayette and my senior year. With all the miles covered, I really saw much of the country for the first time. I have never shied away from long road trips, as subsequent years demonstrated, and even to-day many people are astounded at my super-charged odometer.

Despite my father's enormous success within the company, he attempted to steer me away from a career with The American Tobacco Company, where he worried it would be difficult to chart my own course. I, however, firmly believed American Tobacco offered my best career opportunity to progress. Still, during 1958, my senior year, I explored other opportunities and investigated a wide range of possibilities with some twenty or so other companies. The process was a great learning experience. A group of us had a knack for scheduling recruiting trips to Chicago on Friday and spending the rest of the weekend in the Windy City, which I did five or six times. Sigma Alpha Epsilon had its headquarters near Northwestern University in Evanston, north of Chicago, so we usually stayed in the fraternity house on Northwestern's campus. While these recruiting trips to Chicago were fun, they also resulted in several attractive job offers, none of which enticed me away from my American Tobacco plans.

Under usual circumstances, my ROTC commissioning requirement of service would need to be satisfied shortly after graduation, but I happened to hit the sweet spot when no major conflicts were underway. The conflict in Korea had wound down, and Vietnam was not yet on the scene, so the demand for Army officers was not particularly strong. In fact, the Army was reluctant to take on the expense of personnel they didn't need. Real-izing that my service could likely be deferred if I went on to graduate school, a new idea hatched. I had done well at Purdue, was a member of Pi Tau Sigma National Honorary Mechanical Engineering Society, and had a good resume´. I had favorably positioned myself for advanced studies, and it seemed likely that graduate business school would enhance my career options.

During the January break of my senior year, I drove home to see my parents, who were well settled on Hudson Road East in Ardsley. Not long into the visit, my father asked the typical father-question, "What are your plans after graduation?"

"I think I'll go to business school. The time seems right to go ahead and finish my education now."

"Well," he said, "that's fine, if it's what you want to do. Where do you want to go?"

"I don't know," was my confession. "I think I'll try to go to Harvard. I might as well."

He looked a bit puzzled, but he didn't try to discourage my enthusiasm.

At the time, I knew very little about Harvard Business School except that it was considered the best graduate business school in the country. Presently, there is plenty of competition from other universities, but in the late fifties, Harvard held the top ranking, hands down. The next day, I drove from Ardsley to Boston, where I basically knocked on the door and said that I wanted to attend.

They informed me that requirements included a Scholastic business school test and completed application form, but since I was there, I was welcome to a school tour. That was all fine with me, so I checked out the campus, picked up the application and drove back to Ardsley. After returning to Purdue, I carefully filled out the paperwork, and a couple of weeks later took the required test, which didn't prove too difficult. An officer

John as Head Counselor, Camp Morehead

at The American Tobacco Company made inquiries about whether or not Harvard had received my application. Indeed, they had, and next thing I knew, I was accepted. Later I would learn that only about ten percent of the incoming class was composed of students who were fresh out of college. Almost everyone had at least a few years of work under the belt before entering Harvard Business School, a factor that meant I would be among the youngest and least experienced in my class.

The senior year at Purdue was somewhat glorious as academic demands decreased and there was more time to socialize. Special opportunities arose, like going to Louisville to attend the Kentucky Derby with my uncle and aunt over the first weekend in May. My mother, father, sister and brother-in-law arrived in Indiana for my graduation early enough that we were able to attend the Indianapolis 500 Race a couple of days before commencement. Then there were heartfelt goodbyes and packing up to move on. Purdue played a major role in my development, and I have always been grateful for my experiences there.

In 1965, my parents established a scholarship fund in their names to support students in the College of Consumer and Family Sciences and in the School of Chemical Engineering at Purdue. The scholarship reflects the interests they pursued when they were at the university: my mother's major in home economics and my father's degree in chemical engineering.

Knowing that I was deferred by the Army and would be back in school come fall, I left Purdue after graduation and accepted the position as head counselor at Camp Morehead for my final summer at the camp. It was a great finale in the place I had loved for so long. Years later, our son Jack spent an early summer at Morehead, right before the camp disbanded and the valuable land was sold to developers. Sadly, there no longer is a Camp Morehead.

Chapter 3

Harvard Business School

In early September 1958, I entered Harvard Business School, and began a very, very challenging academic experience that demanded extreme dedication and diligent work. It also was exhilarating, as I met lots of new, exciting people and learned my way around Boston. My studies were motivating and interesting, with professors who were famous in their fields and who inspired me to achieve. I thrived on the hard work and immersed myself in opportunities on campus. Plenty of nay-sayers had warned that I wouldn't be able to handle the academic rigors of Harvard Business School right after college without any work experience. However, I was never one to back down from a challenge. Measured in untold hours of reading and analyzing cases, completing projects and submitting papers, the first academic year at HBS sped by successfully, and almost before I knew it, I had completed the first half of the graduate program.

Having already set myself a career path with The American Tobacco Company, I left Boston for a summer of work experiences in the tobacco auction markets, assuming a position as Foreman in American Tobacco's leaf management training program at Live Oak, Florida. There, I joined others who were working the tobacco market and who had descended on the town and needed housing. We rented rooms at the hotel on Main Street, but only a few of them were air conditioned, so we drew straws to see who would get to sleep in relative comfort with loud but functional window units.

At noon each day we returned to the hotel for lunch, and since it was the only decent choice in town, the judge at the Suwannee County Courthouse, located down the street, also took lunch at the same hotel. In an interesting show of respect, when the judge walked out of the courthouse and crossed the street, the whole town stopped in its tracks. No traffic moved, no pedestrian took a step until he walked into the hotel.

The weather was hot, which did nothing to ease the long hours of these seasonal leaf auction markets. A portion of Live Oak's population was Native American, and some of these hourly workers manned the warehouse. It was my first exposure to a different culture, and I found the Native Americans to be interesting employees. Grateful to have jobs, they were aggressive, but they also worked hard and competed among themselves, which was a boon to production.

After a month or so in Florida, I was assigned to the tobacco auction market in Wilson, North Carolina. I had good experiences there and worthwhile exposure throughout the summer. Working in Wilson gave me an opportunity to meet many additional company veterans, several of whom would be important in my later career. It was a learning process about the basics of the tobacco auction markets, a good place to start training for the company.

Returning in September to Harvard Business School, I launched into a second fascinating year. My two roommates were also Southerners, Wayne Burris, whose family was in the furniture business, and Dan Lafar, from a textile family. Southerners were a minority at Harvard, and it didn't go unnoticed that my roommates and I represented three of the South's most important industries of the time–tobacco, furniture and textiles. Those were the days!

The summer experience I had just completed in the tobacco markets offered me firsthand knowledge that I was able to utilize in my coursework. I wrote two extensive papers that were based on The American Tobacco Company's policies. One was *The Procurement of Tobacco for Cigarettes* and the other was *The Profit Sharing Program of The American Tobacco Company.*

I relished the course in manufacturing, which was taught by a distinguished professor, George Doriot. This exceptional individual was a French émigré who during World War II had attained the rank of Brigadier General and gone on in 1946 to form the world's first publically- owned venture capital firm, American Research and Development. His importance to the academic and business worlds is underscored by the number of publications still extolling his contributions and by Harvard Business School's recent exhibit, *Georges F. Doriot: Educating Leaders, Building Companies.*

Though he taught our large class in an expansive lecture hall, there was nothing impersonal about his course, for he challenged his students in creative ways. Our regular homework was the daily *Wall Street Journal,* weekly *Business Week* and monthly *Scientific American,* with these publications forming the basis for classroom discussions that forced us to consider the world in real time. Doriot emphasized the necessity of our staying abreast of world events because of the impact they inevitably would have on our lives. He inspired us to consider the future as we transitioned into careers. Significantly, he encouraged risk-taking and an entrepreneurial spirit.

Doriot divided the class into small groups with about seven students in each, and he assigned three collaborative projects for completion within these groups. Each project had a distinctive focus so that when all three were complete, every student had researched a wide range of business models. The first project involved a large company, the second studied a small enterprise and the third required an innovative project in manufacturing. In the final project, one test of the innovation's worthiness depended on whether we could sell the idea that we pitched. Could we actually convince someone that our new and unique idea was a valuable commodity? It was a high threshold for graduate students!

The two companies my group chose to research were Plymouth Rubber Company and Bestpak, Inc. I was selected group leader for the innovation project, which we entitled *Plastics as Building Construction Materials.* At the time, the use of plastics in construction was a cutting edge concept with plastics new on the scene and seldom envisioned as a building material. We worked on our project throughout the entire year, solicited assis-

Business School Friends, John – second from right, standing

tance from experienced businessmen, and even secured the help of an architect to help us design a plastic house. In retrospect, it is surprising to remember the positive responses we received from people in the business world whom we approached for assistance.

My project teammates and I collaborated on the researching and writing of our group thesis, managed to have it published and actually sold enough copies to make us all feel like budding tycoons. In the process we gained lasting lessons in entrepreneurial thinking, hands-on experience in innovation and practical applications of salesmanship. Our project was featured in the George Doriot exhibit in Baker Library that Maggie and I visited during a return to my fifty-fifth reunion in May 2015. Four of the seven project group members were in attendance.

I was blessed to have parents who supported me in pursuing college at Purdue and then graduate school at Harvard. Making the most of my opportunities, I ranked in the upper third of my class, was a member of the Finance, Marketing and Southern Clubs and participated in intramural athletics. Everyone at Harvard Business School worked hard, but it was a wonderful place to study, and nearly all of us who were fortunate enough to attend, relished the experience. We were taught not to think about who we were but about who we could be. The professors were unparalleled, and enrichment abounded with outstanding visiting professors and intriguing speakers. Really, the experience was so special that none of us wanted to leave, but graduation day did arrive in June 1960.

The momentous day is etched in my mind, not just because I received a Master's Degree in Business Administration, but because of special memories like meeting then Senator John F. Kennedy, Jr. Young Kennedy was just beginning his run for the Presidency and was visiting the campus of his *alma mater* when he stopped at Harvard Yard and chatted casually with me and others. The commencement ceremony was impressive, and armed with our degrees, we graduates were all off and running.

There was an informal offer to work at American Tobacco, but my first obligation was to check in with the Army for my ROTC assignment. My orders were to report to Aberdeen Proving Ground in Maryland during the first part of September, a delay that provided three months to enjoy as I pleased. The manufacturing innovation project group had seen such success in selling our idea of plastics in construction that some of us decided we should reward ourselves by going to Europe. Figuring we could finance part of our travel with the proceeds from selling our project and with what we optimistically projected for future sales, we bought charter flight tickets for about a hundred dollars each and flew from Boston to London. Then we rented a car and began a summer of travel in England, France, Spain, Italy, Germany and Switzerland.

There were four of us — Dan Lafar, Wayne Burris, Jim Crawford and me — cramped together in a rented Peugeot the whole summer and having the time of our lives. Cell phones were not yet on the scene, but somehow, we were able to meet up with many friends and classmates along the way. I was the only one without a serious girlfriend. I had dated several girls from time to time, and there had been little flings with girls at Purdue and Harvard, but mostly I was too focused on work to become involved. I had attended my share of state debutante balls in North Carolina and even had been a marshall at two or three balls, but always just with friends. Some of the others, however, had interesting girlfriends. My buddy, Wayne Burris, was dating Wendy Marcus, whose father was the Marcus of Neiman Marcus, and Dan LaFar dated Elizabeth Hanford, now Elizabeth Dole, former Cabinet Secretary and Senator.

Harvard Graduation, 1960

Nowadays, it's hard to find a European who doesn't speak English, but in the early sixties, that wasn't the case. We gamely tried to speak the native language wherever we traveled, and one night in France, we ordered what we thought was a small soufflé for each of the four of us. Unfortunately, our French was twisted so that it translated to soufflé for forty! Needless to say, our desserts were shared with the other restaurant goers, and there were no spare eggs in town. When we arrived in Spain, my fellow travelers figured I could handle the necessities since I had taken several high school Spanish courses, but when it took us several hours to talk our way across the border, they knew they had misjudged my abilities.

We ran with the bulls in Pamplona, though since I had no interest in being gored in Spain, my running was more like walking on the sidelines. We attended bullfights in the afternoon, drank red wine with the locals and slept in a field outside the over-packed town. The bull fights were a major attraction, and when the festival was in full swing, the town swelled to many times its usual population. Ernest Hemingway himself was in Pamplona that year, and we spotted him as he sat, sipping wine on the plaza. Trying not to be obnoxious celebrity spotters, we approached as close as we could to his table and then got our nerve up to talk briefly with him about the exciting festival. It was just a year later that he committed suicide.

We crossed one border after another, toured museums, gawked at architectural wonders, tracked down landmarks and without any dictated schedule, made our way – carefree and having a ball – through all the places we should have seen and probably some we shouldn't have. Sometimes we stayed in the nicest places, and sometimes our accommodations were basic or worse,

With Classmates, Summer of 1960

depending on where we were and what our objectives happened to be. The book, *Europe on $5 a Day*, was very popular.

Near the end of our summer, I broke off from the group in Germany and went to Hamburg to spend some time with the Hauni Company, manufacturers of tobacco machinery. They were very welcoming. In fact, at my big hotel, I came down the first morning, had breakfast and awaited my pickup. A group had gathered outside the front portico to speculate on who was being met by a black Mercedes limousine. I joined the group and gawked as well. I kept hearing a page for a Mr. Ager, but paid little attention. My pickup time came and went, and I began to feel increasingly anxious. Finally, I inquired at the front desk, and lo and behold, not only had they been paging me with, "Mr. Ager," but the limousine in front of the hotel had been sent for my convenience. What a transition to the real world of business!

From Hamburg, I went to Copenhagen, visited with the Crone family and toured the Augustinus Tobacco Company – which would be visited again many years later. Then it was on to London for a tour at J. Wix & Sons Tobacco Company. Little did I know that soon afterwards, The American Tobacco Company's ownership of Wix would be swapped for a thirteen percent interest in Gallaher, Inc., a company that would play a major role in my life.

Finally, after this unforgettable summer, we regrouped and flew back to Boston.

It had been an experience to remember forever with good friends and true freedom. More than that, however, my summer of travel as well as my years at Purdue University and Harvard Business School laid a groundwork for my appreciation of the importance of people. I began to recognize how those from different backgrounds, cultures and/or locations reflect varied perspectives. I saw the unique ways they approach problems and issues, and I came to realize that ultimately, the great challenge is to find acceptable ways to work together and to find solutions without ignoring or diminishing inevitable differences. Having the experience of being in so many places with so many, varied people would later be a great influence on my work in the business realm as well as in my public service as a politician and volunteer.

Chapter 4

Completing My Military Service

September 1960 came soon enough, and I reported to Aberdeen Proving Ground in Maryland for the required six months of military service, which began with two months spent in officer training. I attended basic military officer orientation school for a month and supply school for a second month. Then my assignment was Aide to the Ordnance Board. Probably my education at Harvard Business School helped propel me into this latter desk job, which proved to be an interesting assignment. The Ordnance Corps, which is responsible for keeping the Army supplied with weapon systems, ammunition, missiles, electronics, and ground mobility material during peace and war, was comprised of high-ranking officers who governed the activities of the entire Ordnance Corps, with Aberdeen being its hub. During this assignment, I worked with several officers on projects that entailed planning for future demands, modernizing procedures and updating the Corps. In these pre-Vietnam days, the primary focus, as it had been since World War II, was on Europe.

Mine was a fairly lonely existence in Aberdeen, with most of my non-work life spent in the Bachelor Officer Quarters. Often on weekends, I would drive up to New York to see my parents. One or two people usually rode with me, which helped defray the cost of gas. Larry Liebowitz, who lived in New York City, was a frequent passenger, as was Sam Slaughter, a friend from Harvard. We would leave on Friday night and be back at the proving ground by Sunday night – a trip that entailed plenty of driving but took us away from the monotony of the base.

These weekend visits with my parents in Ardsley were always full but relaxed. We watched my father curl at the Ardsley Curl-

John – Aberdeen Proving Ground

ing Club, and I attended Broadway plays in the city with my mother. My folks really enjoyed their twelve years in New York, and it was a treat to have them close enough to visit.

I remember being assigned guard duty on New Year's Eve, 1960. At first it seemed unfair to have such a dismal assignment on that special night, but since there was no steady girlfriend and no big plans, it didn't really matter. I took it in stride and did the job. The next day, we were to attend the Commandant's New Year's party at the Officers Club, an event which sounded great, but required formal dress, which I did not have. Turns out, there was a steady rental business for Army formal dress, and my appearance at the special event was in someone else's fancy uniform.

Soon after, in January 1961, President Kennedy's inauguration was scheduled in Washington, a short train ride from Aberdeen. We were given the day off, so I decided to attend on my own and in uniform. It had been snowing the night before and was still brutally cold when the train arrived in Washington. Some eight inches of snow blanketed Washington, and crews from the Army Corps of Engineers were working at breakneck speed to clear the inaugural parade route down Pennsylvania Avenue. Not surprisingly, there was chaos all around the Capitol as I walked up the hill and right to the front of the VIP platform. I just kept saluting and walking all the way to the senators' section; then I settled myself for a long wait in the bitterly cold, winter morning. Seats around me began to fill, though vacant spots dotted the stands – attesting to the difficulty that many dignitaries experienced trying to reach the Capitol with local airports closed and roadways clogged with snow. Any discomfort was forgotten when the memorable ceremony began. Robert Frost, his white hair tossed by the wind, recited his poem, "The Gift Outright." John Kennedy, dressed in a morning coat and top hat, delivered his dramatic inaugural speech with its famous passage, "Ask not what your country can do for you, ask what you can do for your country." Then I went to the Russell Senate Office Building to warm up and to meet some friends before venturing back outside. By the time the parade commenced, it was so cold that I would watch a bit, then fall in and march a while and then drop out again to watch some more. Around five o'clock, I returned to Union Station and caught a train back to Aberdeen, the end of a remarkable day, all of which had been totally unplanned.

Six months at Aberdeen passed quickly, and by the end of February, it came time to muster out. On my last day, I left the office during lunch to pack my belongings into my car, and upon returning, I was surprised that the office staff had set up a ceremony, with the chief giving me a certificate of commendation. They tried to talk me into staying, but I declined. I had decided to work full time for The American Tobacco Company.

Theoretically, there was a two-year obligation to the Army, but because of the low demand for military personnel, I was on active duty at Aberdeen for only six months. Uncle Sam didn't need my active service any longer.

Recognizing that my early career with American Tobacco would require extensive traveling, the Army assigned me to a reserves control group rather than a unit. It was necessary for me to take specified correspondence courses and to complete requirements that kept me up to speed, but I never actually had to attend meetings or summer camps.

The only time I came close to being called back into service was in the summer of 1961, with the eruption of the Berlin Crisis. By then, I was working in Florida, and though put on alert, never received the call. When I mustered out of the reserves after six and half years of service, I had attained the rank of captain and was given an honorary discharge.

Leaving Aberdeen, I had a free month before reporting to work with American Tobacco. I stayed in New York and tried peddling the books on plastics in construction from my business school project. From time to time I'd meet with success, but overall, interest had fizzled by then, and sales were tepid. Still, it was fun to be free, see friends and to be in New York City. Who would have ever guessed that I would return to New York at many different junctures of my life?

Chapter 5

Getting Started at American Tobacco

My career with The American Tobacco Company officially began in March of 1961. Despite the imposing Hager family record with American Tobacco that preceded me, it soon became obvious my father had made a clear and resounding announcement that I should get no special privileges. Sure enough, his dictum was heeded, and I not only had to make my own way but actually had to work a little bit harder to prove myself.

First I drove to Durham, North Carolina, to register at the Operations Office for the Leaf Department, and from there, it was on to Upper Marlboro, Maryland. For thirteen weeks, I functioned as a foreman in the Maryland tobacco markets, every day, traveling among four auction markets and many warehouses to purchase tobacco, and then returning to work in the little prizery, where the tobacco we had bought was accounted for, packed and shipped. Once a week, we traveled to Baltimore for the hogshead market. I toured around southern Maryland, which is very different from the rest of the state, and especially as the weather grew warmer, I found much about the area to draw my attention. In those days, tobacco areas spread from Marlboro down to La Plata and Waldorf, locations that today are sprawling suburbs of Washington, but at the time, were rural farmland.

Early my first morning on the job, all the tobacco men gathered for breakfast at a restaurant in Waysons Corner, just a short distance beyond Upper Marlboro. Local farmers and warehouse workers also hung out in this hotspot, with its great reputation for breakfasts, and when I walked in, I couldn't help but notice that beer, not coffee, was the breakfast drink of choice. Not only that, but school kids were huddled around slot machines, playing away their lunch money.

What kind of place is this? I wondered. It took a while before I came to realize, despite initial misgivings, that the hardworking locals were not really gambling alcoholics. There was a lot to learn about the basics of the tobacco business, and my Maryland experiences exposed me to a wide range of fundamentals. I also made many friends and formed fond memories. One of my best friends in Maryland was Duke Cassels-Smith, son of a leaf dealer, who would later be one of my groomsmen and who sadly died at an early age after he had a recurrence of a viral infection contracted while hiking the Andes Mountains in his youth.

When the tobacco market in Upper Marlboro closed, it was back to my old stomping grounds in Live Oak, Florida, where I stayed for about a month. Driving south, I swung through Durham, and from there, my mother and sister caravanned in a separate car to Claremont, Florida, where we visited my maternal grandmother, Anna Richter Rabbe. By this time, Grammie, who was in her nineties, lived in a nursing home in Claremont, but in the years before entering the nursing home, she had been a real presence in our lives. Though she used to winter in Florida each year, she spent a month or so with our family and another month or so with her son Willis and his family in Milwaukee. I vividly remember our visit with Grammie in 1961 because it was the last time I saw her. She passed away shortly afterwards.

After I left my sister, mother and grandmother, my drive from Claremont wandered through land that was rural and filled with farming operations all the way to Live Oak, near the Georgia border. Many oranges were on the trees, the first time I had seen the huge orange groves and fruit waiting to be picked.

Arriving in Live Oak, I took a room at the hotel on Main Street, which by this time had slightly improved and expanded its air conditioning system so there was no need to draw straws for cool rooms. The tobacco country was interesting, and during the week, we worked long hours in the sweltering heat. There were few people my age at the auction markets, but I came to know the ones who were there. Some friends from college lived in the South, and on a couple of weekends I took off and did fun things with them. I remember going to Sea Island and playing golf, which was a real treat. There weren't many obligations except my job and still no steady girlfriend, so mine was sort of a vagabond life, but also an exciting one. I had my car, and all my possessions could be packed in the trunk.

In August when the tobacco market in Live Oak ended, it was time to move north to Wilson, North Carolina, which in those days was the site of the largest auction market in the world. My first priority was finding a place to live, not always an easy feat when the markets were open and an influx of outsiders descended on the town. I located a room in a house, which was a common arrangement since townspeople opened their homes and made a little extra money by renting rooms during the market season.

In Wilson, The American Tobacco Company had a large prizery with a significant number of employees. Once tobacco was purchased at the auction market, it was sent to the prizery for inspection before payment was completed. Then the tobacco was packed into wooden barrels, called hogsheads, and shipped to processing plants, called stemmeries. My workday often entailed overseeing the warehouse floors, and then when the tobacco came in, moving to the prizery, where I'd work a shift inspecting tobacco in the factory.

The experience provided excellent training, and there was an opportunity to meet a broad array of tobacco people who worked in Wilson. One weekend in August, I went to Durham and purchased my first new car, an Oldsmobile Cutlass that was really modern for the time. Thinking that I would stay in Wilson through the season, which would end in October, I settled into a regular routine. Suddenly, on Labor Day weekend, I was transferred to Danville, Virginia, another large market.

Once again, I arrived at my new assignment with everything packed in the trunk of my car, this time the Cutlass. My first challenge was finding a place to live. As before, I took a room in a house, the most economical if not the most accommodating way to live.

I don't think this could be construed as a real promotion, but when arriving in Danville, a portion of my job, in addition to work in the factory, was to be the driver for Mac Morton, the market supervisor. As part of the training process, this assignment gave me an opportunity to shadow the boss man, so to speak, and since he was meeting with tobacco people all the time, I too had the opportunity to meet many of the big players. I also drove to various sites as he supervised four buyers and was privy to their discussions and decisions as they adjusted the types and amounts each one bought according to market conditions, availability and needs. As Mr. Morton chatted with people in the warehouses and held lunch meetings, I witnessed these interactions as well. With all this insider exposure, the duties as a driver proved to be an enlightening experience.

In Danville, the opportunity arose for me to be a buyer at the tobacco sale, an experience that was both unnerving and exciting, especially first time around. The buying process was something beautiful to watch and exhilarating to undertake – part art, part knowledge of the tobacco being sold at auction, part skill at the auction process, part gut feel for the fast moving action and part relationships with the auctioneer and other buyers.

I did the buying several times that September and through actual participation became more confident about the process. Buying tobacco was a very competitive arena, one that no longer exists as an auction system as it did in the heyday of tobacco production.

In late October when the market in Danville ended, I took advantage of some time off and drove to New York to visit my parents. Then from mid-November until mid-January, I resumed my duties, this time in Greenville, Tennessee, which is a large, burley tobacco market. At Christmastime, I drove to Durham to my sister's home, where my parents also gathered, then back to Greenville for the last weeks of the burley market season. Another New Year's Eve on the road found nearly everyone who was working in the Greenville market at a big blowout party that one of the tobacco dealers, Sam Calvert, organized.

My father had said, "When you are working in tobacco, the only places to live are the four main tobacco states: Kentucky, Tennessee, Virginia and North Carolina." I think he really meant those were the only four places worth living in the country, period. But for our business, his advice was on the mark, and with the exception of New York, where we both lived for a while, Dad and I always resided in those four states where, at the time, tobacco was *the* big crop.

By the end of my stint in Greenville, I had completed almost a full year of training – beginning with Maryland tobacco in March, then flue-cured in Live Oak, Wilson and Danville from August through October, and burley in Greenville through January. I had learned the ins and outs of three of the five tobaccos that comprise cigarettes. The two remaining types are Oriental tobacco, which is mostly Greek and Turkish and is used in small amounts for flavor, and reconstituted tobacco, which is processed from waste tobacco products and used as a portion of the cigarette blend. Eventually, I would work closely with all five kinds of tobacco and experience them, whether grown in this country or internationally.

In late January of 1962, I was transferred to Richmond, Virginia, to follow tobacco processing through the stemmery, the completion of its entire cycle. In my college days, I had visited Richmond with my parents and had gotten to know their friend, Julien McCarthy, who was American Tobacco's manager in the city. A distinct memory during our visit had been cocktails at the Country Club of Virginia, where we sat on the patio overlooking the golf course and adjoining vistas. That was my first experience at the club, and I remembered it as an impressive place. It certainly never occurred to me that someday I would be an active member and then president of the Country Club of Virginia.

My initial housing in Richmond had little relationship to the West End's rolling hills beyond the country club's terraced patio. First it was in a Southside motel on Jefferson Davis Highway for about a week. Then I rented an apartment in a new complex, a highrise at 5100 Monument Avenue for a couple of months. Fortunately for me, Blanton Bruner, who worked in the Research Department, made numerous inquiries and located a more appealing apartment for me to rent at 3506 Grove Avenue, a brick building that is still there. For the first time in my working life, I had a place to call home.

After three months in the stemmery, I was transferred to the Research and Development Department as the next phase of my training. The department at this time was located in the same complex as the stemmery and storages, on Jefferson Davis Highway about two or three blocks from Hull Street. A billboard at the highway in front of the storages said, "Tobacco Asleep," a sign that people really noticed.

The large Research Department, with a couple hundred employees, was under the supervision of Vice President Hiram Hamner, an extremely capable and knowledgeable individual. It was my good fortune that Mr. Hamner mentored me during my assignment. He regularly called me into his office in the middle of the afternoon, and we would talk about the business for hours on end. I worked in every nook and cranny of the research lab and the flavoring department – a very informative experience.

After months of following a nomadic life, basically living out of my car and moving from tobacco town to tobacco town, I had finally settled into a more stabilized situation, even beginning to furnish the Grove Avenue apartment to suit my taste. I mostly worked a normal eight-to-five schedule – five days a week and had weekends off – which actually meant the possibility of a social life. Even my meager salary had increased. As far as I knew, my whole life would be in Richmond.

By May 1962, I was transferred to the Virginia Branch, the cigarette factory that was located in the sprawling complex which now comprises Tobacco Row at Twenty-fourth, Twenty-fifth, Twenty-sixth and Pear Streets in Richmond's East End. My title was Assistant Foreman, with Foreman being a higher level in manufacturing than the same designation I had held when I worked the markets. I had the opportunity to learn the manufacturing process from A to Z, in no small part thanks to the knowledgeable employees who worked there.

At one point I started my workday at 5:30 a.m., when the Twenty-fourth Street fac-

American Tobacco Manufacturing and Leaf factory.

tory began operations. From there, as tobacco worked its way through the Twenty-fifth Street prefabrication step and then to Twenty-sixth Street, completing the process over a period of two days, I followed along and learned the entire procedure. Thus, my training was completed in both the leaf and the processing ends of the business. I then became familiar with almost every angle of the company's manufacturing operations and met key personnel and working people in all phases of production. I was assigned to specific jobs at Virginia Branch in this next phase of training.

My working at the Virginia Branch completed an exceptional training program in operations. It had been thorough and intense, one that had been uniquely tailored to prepare me for the future. I had certainly done my part to encourage The American Tobacco Company to support my career through my education, my single-mindedness in pursuing experiences, my reaching out to contacts who could enrich a career in the company and my willingness to work long hours, sometimes in difficult circumstances. Even my determination to join The American Tobacco Company right out of Harvard Business School, rather than accept what initially would have been a much higher paying position, say on Wall Street, spoke to my goals of learning the business and advancing in the company. It was a fascinating labor of love.

Chapter 6

Building My Career

I was enjoying Richmond and beginning to socialize with a wide circle of friends. In August of 1963, there was another call to be named Assistant Superintendent of the Virginia Branch factory, so life was looking good. Then to my surprise, almost immediately after the promotion came a transfer to Reidsville, North Carolina. I had hardly had time to enjoy my new role at Virginia Branch before having to leave! On the road again!

It was a tough move, though it was another promotion since the Reidsville plant was much larger than the one in Richmond, and I retained my newly earned title and responsibilities that I had acquired as Assistant Superintendent. From September 1963 until May of the next year, the opportunity allowed me to become familiar with the operations of that site and meet a whole new batch of people, both professionally and socially. I was able to lease an apartment in Reidsville's only apartment building and joined the little Pennrose Park Country Club, a membership that was arranged by the company. There was no active girlfriend, and sometimes weekends found me wandering around to familiar places while also playing some golf again at the country club. I even managed to break my finger in a pick-up basketball game. The company doctor, Cliff Payne, left a cocktail party to tend to me, and then we both went back to the gathering together.

One of my vivid memories was of the day I was working in the factory when the news broke of John F. Kennedy's assassination. I was on the production line at the time and watched with astonishment as the news of our President's death passed from person to person. All of us were shocked in disbelief! The next week included time off from production so that all the workers could watch the funeral.

The manager in Reidsville was Henry French, who became a dear friend. He took me under his wing, introduced me to important contacts and taught me a great deal. We worked closely together, and there were many dinners at his home. I would often spend an hour or so chatting with him in his office before beginning my ten-hour second shift, which for a time ran from four in the afternoon until two o'clock the next morning. During that period, Ken Howard, the scheduler, and I would leave for dinner at the Family Diner, lugging our bulky, early model bag phones in case there were developments at the factory. Those were long workdays, but I never begrudged the time spent with Mr. French or on the job. He taught me the value of each and every employee. Little did I know that subsequently I would work with him as his assistant when he became Director of Manufacturing.

Those were the times of big changes in the tobacco business. The Surgeon General's warning came out for the first time in late 1963, and with it came pressure to convert from non-filtered to filtered cigarettes, though there were many challenges to overcome before the transition could be made. We never were able to accomplish the necessary conversions as quickly as we hoped, and the Research and Development Department labored under considerable duress to make it happen sooner rather than later.

In July of 1962, American Tobacco's Board of Directors released the news that the company's Chief Executive, Paul M. Hahn, would be retiring, and my father and Robert B. "Barney" Walker were both nominated to assume the vacated position. Mr. Walker was the marketing chief, and my father was the manufacturing chief, both very well liked and both fully qualified to be CEO. At the next board meeting, a tie vote ensued. For the next month, there was quite a bit of uncertainty about the selection, but during the monthly meeting of August 26, 1962, a director who had been absent from the July meeting cast a vote for Mr. Walker and broke the tie.

Though my father finally lost the presidency, when positions were announced, he was named Executive Vice President, certainly a prominent position, which was made official in February 1963. As Executive Vice President, he was responsible for a huge chunk of the company and a whole host of subsidiaries. My father took his brush with the top job and subsequent appointment as Executive VP in stride, but the fact that he never talked about it is probably indicative of real disappointment.

One of the other rising stars at American Tobacco was Bob Heimann, who assumed a marketing role under Barney Walker. In May 1964, just as I was settling into my work at the large Reidsville plant, Mr. Heimann traveled to North Carolina to meet with me. He broke some news: "We want to promote you and transfer you back to Richmond. We are going to involve you with new products and call you coordinator of a brand new division that we will create, the New Products Division of Research and Development."

Mr. Heimann was very persuasive, and I assumed that this move would occur in the near future, but I wouldn't have guessed just how near that future actually was. "When do you need me in Richmond?" I asked.

"Tomorrow," he answered.

Mr. Heimann had an agenda. There were real needs to be addressed and no shortage of ideas for the envisioned but still unorganized New Products Division of Research and Development. He enthusiastically described to me the new facility to be built outside Richmond at Bermuda Hundred in Chesterfield County. It would be constructed on a 600-acre parcel, bordering the James River, where the company had already built an innovative reconstituted tobacco plant that functioned like a paper mill. The new building would be on Enon Church Road and would be designed as a state-of-the-art, modern facility to take the company into the future.

Much as Mr. Heimann had described, in November 1965, the New Products Division moved to the Bermuda Hundred site and into the facility which was dedicated in April 1966. Later, the whole Research and Development Department was consolidated into this new complex, and an additional building, the Process Development Laboratory, was added.

Though it was a little tricky making the transfer with no prior planning, I left Reidsville in May 1964, the day after my conversation with Mr. Heimann. I was fortunate to have a good friend, Mary McGeorge, who was married to my close buddy, Winston "Winky" McGeorge, and a week or two after my quick departure, Mary went to my apartment and packed all my belongings so they could be moved.

In Richmond, I began a grueling work schedule in the newly created position as Coordinator of New Products in Research and Development. Having known people during my last assignment in Richmond, I resumed contact with several contemporaries. My closest relationship was with Dick Irby, who was named Director of the New Products Division.

I made arrangements to live in the Georgetown Apartments, a relatively new complex in Richmond's West End. Joining the Westwood Racquet Club, where a lot of young professionals played tennis and relaxed, was the next step. At the urging of my friend, Julien McCarthy, I had previously joined the Country Club of Virginia back in 1961, and that proved to be a base for many social connections.

It was easy to resume a social life with my friends, and there were many bachelors and single girls who shared activities together. The Bachelors' Club sponsored dances, and as my new assignment in Richmond would extend over four years, there were opportunities to connect with young women in a social setting. Even though I still didn't have much in the way of free time, it was stabilizing to live in the same place for more than a few months, and the social scene was lively and fun.

A group of us bachelors had some exciting weekends at Virginia Beach during those summers. We collectively rented a house and used it on the weekends or whenever we could get away. There were several couples going together, but it was an ever-changing scene and quite tame by today's standards. It was all great fun and reasonable since we tallied up our expenses at the end of the summer and split the bill.

I began to go back and forth to New York fairly often on business with involvement in numerous priority situations and projects within the company. From his New York office, Mr. Heimann was quite a taskmaster, and as time went on, he began to think of our division as the place to turn to get things done. It was a very busy time. Although my title was Coordinator of New Products in Research and Development, I routinely worked with people from the Research, Manufacturing and Marketing Departments and participated in several projects with other divisions. With various degrees of success, we tried numerous new products, and I was involved in all of them. In fact, there were so many product introductions over the next couple of years that in New York, President "Barney" Walker, became known on Madison Avenue as "Brand-A-Month Barney."

Through Winky and Mary McGeorge, I had opportunities to go fishing on the Rappahannock River, sometimes with Winky's neighbor, Bill Grinels, who had an offshore boat. In the summer of 1966, Bill invited me to fish out of Morehead City, which was great fun. In fact, I caught a white marlin, a very exciting feat and no easy accomplishment as my prize exceeded the fifty-pound citation mark. In those days, they actually shipped the fish to Florida to be mounted. Years later, Maggie was somewhat unnerved when we unpacked a big box to reveal the mounted fish. It seemed destined for the trash heap until our son Henry took a liking to it, had it refurbished and found a spot for it on his wall.

The next summer, Winky and I went to Hatteras with Bill, and while we were fishing offshore, we received a call on the ship-to-shore radio saying that at the end of the day, I should check in with American Tobacco. It was late by the time we hauled in our fishing lines and headed back to shore, and to my surprise, I found that the company had sent a plane to pick me up and fly me directly to Richmond, where I was to meet Dr. Hamner of Research and Development. The plan was that we would continue on to New York City by train that same night.

When we landed in Richmond, I had barely enough time to run to my apartment and grab some clothes. That was about all the preparations I managed before we headed to the train. I couldn't sleep much during the trip, and I knew little of our mission. In hurriedly washing my hands in the compartment's foldout sink, I accidently lost my gold Purdue ring. Amazingly, months later, the railroad company tracked it down in the elbow under the sink and returned it to me.

When we arrived in New York, we were driven directly to New Jersey. There was a man named Robert Strickman, who claimed to have designed a new cigarette filter that would be the miracle to save the smoking world. It was composed of a powdery substance, and the revolutionary design was purportedly more effective than any of its predecessors. This supposedly major development even made the front page of the *New York Times*. My assignment was to stay in New Jersey and work closely with Mr. Strickman.

We planned a press conference to announce the product, and I began what turned out to be about a month with Mr. Strickman. Keep in mind that this was an assignment that commenced without my packing much of anything and with my leaving Richmond without any goodbyes or fanfare. I purchased the bare necessities that I hadn't included in my hurried packing and settled into New Jersey life.

During my time there, I came to know Mr. Strickman well, became acquainted with his workers and his girl Friday and nearly all the ins and outs of his life. A couple of weeks into the relationship, however, I became convinced that his filter was not the phenomenon it had been touted to be. After all the hype and hopes, it proved quite unremarkable, and once we demonstrated to the company that his claims were overblown, we moved to lessen ties with him.

The Strickman incident was just one of many that I experienced, though that particular one happened to be high profile. We were always pursuing an array of new ideas and products, and in conjunction with them, I traveled frequently, so that although I lived in Richmond, it took on the feel of a home base as I ventured in many directions, working with projects that were assigned to our new products division. Of particular interest were several research projects that were tested at Arthur D. Little in Columbus, Ohio.

My parents were still living in Ardsley, New York, and one highlight each year continued to be our Christmas family gathering in Durham with my sister's family. Uncle

Jack in Louisville retired, and there was a grand dinner there to bid him farewell. Meanwhile, despite the frenetic pace, unpredictable schedule and frequent travel, there was a near certainty that I was moving upward in the company. I enjoyed the support of many people. My salary had increased, which was satisfying, but as a full-fledged workaholic, my time was never my own.

In late 1967, the company's master labor contract at all the manufacturing and leaf plants came due for negotiations. Julien McCarthy and Henry French, my prior bosses and close associates, headed labor relations, an important part of their responsibilities. They had held negotiations for about three months with no perceptible progress, and then, though my position as Coordinator of New Products at Research and Development had nothing to do with labor negotiations, I was suddenly assigned in December to a reduced size negotiating team. I began working full-time with the team as we commenced intense sessions that lasted all day and late into the night in an effort to forge an agreement. Starting early each morning, we grappled with issues, took a break to grab dinner and then continued well into the evening. Fortunately, we were in Richmond, so my apartment served as my home base, not far from the site of negotiations in the old Hotel Richmond, which is now a state office building at Ninth Street. The routine was to drive home and snatch a few hours of sleep before heading back, day after day after day. As Christmas approached and passed, it appeared we would never come to an agreement, and sure enough, on January 1, a strike was called in all four of The American Tobacco Company's huge cigarette factories, the stemmeries and the smoking tobacco factory.

I had planned a New Year's Day party at my Richmond apartment, but shortly before the strike began, a call from Julien McCarthy came. "You need to be in New York the first working day of the year, when the labor contract expires."

All planes were booked because of the holiday, so the only way I could get to New York was by train. So much for my party! It had just gotten underway when I had to say my goodbyes, rush to the train station and commence my late night journey to New York City. Some of my friends offered to take over the hosting duties, and with Hager missing from the Hager party, they made sure everyone had fun, cleaned up afterwards and locked the door behind them. We were all foot loose and fancy-free in those days, and our close friendships made it work.

Next morning, I arrived in New York very early, tried to clean up and then headed straight to Mr. Heimann's office. I was anxious to call around to the factories and be sure that no strike-related violence had erupted overnight. As soon as he arrived at the office, I reported to Mr. Heimann, whose first question was, "How are things going with the strike?"

"Okay," I assured him. "I think we can work things out eventually, and there are no big problems right now."

"Well, what are you doing here?" he barked. "You need to be in Richmond, working on it!"

So I spent exactly two hours in the New York headquarters before I turned around and took a taxi back to LaGuardia Airport for the flight home. I wasn't in charge of negotiations, but eventually I was one of three from management at the table, and Mr. Heimann trusted me to be an effective part of the team. He wasn't the top man of the company, but he was in charge and upset at this disruption.

We negotiated for another entire month. Finally, my father flew in from New York to join us, and he was the one who really settled the strike at the end of January 1968. By that time, I had spent over two months in the negotiating process and learned a whole lot about the process and the people.

My duties had shifted so often between negotiating and other responsibilities that I began to feel there was a contest for my time. Early the next month, I was named Assistant to the Director of Manufacturing. Other people were assigned the responsibilities I had handled in research, and soon the company appointed my friend, Sonny Kern, as the Coordinator of New Products.

My superior in manufacturing was Henry French, whom I had come to know so well in Reidsville, and my office was at Virginia Branch in Richmond. I had progressed from Assistant Foreman to Assistant Superintendent to Assistant Director of Manufacturing — this last a position that gave me oversight of all the company's factories, where my role involved supervision and working with the managers. During a year of exciting strides in manufacturing, from January 1968 to 1969, I remained in the position of Assistant Director and traveled literally all the time, going from factory to factory — four cigarette factories, five cigar manufacturing plants and one smoking tobacco plant. I also traveled for the company to Europe and elsewhere as needed, visiting various suppliers and partners. Working with The American Cigar Company was a new venture as they had been folded into American Tobacco. In addition to close coordination with the managers, I was involved in project work. Despite the rigors of the job, I enjoyed the challenges and appreciated the opportunity of working with Henry French and Julien McCarthy, who by this time was a vice president and assigned to the New York headquarters.

During May 1968, I traveled to Durham to visit old friends, Henry and Cary Stoever, in whose wedding I had been a groomsman. After medical school, Henry had served in the Army in Vietnam and while in Southeast Asia, had contracted an illness that led to a brain tumor. He was hospitalized in the Veterans Administration Hospital in Durham, where I went to see him. At the time, his wife Cary was very pregnant and ready to give birth. Tragically, Henry passed away the night before their baby, Brude Stoever, was born — a happy but sad time. I remember carrying roses to Cary at Duke Hospital, and the nurses thought I was the father. Cary lives in Richmond now, and we continue to stay in touch, especially through Kiwanis Club meetings.

In late 1968, I oversaw an exhibition of tobacco memorabilia at the Valentine Museum in Richmond. Objects were sent from New York for the exhibit, and I compiled information and materials which traced the long history of tobacco in Virginia and beyond. I felt strongly the need to save, maintain and display memorabilia, so my efforts in helping assemble the exhibition were especially satisfying. Many of the items continue to be located at the Valentine Richmond History Center and some are presently on display.

During 1968, *Outstanding Young Men of America* recognized me, though being on the go so often, I hardly had time to consider any achievement. My career was moving at breakneck speed, and I was loving every minute of it: endless workdays, constant travel, unexpected challenges, varied projects, interesting people and all.

Chapter 7

The Big Apple

In January 1969, I received an unexpected promotion to Marketing Coordinator, a position that entailed a transfer to New York City. After a rousing going-away party at Dewitt Casler's house, I moved to the Big Apple at just about the time my father's retirement was scheduled, July 1, 1969. The company's board threw a huge retirement party at the new Pan Am Sky Club on May 23, an extravagant finale for my father's influential, lifetime career. Upon retirement, he and my mother planned a move back to Durham, and as a gift from American Tobacco Dad received an English setter named Lady to meet them after the move.

At his lavish retirement dinner, a carefully crafted display included elaborate easels with blown up pictures accompanied by the following script that caught some of the background to my father's American Tobacco legacy:

"Tribute to Duke" (Dad's middle name)

Finzer Bros. was the name
From which our hero's father came.
He ran the show in his great day
And wed Matilda Coldeway.
John G. Hager, tobacco man,
Is where this story all began
He had tobacco 'neath his skin
And rubbed it off on all his kin.
He liked Buck Duke and so he proved:
Upon our hero's birth he moved,
"Call him Duke" — Matilda approved.

'Twas in the year of 1905
That Virgil Duke came alive,
And since that time as you will see
He's had effect on you and me —
And made his mark in history.

Stanley Steamers — dangerous then —
Were only mastered by real men,
But here you see him in the stern
Showing all intent to learn
To maneuver that next turn.

He invented Rock'n Roll —
I never knew it was that old.
But here's my proof: guitar in lap
On his way they say perhaps
To start the generation gap.

Lord Fauntleroy was ne'er so cute
As Virgil Duke in this new suit.
A football was his posing prize,
For dressing up in his disguise
Was quite a painful exercise.

Bonnycastle football team
Was the product of his dream.
'Twas semi pro and made some dough,
And bought a field and gave it though
To Louisville to make it grow.

Here our hero rows a boat
And makes it fly, instead of float.
He little knows that his great skill
Prepared him well to fill the bill
To paddle Jack some fish to kill.

Now Duke was a swimmer too,
And when with paddle he was thru,
He went ashore his clothes to peel
And put away Jack's rod and reel —
To dive and catch the slippery eel.

Now off to Purdue went our man
To swell the pride of his whole clan.
He mastered books and maids and men;
He learned expression with the pen
And played a little now and then.

Here he is — quintet I guess —
Looking dapper more or less
And later in the month of May
We found him here on Family Day
In the midst of this foray.

When Duke appeared in senior cords
(Purdue's pants for upper lords),
The fashion was set for many a year
And many a gal shed a tear,
A toast to the Duke — Here! Here!

Ah, Bliss! The day of wedding came.
Ruth Rabbe had ruled to change her name.
October 6th of twenty-eight
Was the day she took the bait
And was hooked — our hero's mate.

Here's to Ruth, we've known her well
And on her attributes could dwell.
No man could wish a finer bride
She's always at our hero's side.
Long may her happiness abide! — Here! Here!

Here Duke has grown as big as Jack,
Said you row down and I'll row back.
And as they fished at Currituck,
This picture proves they had good luck
And Duke caught these — I'll bet a buck.

Our Virgil is a curler too,
And I suggest when you are thru
You come and read what Ashley said
How Virgil forged the team he lead
And ended season way ahead.

Now to international fame —
Order of Phoenix is the name
Of highest medal earned in Greece
In honor of his expertise
And vigor that will never cease.

A handsome one of him with Barney —
Trust in me the talk's not blarney,
Annual meeting, resolution,
Here they talk of a solution
To prevent income dilution.

At the Waldorf for stockholders
Barney did not need the folders
To express his sincere feelings
For his Virgil Hager dealings.
The applause was most revealing.

Duke: To you we pay tribute!
There's nothing we could say would suit —
Anymore you might think corny
And perhaps would smack of Blarney,
Will you take it over — Barney?

What a night it was, and while my parents were leaving New York, I was arriving! I gave up my apartment in Richmond and leased one in a Manhattan high-rise on Seventy-second Street. Mother helped me get settled and gave the apartment some decorating flair. Then I immersed myself in two incredible years of working in New York City. Our offices were in a very fine, newly completed building at 245 Park Avenue. As Marketing Coordinator, I frequently met with agency people, and in the process learned a great deal about advertising, sales and marketing research. I continued to be project-oriented, and of course, with my previous work experience, held a thorough knowledge of our tobacco products and their origins. The marketing world seemed to revolve around an incredible number of meetings, so my work life became even more hectic than before. I plunged into a wonderful and unusual opportunity to work with many company department heads and suppliers. There was a great deal to be learned about packaging and a multitude of other aspects of the business.

Occasionally on the weekends, I drove out to Ardsley to visit my parents before their post-retirement move to Durham. I joined the Ardsley Curling Club, which my father had enjoyed during the New York winters, and I participated there for two seasons. Networking with other young professionals, my circle of friends in the city widened. I was working hard but enjoying life.

At the time, The American Tobacco Company had a small holding of about thirteen percent of Gallaher, Inc., a company in London that had been acquired through the exchange of J. Wix & Sons' stock. When Philip Morris attempted to take over Gallaher by purchasing shares in the open market, President Heimann countered by flying to London and buying shares of Gallaher for American Tobacco. He succeeded in thwarting Philip Morris' takeover attempts, raised the company's ownership of Gallaher to a majority and

John with father in his office, 1969

eventually acquired all the outstanding stock. With so much at stake, he decided that American Tobacco needed help in overseeing its interests in London.

Though my title was Marketing Coordinator, which doesn't suggest any relationship to our London subsidiary, Mr. Heimann did not worry a lot about titles, and in January 1969, I was named a director of Gallaher, Inc. In this part-time capacity, I began to fly back and forth to London. I usually stayed about a week, coordinating with the people there and keeping a watch on our investment. Interestingly, the Chairman of the Board of Gallaher, Inc. was Mark Norman, who had married a Richmonder, Helen Bryan, and their daughter, Selina Rainey, and her husband Gordon presently live in Richmond. It was my good fortune that Mr. Norman took a liking to me, so that I was a protégé to him, and through him, I was able to learn the ins and outs of the British company.

Gallaher was a diversified cigarette company with all sorts of tobacco products, but it was also involved in wholesale and retail businesses. They owned store chains that carried their tobacco products, and since these stores carried many other goods, Gallaher dealt with non-tobacco merchandise as well.

In a similar manner, American Tobacco reorganized as a division of American Brands, Inc., with Barney Walker assuming the chairmanship and becoming CEO and Robert Heimann becoming President. The move was conceived as a step towards shaping public perception of a diversified company under the American Brands umbrella, and it had become official on the same date as my father's retirement. Since the company had bought Sunshine Biscuit, Duffy-Mott and Jim Beam companies, the new name reflected the multiplicity of its holdings, and it was no secret that even more diversification was planned.

In my positions as Marketing Coordinator and a director at Gallaher, I continued to work on exciting projects and to travel frequently. Though I was working longer hours and harder than ever in a wide range of responsibilities, it all seemed manageable and the non-stop action was both stimulating and exciting. I balanced the demands of travel as required, continued my involvement in marketing and also worked with company lawyers in various assignments. Generally, I had experienced about every possible facet of the tobacco business within the recently renamed American Brands, Inc. After the corporate lawyers became worried about tobacco anti-trust implications about a year later, I, along with two others, was asked to resign as directors of Gallaher, a move that alleviated some of the demands on my time and kept American Tobacco more at arm's length.

I remember one occasion in October 1969, when I flew back to New York from London to attend the wedding of my friend, Jeff Walker, the son of CEO Barney Walker. I happened to be seated behind Mr. Heimann in the church, and he leaned toward me and cautioned, "You probably thought last week was a holiday. Wait until you see next week!"

I couldn't imagine what was up, and there were so many crash-bang weeks during this time that I didn't worry about this particular warning over the weekend. It seemed that every week held its own set of opportunities and challenges.

When Mr. Heimann called me into his office Monday morning, he informed me that he wanted me to serve as Assistant to the President, a position that involved my working for him in an even wider variety of capacities. This was exciting news indeed, as I would be working across the whole company and reconnected again with operations. At the time, another young executive in the company, Dick McKeever, who could have been considered a "rival" as I climbed the corporate ladder, also received a promotion and was named Marketing Director, an equivalent position.

These were interesting times as the company was rapidly changing and remaking itself. In an attempt to remain competitive, we struggled mightily to transform the tobacco company, but we were always under a certain amount of stress because more people were beginning to question cigarettes, and despite our efforts, it was impossible to convert quickly enough to filtered options. Meanwhile, diversification, which the company had pursued, gradually began to dominate and blossom.

Personally, my career was very satisfying. I was used to working hard and never resented the long hours or the challenges of my diverse responsibilities. I felt fortunate to be recognized within the company, a distinction shared by few others. I had become familiar with New York City, loved living there, and had made a wide range of wonderful friends.

Weekends outside the city were special. Summers on Long Island usually involved activities at the Rockaway Hunting Club and Lawrence Beach Club, both of which offered "Joint Junior Memberships," a program designed to attract young members by allowing them to join for the summer months to enjoy the amenities of both facilities. Through these clubs my social life ratcheted up as I played golf, went to the beach, met many people and mingled with lots of upcoming young ladies. I had a small car in New York, a Corvair, which had been my father's commuter car, and was an asset when I wanted to leave Manhattan. It wasn't very attractive, but it suited my life in the big city.

Usually, it was parked on the street or in a lot on the East River, and remarkably, I never got a single ticket – an impossibility today.

One spring night, I was invited to attend the Junior League Ball at the Waldorf Astoria's ballroom, and the party continued quite late. Rising early the next day after a few hours of sleep, I returned to work and realized that American Brand's annual meeting would soon be taking place in the exact same ballroom where we had partied into the wee hours of morning. I was recruited to help set up for the meeting, a very different affair from the Junior League Ball.

Annual meetings were always challenging, and under the ensuing pressure, everyone in the company grew tense during the preparation period. Once the meetings were underway, however, everyone relaxed, for the proceedings usually went smoothly, and the attendees, who received gifts and attention, reacted positively to American Brands' presentations.

Though a confirmed bachelor, I had experienced a couple of flings in Richmond. Relationships could only progress so far because I was always packing my bags for another business trip or a full-fledged move. In New York as a single executive, there were exciting opportunities through American Tobacco. Whenever there was a function that required representation from the company, I was given the assignment, and as a result, my calendar was filled with plenty of interesting events and dinners.

One evening I became involved in an off-beat situation that probably could not have happened anywhere except in New York City. I had gone with a date to dinner on lower Park Avenue, and calling it an early evening, we hailed a taxi to drive us home from the restaurant. As we made our way up Park Avenue, another cab rear-ended ours with enough force to throw both my date and me forward to the floor. These were the days before seatbelts, and while I emerged from the crash feeling okay, I was worried about my date. It didn't take long for the policeman who came to our aid to see that our cabbie had no license and neither he nor the other driver spoke English. The officer dutifully took down information, and then loaded my date and me into a paddy wagon for the bumpy, wild ride to Bellevue Hospital. There, we checked into the emergency room and took our place with a noisy crowd of street people, drug addicts and a few folks with injuries.

Hours ticked by before we were finally seen, but eventually, the doctors decided to monitor my date overnight. I, on the other hand, was free to go. It was about three in the morning when I left the hospital, and there wasn't a cab to be seen. I had to walk all the way from Bellevue back to my apartment on Seventy-second Street — about thirty or forty blocks.

Next morning, I contacted the company's top lawyer, Arnold Henson, who heard my rendition of the night's events and predicted that I would never hear any follow-up about the accident. Sure enough, my date was released from the hospital, and we never received any bill, never got a call from the policeman and never heard anything from the cab companies. It was as though the accident had never happened.

Despite such oddities in New York, the fast-paced life and working on Park Avenue were an exceptional opportunity. Employees loved the new building, and amid the glitter and splash, they were proud to work for American Brands and American Tobacco. My office was fashionable, and the company had a fabulous private dining room for officers to enjoy.

During early 1970, Mr. Heimann asked me to prepare a paper detailing our needs within the Research and Development Department and highlighting the importance of strategic planning. Little did I know that in June 1970, as a response to my findings, I would receive another promotion, this time as Research and Development Director. I would be in full charge of a whole department for the first time in my career, a promotion I would have embraced had it not also necessitated my moving.

Happily situated in New York, I was pretty much devastated at the thought of a transfer. Furthermore, I didn't want to leave my position as Assistant to the President, which I believed was progressing very well. Of course, it was precisely because of dependability that I was promoted, but I fought it tooth and nail.

"I can't leave. There are too many important things going on here," I protested.

"Don't worry. We will find some others to pick up your work," they countered.

"But I have an apartment, and I can't back out of the lease," I tried again.

"We'll take it over. We're moving Jack Behr, the President of Sunshine Biscuit Company, from Chicago to New York. He's a bachelor, and your apartment will suit him perfectly."

I gave up my protest, hired a mover, packed my Corvair with as many of my belongings as could be crammed in — plants, most of my clothes and papers. Off I drove to Richmond, never guessing that this would become my hometown city for the rest of my life.

Chapter 8

Back in Richmond

People said that my mistress was American Tobacco, and my devotion to the company didn't belie that view. Being less than happy about leaving New York, I consoled myself with the realization that I already knew people in Richmond and there would be ready social outlets thanks to memberships in various clubs. It was a plus too that mine was a well-respected job. My Corvair had made the trip without any problems. Then, as a department director, the company gave me a brand new 1970 Oldsmobile 98, a behemoth of a model by today's standards. I had two cars but was still living in the Holiday Inn – some irony!

I returned to Richmond in July 1970. I checked into a Holiday Inn off I-95 in Chesterfield County, near the Department of Research and Development. "I need a room," I said, "and I suspect it will be for a long time."

The assignment at Research and Development was daunting. For some time before my arrival, Mr. Heimann had not been pleased with the progress of the department. The budget was too high, and some of the new products had not panned out as expected. We had a big job ahead, and the next three years would prove to be challenging and eventful, to say the least.

By this time, the Research and Development Department had relocated to Bermuda Hundred, had consolidated with the New Products Division and included some 200 or so employees, all of whom I knew by name. Work covered a broad range of activities with emphasis on new products, and sometimes the responsibilities were quite tedious. Among our external projects were the development of packaging for Sunshine Biscuits during the PCB chemical crisis and engineering work for Beam during environmental challenges within that company.

In a lucky turn of events, I was downtown and walking along Main Street shortly after my move, when I ran into Beverley Crump, a lawyer and acquaintance from my previous time in Richmond. "What are you doing here?" he asked.

"Well, I've been promoted and am back in Richmond," was the explanation.

"Hey, I'm getting ready to attend tax law school in New York for a year. My wife Susan and I are leaving next week," he told me. "Why don't you move into our house and be our house sitter while we're away?"

"That's an interesting idea," was my surprised answered. "I haven't lived in a house for a long time, not since starting to work ten years ago."

Enticing me further, he added, "We are taking a few things with us and putting the rest of our furniture in storage. You would have room in our house to put your stuff."

During my two years in New York, I had accumulated a fair number of possessions. With no other immediate options, it made sense to agree with Bev's proposal.

I walked on down the street and met another old friend, Tom Jarman. "What are you doing here?" he asked.

Again, my promotion and return.

He said, "Well, why don't you open an account with us at United Virginia Bank?"

It was because of that encounter that I closed my bank account in New York and began a relationship with United Virginia Bank, which over the years has evolved into SunTrust Bank and still retains my business. As I settled into the Crumps' house and put down roots, it seemed possible that my life in Richmond could take shape.

The work at Research and Development was time consuming as we undertook what today would be called reimagining and reengineering. We went through every part of the organization and made significant changes to improve efficiency and productivity. Of course, there were never- ending projects as well. This career move dominated my life, but it was necessary, and there was lots of support.

Even I couldn't work all the time, and I started playing tennis and golf at the Country Club of Virginia. One August afternoon in 1970, some friends, all about my age, met for tennis and dinner in the Grill, and as luck would have it, "Maggie," Margaret D. Chase was part of the group. Like me, Maggie had been living in New York, but her mother had prevailed on her to return to Richmond, and she was transitioning back. Someone in the group said to me," You know Maggie, don't you, since she lives in New York?"

"No," I answered. "I've met her sister Sally but never met Maggie."

Meanwhile across the room, someone was asking Maggie, "Don't you know John? He lived in New York — just moved back last month."

And she answered that no, she didn't know me. Before the night was over, we did chat briefly, but that was all.

The next day I was flying back to New York, and as it happened, Maggie was going back also. To make a long story short, we started dating. She soon moved to Richmond, lived at her mother's house on Three Chopt Road and began working in horticulture for a tree surgeon, Mr. Campe. We started seeing each other from time to time during August.

When Labor Day weekend approached, Maggie extended an invitation. "I'm going to my mother's house in Martha's Vineyard. Why don't you come too?"

I hesitated. "It's a long way to go for a weekend. I'm not sure how to get there and back."

"Oh, we can work it out, "Maggie said." My sister Sally and her husband, Bobby Daniel, have invited the Brockenbroughs. They have access to a private plane that Jim McGeorge is going to fly, and we can return from Boston."

At the time I was extremely focused on my work at American Tobacco. I had the new assignment and was trying to reorganize the Research and Development Department, control the budget and produce some good work. But with a private plane in the picture, the weekend in Martha's Vineyard seemed do-able. I agreed to fly up on the plane and during the trip, came to know Maggie's sister Sally and her husband, Bobby Daniel, who later would serve in the U.S. House of Representatives and was quite a personality. The flight went smoothly, and when we arrived, there was this woman, standing smack on the runway, my first view of Maggie's mother, Sally Todd. Enough said!

We had a fine weekend – full to the brim with playing tennis, mingling with other young people and relaxing. Late Sunday when it came time to think about returning to Richmond on Monday, the weather turned threatening. Foghorns started sounding as the area was engulfed in fog, and my connector plane the next day, Labor Day, was grounded.

There was no way that I was going to call work on Tuesday and say that I was relaxing at Martha's Vineyard. "I really need to make this flight and be back at work," I fumed.

We began looking at options. "How can I reach Boston to catch my flight from there to Richmond?"

The process wasn't easy. "Well, you take the ferry and then a bus, which will carry you to a second bus that runs to the airport. Then you can fly out on your scheduled flight."

"That's what I'll do," I declared. "It's going to be a long journey, so I had better get going."

Maggie's stepfather, Verser Todd, suggested to Maggie, "You can stay here and return to Richmond later in the week."

"No way," Maggie spoke up. "I'm going back with him."

That was the bond that put us together, and eventually, after the ferry, buses and plane, we did make our way back to Richmond. We began dating steadily, and together we drove to Durham so Maggie could meet my parents. In November, we became engaged and set the wedding date for February 27, 1971. The two of us gave ourselves over to the hubbub that led up to the wedding, beginning with a big engagement party in Richmond.

The work at Research and Development kept me very busy, and there was little free time, but the Crumps' home worked out well and served as a retreat. I began considering which friends to include in the wedding, but as usual, the bride–to–be and her mother were in control of most of the wedding plans.

Although our wedding date was at the end of February, the day arrived with unseasonably warm temperatures, about 70°. The ceremony was a large one at St. Paul's Episcopal Church in downtown Richmond. My father was my best man, and I had eight groomsmen, including Kenan Rand, my brother-in-law, and the others chosen from my close circle: Bill Lamb, a long-term Richmond friend; Harold Work, who was employed at Dupont in Richmond and is now deceased; Austin Brockenbrough, whom I had come to know in Richmond; Winston McGeorge, who worked at American Tobacco and whose wife Mary had helped me move back to Richmond from Reidsville; Bill Ballou, also

John and Maggie on their wedding day, February 27, 1971.

from American Tobacco and now deceased; Duke Cassels-Smith, who was my friend from the Maryland tobacco market days, now deceased, and Sonny Kern, a lifelong friend from Durham and the colleague from American Tobacco who took my place as New Products Coordinator. During the reception at the Country Club of Virginia, my groomsmen tried to pull a prank and jack up our car at the club's entrance. Little did they know that I had anticipated some sort of trickery and had hidden a second car on St. Andrew's Lane.

There were two drivers at American Tobacco, Alvin and Calvin, and both of them were on hand for our getaway. Calvin was stationed as a decoy at the club's front door, and Alvin was hiding in the bushes to drive the actual get-away car. While I was changing clothes, the groomsmen managed to ambush me and chained a bucket to my neck. A placard on the bucket said, "No Smoking," and it was full of ice and a bottle of champagne. Maggie claims that by the time I reached the balcony, it looked like I had nearly been killed. What a splash to end on! Maggie and I ran past Calvin, out to the second car where Alvin waited, and in we jumped. Alvin, who weighed about 300 pounds, put all his weight on the accelerator, and the car practically jumped off the ground. Away we went.

We were both exhausted, and we spent our first night in Williamsburg in one of the Colonial houses. Next day, we drove to Dulles and flew to Barbados, where we played a few days, and then to St. Bart's, where we had rented the house of one of Maggie's friends.

On our way to Barbados, we flew to Puerto Rico to connect to our island flight. We had just deplaned when there was a sudden uproar as a friend, Julio T. "Speedy" Gonzalez, accompanied by two "island ladies," came roaring across the airport. He shouted, "John Hager! John Hager!" several times and certainly got everyone's attention. "Speedy" was a tobacco machinery salesman from Baltimore, and he had planned his business trip so that he could intercept us at the airport. During the layover, he drove us around the sights of San Juan. Sadly, "Speedy," one of the most colorful characters I have ever known, passed away in 2015.

By the time we reached St. Barts, Maggie and I were ready to enjoy the island. We toured around in a rental car and drove through a huge rainstorm, strong enough to wash out the driveway. There were great restaurants and long beach jaunts. One afternoon, I rented a Sailfish and stayed out so long that Maggie worried I had disappeared forever. It was a real honeymoon.

When we returned to Richmond, we settled in the Crumps' house on Brookside Road, where we stayed until late summer. Knowing that the Crumps would be returning to Richmond, we began looking for a place of our own and bought our first home at 5407 Tuckahoe Avenue. We moved in September 1971. Meanwhile, we enjoyed a wide range of friends in Richmond, periodically visited my parents in Durham and occasionally on weekends, joined my sister's family at Buggs Island Lake.

I continued to travel extensively for American Tobacco, sometimes on the spur of the moment. I remember coming home and saying, "Maggie, I'm going to be leaving on a business trip."

She asked, "Where are you going?"

"England."

"When do you leave?"

"Tonight," was my answer. Before the evening was over, I'd driven to Dulles and boarded a plane for England to work with the Gallaher people.

On another trip, Maggie was able to accompany me as we returned to England and went on to Denmark and Holland. The shared trip proved to be a wonderful and memorable experience in so many ways. Our friendships with so many contacts lasted for years.

On January 17, 1973, Barney Walker, Chairman of American Brands, passed away, and company officials attended his funeral in Darien, Connecticut. It was the first, big-time funeral I had ever witnessed, with an impressive array of well-connected and influential men and women on hand for the service.

Maggie had become pregnant, an exciting development, and as the due date approached, my job also took a significant turn. The company made clear that I was going to be promoted again and moved back to New York. There was a great deal of buildup to the promotion, and my responsibilities required my being in the New York offices more and more frequently. In preparation for the transfer, we needed to sell our home on Tuckahoe Avenue and locate a new one in New York. As though that were not enough to keep me busy, Maggie's sister began having problems with her marriage, and with her home at Brandon Plantation located close to my work at Bermuda Hundred, I often stopped by and tried to help. I had always kept long hours, but during this period, I was even later than usual getting home from work.

Our son, John Virgil "Jack" was born on May 21, 1973, an exciting event but also a difficult birth that necessitated a long hospitalization for Maggie. Maggie and I were still adjusting to new parenthood when on May thirtieth, a week after Jack's birth, the company announced that both my old friend from Richmond, Julien McCarthy – who by this time was in New York – and I were being promoted to Executive Vice Presidents. I was to prepare promptly for the move to New York, but until that could be orchestrated, I would need to commute regularly back and forth to the New York office.

When Maggie was strong enough to travel, we went house hunting in and around New York City. After an extensive search, we settled on a one at 336 Stanwich Road in Greenwich, Connecticut. The charming house had a great deal of history. In addition, it had some land and its own red barn, which according to Maggie was my favorite feature. The public schools in Greenwich were good, and I would commute to New York as my dad had done from Westchester County. All in all, it looked like the perfect home for us, one that would provide the backdrop to a happy situation for a long, long time. We could envision our son Jack growing up there, and the Hager family settling into a Greenwich-New York lifestyle.

Chapter 9

The Curve Ball

With so much going on in our lives — adjusting to life with a new baby, preparing our Richmond home for the market and locating a new one, transitioning to a new job — my stress level skyrocketed. Someone said that on a stress scale of twenty-one points, mine would have registered about nineteen. I wouldn't have disputed it, but it seemed manageable. I knew I was running at a frantic pace and didn't feel great, but I charged ahead.

Maggie and I were both excited about our move, and over the July Fourth weekend, we flew to New York to finalize arrangements for the purchase of our new home. The first morning in New York, I awoke feeling stiff and stayed in bed later than usual. In fact, Maggie, who then was the late riser in our family, was up before I was. Strangely, I was pale, as though all the color had drained from my face. But I was determined to seize the day, and so off we went in our rental car to Greenwich. By mid-morning, my body was racked by tremendous pain, and when we stopped for gas around eleven, I could hardly manage to pull myself out of the driver's seat. It was a relief when we arrived at 336 Stanwich Road, signed the papers and took steps toward the purchase.

I had planned for Maggie and me to spend the night at the Rockaway Hunt Club on Long Island, and by the time we arrived there, I was in enormous pain. Maggie suggested soaking in a hot tub and resting.

So I lay in the deep, old fashioned bathtub and let the hot water keep running over my aching body. Eventually, there was some relief, enough that we were able to go downstairs for supper and watch the Independence Day fireworks. I struggled through the rest of the weekend and awoke every morning hoping that the aching and pains would diminish.

Returning to Richmond, Maggie and I worked on our Tuckahoe Avenue house and put it on the market. It sold right away, which was a good thing but necessitated our accelerating the pace of our packing.

Though the pain subsided, it did not really go away, and I continued to look paler than usual. Our friends were very supportive of our returning to New York, and they threw several going-away parties. Some of them remarked to both Maggie and me about how pale I looked, but I dismissed their concerns and attributed it to stress.

On Monday, July 30, 1973, an article appeared in the *Richmond News Leader*, highlighting my rise at age thirty-six to Executive Vice President of The American Tobacco Company. Written by Tyler Whitley, the article was entitled, "Young Man on the Move Nears the Top," Tyler described me as "a man who gets things done, whom success follows." He highlighted my promotion by adding, "The betting at American Tobacco is that he will be President of the billion dollar-plus tobacco operation within a year." The article detailed my background and experience within the company as well as my management philosophy and determination to "try to get [the company] back into a real leadership position." It was so flattering that it was almost embarrassing. It also proved to be an ironic highlight before the dramatic plunge that followed.

On Tuesday, the day after the article appeared, I went for an early morning jog down Grove Avenue. Following my usual course, I was running along when, without warning, I fell down. In fact, I hit the pavement so hard that I knocked myself out for several minutes. Eventually, I regained consciousness, stood up and made my way home. I showered, but couldn't explain what had happened to trip me.

On Wednesday, I was scheduled to fly to New York, and I awoke feeling so stiff that I had to stand up to eat breakfast. Still, I pushed through and spent the day at the New York office. By the time I got to Newark for my return flight, the stiffness had progressed to excruciating pain. I called Maggie from Newark. "I'm just crumpled over in the phone booth. I don't seem to be able to move. I'm in such intense pain," was the message.

"You stay there," she said in a panic. "I'll put the baby in a basket and drive to Newark tonight to pick you up."

What a nightmare that would be, but I couldn't have her do that and insisted that somehow I'd make it. And I did. But the stiffness and pain continued. We tried to find a logical explanation for my symptoms and decided the problem must be centered in my back. Without delay, we consulted an orthopedic doctor in Richmond the next morning, and he assured me that there was nothing wrong with my back. He suspected that I had a urinary tract infection. "Drink lots of water, just to be on the safe side," he recommended. If only it had been so simple...

That Friday was my final day at the Research and Development office, a grand finale that was to be capped by a going-away party in my honor. I never made it to the festivities. Such enormous pain and stiffness racked my body that I stretched out on the floor behind my desk to try and make a few phone calls. Our top administrative assistant entered my office and found me prone on the floor. "There is something seriously wrong with you," he said. "You have to go home."

He insisted that I skip the farewell party and have Calvin drive me directly home, and as disappointing as it was to miss my own party, I knew that was the only sensible thing to do. I was walking up the front steps at home when I inexplicably stumbled and fell. I struggled up the steps with my elbows. Later we learned that Calvin was so worried that he parked the car down the street and waited for Maggie to arrive home. "There's something wrong with him," he warned as she entered the house with Jack.

Maggie found me lying in bed, and over the next eighteen hours, paralysis gradually crept up my body — beginning at my ankles, then through my calves, on to my knees, steadily moving upward until I was paralyzed from my neck down. The pain continued, really excruciating pain joined by this frightening new condition of being unable to move. At the time, I was under the general care of Dr. Charles McKeown, the physician at American Tobacco, so we telephoned him, and though he came once to the house to check on me, he had no diagnosis and no solution. As I lay in this painful and bewildering state, Maggie tried to care for my needs and at the same time to nurse and tend to Jack, just two months old. By early the next day, Dr. McKeown called for the West End Rescue Squad to rush me to St. Mary's Hospital, and thus began a grueling several-week hospitalization and the frustrating search for the source of my paralysis. The referring physician, Dr. McKeown, made it very clear that once we entered the hospital, his jurisdiction over my case ended, and he emphasized, "You are to be seen by St. Mary's doctors from now on."

Mind you, on Monday morning, the sixth of August, just one week after the glowing newspaper article had appeared, I was due in New York to begin my new position as Executive Vice President. I was still under the delusion that all might be cleared up over the weekend.

A group of neurosurgeons was called in, though many doctors were on vacation that Saturday in August. The neurosurgeons included Dr. Robert Singer and his team. Their first step was to drain my bladder, which had shut down as the paralysis worsened. Because I could not pass water, my stomach had extended so far out by the time of my admission that I was actually in danger of popping. Once that crisis was averted, a myelogram, the precursor to today's MRI, was performed. According to Dr. Singer, the myelogram indicated that disks in my back, possibly pushed by a tumor, were out of line, a diagnosis that would later prove completely incorrect. The recommendation was that the ruptured disks should be removed in the hope of stopping the paralysis. It was a serious operation, and Maggie was required to sign paperwork stating that three disks would be removed from my back, and the doctors would not be held liable if I did not survive the procedure.

Maggie agreed to sign the paperwork with the provision that the doctors promise to keep her informed of the operation's progress. They assured Maggie that they would find her in the main waiting room and would give her updates on my condition and reassure her that I was still alive. The situation was that dire, and no one was making guarantees. She had engaged Mrs. McElwaine, a dependable babysitter, to stay with Jack, and she took a seat in the waiting room as the operation proceeded. Hours ticked by with no news. No one came to her. Night fell, and the cleaning crew washed the floor, but no one came. They turned down the lights, and still no one came. Maggie assumed I was dead.

Finally, she found the stairs to the basement and started going down the corridors, opening every single door as she went, determined to see if she could find me. At last, she opened the door to the recovery room, with its blue lights shining down on me, still under sedation. I had made it through the operation, but no one had bothered to tell Maggie. The nurses assured her that they would be sending me up to the fifth floor, and that would be the best place for her to wait.

Maggie made her way as directed, and it was from the fifth floor that she heard a gurney approaching, but mostly she heard my screams of agony. The back operation had created waves of intense pain. Despite my desperate condition, I was wheeled into a semi-private room with another patient. Only then was I administered intravenous drips, which included pain medications. Maggie stayed with me all through the night, the beginning of a long vigil that she maintained, some eighteen hours a day during my initial recovery. She wasted no time in securing a private room, and she was vigilant in guarding against missteps.

Dr. Singer, the surgeon, Dr. Laurie Rennie, a neurologist, and the others in the group could not understand why the paralysis had not disappeared with the operation. They still had no idea what was wrong, but they realized that the extensive and danger-ous operation they had performed on my back was a mistake. They had trimmed three disks, but there was no tumor, and the bulge they saw in the myelogram was probably a result of the fall I had taken while jogging. Still unable to pinpoint the cause of the paralysis, they were at a loss for treatments, and they held little hope for my recovery. Then the team of physicians recommended that I be transferred to McGuire's Veterans Hospital for further care.

Maggie knew that such a move would dishearten me. It would sap my hopes for re-covery and could be disastrous to possibilities for recuperation. In the face of my doctors' insistence on such a move, Maggie decided to confront Dr. Singer and his team head on. She heard them approaching my door and planted herself in the middle of the hallway with her legs and arms spread wide, blocking their way. Maggie is not a large woman, but she made a formidable obstacle to the group, and she spoke with a fierceness born of desperation.

"You shoot first," she ordered. "I'm an easy target. You can shoot me, but you are not moving my husband to McGuire's Hospital. It's a very easy choice...shoot me or stab me with whatever you've got, but you are not going into his room until you give me full promise that you are *not* sending him to McGuire's Hospital."

They got the message and dropped the threat of a transfer.

On the night of August fourteenth around ten o'clock, Maggie was still in my room when Dr. Read McGehee, a pulmonologist doing research at the Medical College of Virginia Hospital, entered. He lived in our Tuckahoe Avenue neighborhood, and by co-incidence, we had met him at a neighborhood gathering we had hosted. He approached my bedside. "I have seen on the chalkboard down in the basement by radiology and the operating rooms, the name John Hager and a question mark. Day after day, the big ques-tion mark stays. I came up to find you. What can we do to help you?"

"Find out what's wrong with me!" With my voice reflecting the desperation that weeks of uncertainty had wrought, I told him, "I have my brain, but I've been paralyzed to the neck."

"Have all the vital specimens been taken for further testing — blood, urine, wax in the ears, saliva, skin — that sort of thing?" he asked.

Maggie answered that none had been called for.

He laid out a plan. "I will have the orderly come in to take samples. You stay here, Maggie, to be sure it is done correctly. I'm not a doctor for you, but I think you need these specimens."

Maggie assured him she would sign him in as a doctor on the team.

He warned us that tests on specimens are most effective when the samples are taken immediately after the onset of the condition, and since that had not been done in my case, it was highly unlikely that whatever was in my system would still grow or manifest itself. Nonetheless, it was worth attempting.

"We have to try everything," he said. We agreed.

A large number of specimens were gathered and sent to the state labs. In keeping with procedural regulations, three classifications were made for the tested specimens. One was for the growth and experiments to see what developed from the specimens, a second was tagged as an extra lab specimen, and a third was locked away as a back-up, accessible only to the lab administrator.

Meanwhile, the realities of life continued beyond the hospital room. We had agreed to vacate our house on Tuckahoe Avenue for the new owners by the end of August, so Maggie and Jack moved to her mother's home on Three Chopt Road, thankfully not too far away from St. Mary's Hospital. Having been advised that I would soon be up and around, Maggie packed for Jack, herself and me as though the move would be for just a short time — a suit and dress shirt for me, a couple of changes of clothes for her, and Jack's crib and a few baby items. She sent everything else to storage.

On August twenty-eighth, my birthday, Maggie oversaw the movers emptying our house, a day for which she had spent hours packing. It also fell to her to go to Greenwich for the closing of the house we had purchased there and to arrange to store our furniture in Rye, New York. My father took this difficult trip with her.

Unfortunately, my situation had not left Dad unscathed. He had experienced such anguish when he learned of my paralysis that he had suffered an accident at his home in Durham. He loved cutting the grass, a process he found relaxing and one that seemed, at least temporarily, to soothe his sorrow over my situation. On one of the August days when I was still hospitalized, his lawn mower was slow starting, and in frustration, he kicked it. When it still wouldn't start, he reached under the mower, and the fingers of his left hand were partially cut off by the blade that he had not realized was rotating. What a disaster, caused by my curious situation.

For me, there was basically nothing happening beyond a modest amount of physical therapy. Physically, I felt slightly better and the paralysis had regressed some, but the doctors seemed no closer to a diagnosis than when I had first arrived in the hospital. The helplessness of not having answers and not knowing what to expect weighed on my spirits. They could say only that I had myelitis, a very general term for paralysis and nerve damage, rather like saying *food* instead of *fruit, meat* or *vegetable*. So they began to say I had myelitis, but they had no other diagnosis.

In hindsight, probably one thing that helped me through the ordeal was not know-ing what was wrong. Remaining ignorant of the truth, I could believe that I had something that would be cured and that eventually, I would resume my life the way it had been before being knocked down.

A great source of strength was the stream of visitors who stopped in to see me throughout my hospitalization. Friends seemed to appear just when I needed them most, and their support helped bolster my spirits. Colleagues from work, co-workers and laborers from the plants, work contacts from out of town – so many thoughtful souls made their way to my hospital room, and their visits sustained Maggie and me.

About the third of September, Maggie had the brilliance to remember that seven years earlier in Philadelphia she had been maid of honor at her friend Ethel Benson's wedding. The best man had been a physician, Henry Betts, who by this time was running the Rehabilitation Institute of Chicago. His position was an outgrowth of his earlier work with Dr. Howard Rusk, who is considered the pioneer of rehabilitative medicine. Once Maggie recalled that Henry Betts had assisted Howard Rusk in running the Rusk Institute — part of New York University Hospital — she called him in Chicago and explained my condition.

She described the onset of paralysis and informed him that there had been limited signs of recovery but still no diagnosis. Dr. Betts promised to initiate immediately an effort to have me admitted into the Rusk Institute. Because it was the top rehabilitation hospital in the country, there was a massive waiting list at Rusk, but not long after their initial conversation, Dr. Betts called Maggie and said, "I've located one bed in the research wing, and we've reserved it for John. It will be available by the middle of October. There's no way I can help you with a diagnosis, especially because myelitis is such a general term, but you all hang in there, and we'll arrange for his admittance as soon as possible."

September was a tough month. Maggie assisted with my care, and one day as she helped me roll over, she realized that gangrene had set into the wound that was still on my back from the unnecessary operation that had been performed. No one except Maggie had checked my stitches. In fact, during this period, I was receiving little treatment with the exception of physical therapy by Peggy Chappell.

Peggy would prove to be an important individual in my progress. While my doctors had neither the background, the experience, nor the tools to deal with my problems, Peggy, as a physical therapist, was familiar with poliomyelitis, and she treated me as she would have if a polio diagnosis had already been made. She and her assistant, Tim Austin, placed hot compresses on my legs. As my arms gradually regained motion, she forced me to move them in any and all ways possible. At one point, she pulled Maggie aside and confided to her that she was certain I had polio. Beginning with the way the disease had demonstrated itself at the onset, including the 104° temperature I had suffered, and because I had paralysis but full feeling — suggesting a loss of the motor nerves but not the sensory nerves — she was sure beyond a shadow of doubt that I had polio. "The doctors won't make a diagnosis," Peggy Chappell told Maggie, "but I am sure."

I had not yet heard Peggy's opinion. Maggie kept the information to herself until it could be officially confirmed, which actually was much later when the findings were scrutinized twice because the medical experts couldn't believe that the first positive polio result was correct. It must have been a harsh reality for Maggie to face alone, though by this time we both had faced a great deal that we would have considered unthinkable two months earlier.

I could not fathom life without work. From my hospital bed, I telephoned colleagues at American Tobacco, but no one knew what to say. It was surreal. I was just out there in never-never land, lying flat on my back and waiting for some semblance of normalcy to return.

Days continued to grind by as I remained in the hospital bed at St. Mary's. My feelings of helplessness turned increasingly into feelings of despondency. Dr. McGehee and Maggie stayed in contact about the specimens, though there still was no word from the state lab. Replacing Dr. Rennie, a neurologist on my team, Dr. Frank McGee became our trusted point-person — a professional with whom we could really collaborate.

We utilized a sling to lift and put me in a wheelchair, and after that laborious process, Maggie occasionally rolled me around the grounds. Many relatives, friends, acquaintances and company employees had been supportive throughout our ordeal, wanting to help in every way possible, but not knowing what to do.

I was determined to attend some of the National Tobacco Festival events, especially because I had been elected to lead the organization as President in 1973 — the twenty-fifth anniversary year. At the time, the Tobacco Festival was a huge, annual program for Richmond, drawing people from around the area as well as celebrities brought in from outside. It involved an entire week of events, beginning with a formal ball and including a fashion show, tours of tobacco companies, luncheons, and a parade. The week culminated with the Tobacco Bowl, a college football game at City Stadium. While I did not attend all the events, somehow I made an appearance at the main ones — the black-tie Grand Ball, the parade, and the Tobacco Bowl. Seeing me wheelchair-bound, people were curious but supportive. Most thought, as I did, that I would eventually recover.

Shortly after the festival, we received a call from the Rusk Institute informing us that a bed would be ready for my arrival on October fifteenth. Our immediate responsibilities were to accept the bed and to obtain from my doctors an official release from St. Mary's. What should have been a simple matter of paperwork became complicated because no doctor on the team — neither the neurosurgeon nor the neurologists — came forward to sign the release. Finally, Frank McGee, the young neurologist in practice with the others, agreed to sign the essential release papers despite the animosity this must have caused among his partners.

Perhaps the other doctors realized that if I entered another institution, truths might come out: that they had incorrectly read my myelogram on August fourth and subsequently had performed an unnecessary operation on my back. In fact, when the myelogram did arrive at Rusk Institute with my other records, the lower area was so smudged and unreadable that a new myelogram had to be performed. Maggie and I speculated on how it had come to be damaged.

Once we knew that I would be leaving for New York, Maggie and I felt strongly that our son Jack should be christened before my departure, so on October fourteenth, his christening took place at First Presbyterian Church. Maggie's mother hosted a luncheon in her garden for our friends and family, including out-of-town relatives. To be able to attend, I was lifted by sling and placed in a wheelchair that Maggie then pushed. It was a special occasion, but bittersweet.

On Monday, we went through the process of placing me in a wheelchair and preparing me for the flight on Eastern Airlines to Newark Airport. The assistant minister from First Presbyterian Church, Mac McCord, as well as my parents and aunt and uncle, were at Byrd Airport in Richmond to send us off. Baby Jack stayed with Maggie's mother.

When we arrived in Newark, airline personnel came to lift me from my seat, and in the process, they dropped me. The stitches from my back operation tore open in the fall. For me, it was an excruciating blunder that necessitated new stitches being inserted once I arrived at Rusk. Still more complications from the unnecessary operation.

An ambulance met us at the airport and drove us through New York City during lunch hour. Shortly after we had started on our way, the emergency medical technicians turned on the siren and lights as we zoomed along the street. An already unnerving situation became even more frantic. "What's going on?" we asked.

"Oh, it's time for lunch. We have to hurry so we can get something to eat!" they replied.

We arrived at Rusk Institute, and one of Dr. Henry Betts' associates met us there. She told us that very soon, in addition to undergoing extensive medical evaluations, I would begin working to gain self-reliance. These were the early, pioneer days of rehabilitative medicine, but the goal of facilitating patient independence was just as entrenched as it is today, and almost immediately, this new phase of recovery began.

The whole philosophy at Rusk Institute involved invigorating the patients to move and do things for themselves. I was given a wheelchair with a schedule taped to the arm, and, from the beginning, I was expected to adhere to the planned activities outlined there. No one worried about giving me time to adjust to my new surroundings. In the mornings, I would dress by myself, have breakfast, and then follow a regimen that kept me busy all day – boot camp style. At first, the tasks seemed daunting as I tried to accomplish what used to take little thought, the tasks that would ensure my self-reliance. There were sessions of physical therapy and occupational therapy, both of which focused on activities of daily living, and then to reinforce these sessions, there were exercises that I was expected to practice on my own. I plunged directly into the Institute's rigorous routine, or perhaps more accurately, it was thrust on me. I always understood the value of my rehabilitation, but that did not diminish my occasional feelings of frustration, helplessness and ineptitude. Meanwhile, my treatment in Richmond was evaluated, and in short order, all the medications and prescriptions from my Virginia doctors were unceremoniously tossed aside as useless or ineffective.

I underwent an elaborate series of tests, including some that were related to my mental health. My meetings with the psychologists did not go smoothly as I obstinately balked at their attempts at analyzing my state of mind. About the last thing I wanted was someone telling me how to feel or worse yet, telling me I was a screwball for feeling as I did.

Caregivers were very kind and supportive, but the routine at Rusk Institute was rigorous and exhausting. After the weeks of inactivity at St. Mary's, I was engulfed in a whole new universe with a completely unfamiliar approach. Every aspect of my care, no matter how difficult, was presented with confidence that I could meet the goals before me. Each day was devoted to the pursuit of self-reliance, and while I willingly worked hard, the total immersion in the rehabilitative schedule left me feeling more and more distanced from the world I once had known. It was as though I had entered another realm, where I was expected to strive tirelessly to accomplish the tasks at hand. There was little time to ponder what I had lost or how my life would evolve after Rusk Institute. I was consumed with maneuvering through the day-to-day activities that once had been so easy.

I eventually learned to drive using hand controls, but more, I learned to handle with complete independence the entire process of taking the wheel. True self-reliance came when I could transfer myself without assistance from the wheelchair into the car, could retrieve my wheelchair and store it in the backseat, and finally could drive without use of my feet. I remember calling my father and saying, "Guess what I'm doing today, Dad. I'm learning to drive!"

"Well, where are you?" he asked.

"I'm in New York City. I'm learning to drive on the streets of Manhattan."

He was flabbergasted.

By this time, it was becoming evident to Maggie and me that although the paralysis had receded, it was not going away. Emotionally and personally, that was a difficult reality to face. It was a crushing feeling to ponder life in a wheelchair, but I attempted to remain optimistic. By November, I was fortunate that my plumbing returned to normal function — an important progressive step.

Maggie stayed for a week at a time in New York, and between her stays she returned to Richmond to care for our son Jack. American Brands had a suite at the Berkeley Hotel on Forty-eighth Street, which they offered for her use while she was in New York. Because Rusk Institute was at Thirty-fourth Street, Maggie soon became familiar with subway routes between the hotel and the hospital. She had friends in New York City who visited me at Rusk. I even left the hospital for a few hours to spend Thanksgiving with thoughtful friends who invited me to Connecticut. Slowly but surely, I began regaining my strength and independence.

I hadn't been in New York very long before getting to know Dr. Howard Rusk himself. He was directly involved in my case and usually arrived at my room with a team of young doctors in tow — interns he was instructing. By mid-November, they had performed a second myelogram, but we still could obtain no diagnosis. Dr. Rusk enlisted the help of Dr. Ransohoff, head of neurosurgery at New York University. Dr. Ransohoff happened to be a friend of my father's best friend in Durham, Dr. Guy L. Odom — Dean of Neurosurgery at Duke University. With that connection linking us, Dr. Ransohoff began coming to my room every day, and, like Dr. Rusk, he was determined that I would fully recover and regain a vital life. These men were saintly in their dedication to my case.

Dr. Lauder, one of my physicians at Rusk, approached Maggie and me to discuss the reality that he and my other doctors continued to be confounded by my condition and were unable to make a clear diagnosis. He proposed another, complicated test that could be an important tool. "We are going to have to put electrical charges on your legs and body," he described. "It is a painful procedure, but we feel it is necessary to help us identify a diagnosis."

Maggie asked Dr. Lauder to allow her time to return to Richmond and glean any information possible from the Virginia state laboratory before he performed the test. Hoping that we could avoid the procedure, Dr. Lauder agreed. Returning home, Maggie went to work. She contacted Drs. Read McGehee and Frank McGee and explained the urgency in obtaining results from the state lab. They intervened and located my specimen, which had been stored in the locked area. The cultures clearly indicated poliomyelitis, and staff personnel were so surprised that they had repeated the test. The evidence and second test left no doubt. Immediately, the results were rushed to Rusk Institute, and by the time Maggie returned, they had broken the devastating news to me. It was a bitter pill to swallow, but at least we had an answer. At this time, the Richmond newspapers published an article pinpointing the diagnosis.

Later we would learn that tags on the first and second classifications had been clipped. Consequently, as far as the technician in the state lab could tell, there was no specimen at all for John Hager. Only because Drs. McGee and McGehee were granted access to the third specimen, which had been locked away as a safeguarded record, were we able to view the results. Though the specimen was weakened from time, the polio virus had grown.

At this point, Maggie and I realized it was highly unlikely that I would regain any further use of my legs -- a crushing blow. Still the medical people were exultant. Dr. Rusk encouraged me, "You are so lucky. You have something you can deal with. You don't have multiple sclerosis or a spinal cord injury. You are in great shape, and you are going to be able to go on and master this. Polio is not a debilitating disease."

"Lucky?" It didn't feel that way to me. At best, for Maggie and me it was a bad news/good news situation. Especially difficult to dismiss was the reality that if I had been correctly diagnosed from the beginning, I would have begun rehabilitative therapy earlier, and most likely, more muscles in my arms and legs would have regained function. The misdiagnosis and back surgery and then the ensuing complications, like gangrene and torn stitches, all made rehabilitative therapy difficult for long stretches of time. Sadly, much of my hospitalization in Richmond involved a struggle to learn the truth. Thank goodness for caring doctors who stepped forward, and thank goodness for Maggie's persistence.

With a diagnosis in hand, we began to unravel the mysteries of my exposure and subsequent infection. There were two polio vaccines available at this time in the United States. One was an oral vaccine with live polio virus that was developed by Albert Sabin. The other, the original — an injected vaccine with dead polio virus — was developed by Jonas Salk. Though the Salk vaccine predominated in the 1950s and had lowered the U.S. incidence of polio by some ninety-five percent, it fell out of favor due to the politics of treating large numbers of children "who would not take a needle shot." The Sabin vaccine, largely at the urging of the American Medical Association and because of the ease with which it could be administered, began to displace the Salk vaccine in the 1960s. Ominously, even as it gained usage, the Sabin vaccine became linked to new polio cases. Numerous studies indicated that the live vaccine itself was the principal, if not the sole, cause of all polio cases reported in the United States in the 1960s and '70s. Definitive studies conducted in Norway and Finland confirmed the danger of the Sabin vaccine. Still, the United States condoned the live-virus vaccine, and Pennsylvania went so far as to mandate its exclusive use in the state.

Just two weeks before I contracted polio, Jonas Salk had written an Op-Ed article in the *New York Times* in which he stated that more polio cases in the United States were caused by the Sabin vaccine through contact than by natural causes. The Sabin vaccine was perpetuating the disease. He predicted in his article that people like me, individuals who were healthy and in their mid-years would be struck by the disease because of the live-virus vaccine. And in fact, that is exactly what did happen, though many people were not lucky enough to be correctly diagnosed and treated. Despite evidence to the contrary, government agencies in the United States turned a blind eye to the dangers their policies imposed. The ease of administration in the inner city won out over caution. It was an epiphany to me that a political decision could be so destructive. That realization would later germinate into my active interest in politics.

In my case our son Jack, who was two months old, received a dose of the Sabin vaccine (which we learned later had excessive neuro-virulence) from his pediatrician, Dr. Gayle Arnold. Jack slept in the room with Maggie and me because it was the only place in our house with air conditioning, and during the night after his inoculation, he threw up excess of the vaccine he had received. Somehow, in cleaning up, I came in contact with the live virus at that time, and though it would be days before I felt the effects and months before I was diagnosed, in that dramatic moment my life turned upside down.

I had hardly come to terms with the diagnosis before The American Tobacco Company, which learned of my diagnosis shortly after I did, sent a representative to inform me that I should retire once my sick-leave compensation ended. There was not much sensitivity or finesse in the ultimatum. They recommended returning to Richmond, and by then most of my work had been transferred or was being reassigned to other employees. My career, which had soared to the top, suddenly plunged to the bottom! Financially, they had helped considerably. But the reality of my imposed retirement was devastating.

With this news, Maggie and a team from the Greenwich Hospital evaluated the house we had purchased just weeks earlier to determine whether it could be modified to accommodate my special needs. As they surveyed the possibilities, they concluded that it would be impossible to reconfigure the historic structure sufficiently to allow wheelchair access. Maggie and I had to face the truth that we would never live in the beautiful farmhouse we owned. It had been a real financial stretch for us to make the purchase, and now it was unlivable for me. We had no home anywhere.

These were dark days. Maggie and I had not yet been married for three years. The active, robust executive she had married was wheelchair-bound and jobless. Our son Jack, just seven months old, hardly knew his father. It had taken more than three months – 100 excruciating days – to receive a diagnosis, and we had to face the reality that polio had twisted our dreams and rearranged our lives.

Chapter 10

Picking Up The Pieces

It was Maggie who shouldered the task of locating an adequate place for us to live. She returned to Richmond and began searching, but nothing seemed to provide the space we needed, both for our family and for my wheelchair. Fortunately, our friend, Joe Stettinius, recommended the Berkshire Apartments at 300 West Franklin Street, and with two apartments on the twelfth floor available, Maggie signed short-term leases on both. We planned to store our belongings in one and set up housekeeping in the other large, very pleasant unit. Blessedly, at the Berkshire, we were reunited with Jack and returned to living as a family, albeit within the new-normal.

Our final goodbyes at Rusk Institute came on December 7, 1973 — a cold, damp, grey day — and together, we flew to Richmond. I had lost weight but gained strength in New York, and I soon began putting to use the life skills I had practiced. There were plenty of frustrations along the way as we grappled with the logistics of maneuvering a wheelchair around furniture and Jack's toys, to say nothing of a city that offered little accommodation for wheelchairs, and though these were often difficult and discouraging days, they were first steps in the process of functioning independently. Since the Berkshire was equipped with an elevator, I could navigate from the lobby to the twelfth floor, and I promptly mastered the challenge of driving into the basement garage, exiting my car and taking the elevator up. It was also wonderful to be with Jack, who was already showing his own little personality. Somehow we managed to make it through Christmas, and though it wasn't really jolly, it was important that we were together as a family. Slowly but surely, we were learning to cope with my being in a wheelchair and all the other changes involved.

My predominant feeling was that what was done, was done. The botched initial diagnosis and unnecessary surgery, the weeks languishing without having a confirmed name for what had crippled me – it was all in the past. More than anything, I wanted to move forward and beyond that history. While I was disappointed that American Tobacco did not restore my vice presidency, those feelings were tempered by the pervasive attitude of the time that physical limitations equaled diminished potential. American Tobacco was no different from most other business in its inability to look beyond a wheelchair. In the early seventies, there were no laws or policy statements protecting the rights of disabled individuals and no ready benefits for workers like myself. I was just thankful that despite having no legal obligation, the company had generously compensated me during my hospitalization, thus keeping my family from serious financial straits. The company had provided for much of my medical care and named me a consultant, with adequate salary to keep us afloat. It never occurred to me that I should sue for further benefits or seek government assistance to ease my plight. More than anything, I wanted to be self-reliant, and I was willing to work hard to achieve that goal.

The weeks of rehabilitation at Rusk Institute, with doctors and caregivers who were giants in their fields, were nothing short of a blessing. In Richmond, people continued to be supportive – family, friends, acquaintances, physical therapists and medical personnel. Whenever I felt disheartened, there always seemed to be someone who would offer encouragement.

I resumed physical therapy with Peggy Chappell, whom I called St. Peggy, and worked with her three days a week at St. Mary's Hospital. With total confidence in this remarkable woman who had diagnosed my illness months before anyone else, I embraced a rigorous schedule, which consumed a great deal of time but further strengthened my body. Whether during this period I was still holding out hope to walk again, who knows?

Peggy's training and strength building exercises enabled me to begin the strenuous process of "walking" on crutches. With long leg braces and my weight supported on crutches, I could swing my legs and propel myself forward. The motion was precarious and depended on my maintaining balance on the crutches while bearing the weight of my body on them, so there was an ever-present danger of falling. The reward was the pleasure of standing upright and moving forward with motion that resembled walking.

Sometime after Christmas, I received a visit from a wonderful gentleman, O. D. Dennis, who owned Dennis Oil Company in Richmond. Years earlier, he too had been stricken by polio, and the disease had left him using crutches. When he learned of my situation, O.D. tried to encourage me, "Oh, you will be fine. The only thing you have to remember is to take care of yourself. Take a nap every day and stay healthy."

After he left, I tried to picture myself taking naps. I had always been the one whose stamina was the envy of the group, the one who could out-last and out-perform the competition. *Enough of this crap!* I thought. *I will never again take a nap. Wheelchair or not, I'm going to charge ahead full blast.*

It was a turnaround moment. From that day forward, involvement was the name of the game! If American Tobacco wouldn't restore the title of vice president, then the search was on for other meaningful ways to contribute, either within the company or elsewhere. Having always held the philosophy that it is better to be part of the action than to sit back and watch, I would not change my outlook because of a wheelchair. Active involvement became my mantra, and while the laborious recovery process continued for several years, and surely there were ups and downs, I resolved that instead of settling into a sedentary life – naps included – I would be, as I always had been, a doer and not an observer. This strong impetus to regain an active, contributing lifestyle began on that winter day in 1974 and never diminished.

The news out of New York was mostly silent, but at least with my forced retirement in January 1974 and the company's engaging my services as a consultant, I retained a lifeline that loosely tethered me to the company. The position was ill-defined and involved little real responsibility, but I viewed it as the first step in the process of salvaging my career.

I started a routine of going into the American Tobacco offices at Bermuda Hundred three days a week, riding with Ed Martin, who also lived in the Berkshire Apartments. Gradually, I began catching back up on company news and interacting with old associates. I even did some projects with packaging and research, though my work didn't come close to involving the same intensity or importance as the responsibilities I had manned before.

While company officials had forced me into retirement, they had a hard time ignoring my willingness to contribute whenever possible with genuine effort and hard work. I never turned down any sort of project, no matter how insignificant or how inconvenient it might have been. In fact, when offered the opportunity, Maggie and I drove to New York seven different times so I could work on various assignments with company lawyers. That sort of independence, tenacity and involvement was difficult to dismiss.

In August 1974, I officially resumed full-time work at Bermuda Hundred with the title, Coordinator-Leaf, another ill-defined position, but one that involved interesting assignments as I worked with research and development, consulted with the legal department, and coordinated with people in tobacco buying, tobacco processing and at the reconstituted tobacco plant. The job would evolve over several years as I helped shape the responsibilities.

Over time, my work became focused on computer operations and information technology so that while I was not exactly an IT Department, I was able to highlight the necessity of adopting company-wide technological systems into our operations. I became the bridge between the technical experts in New York and the local operating experts, who would eventually benefit from the inclusion of technology in various processes at our plants. I also assumed an advisory role for some of our subsidiaries, one of which was Golden Belt Manufacturing Company, located in Durham, and began working some with The American Tobacco Company of the Orient. In conjunction with company lawyers at Chadbourne and Parke in New York City, I extensively supported preparations for some class action leaf lawsuits that the company faced. This legal involvement provided my first exposure to government agencies in Washington as we met with the Department of Agriculture and others on numerous occasions.

Mine was an odd-ball assortment of duties and projects that needed to be done. Someone had to do these things, and from my standpoint, the important aspect was that I had returned to a schedule of working every day and could utilize my skills. Gradually, people within the company realized that I could again handle responsibilities and be trusted with important decisions. I retained the title, Coordinator-Leaf until August 1982, when I was named Leaf Services Director, a much higher title. This promotion entailed a heavier workload that involved extensive duties with the overall leaf work and the coordination of operations. Additionally, during this period, I became more involved with labor negotiations. It was good to be back at work on a daily basis, to see that colleagues were regaining confidence in my role and to feel the trust and respect that fol-

Family in golf cart, 1981.

lowed. Unlike the early days, however, there was balance so that my devotion to company work did not preclude family time.

In the spring of 1975, Maggie and I attended the wedding of her good friend, Flossie Bryan. In the course of the festivities, Flossie asked where we were living, and when we told her, she immediately declared, "You should move into my house at 325 Charmian Road! I don't want to sell it, but I'm moving to Maryland, and I'd love for you to live there. It is modern and almost all on one floor."

We were carrying a month-to-month lease at the Berkshire Apartments, easy enough to terminate, so Maggie and I went that very day to see the house on Charmian Road. It seemed ideal, so much so that we signed the rental papers on Flossie's wedding day and moved in that June. The contemporary house was situated near the canal in Hillcrest, provided a view of the James River and had a nearby pond with great potential. Its single story design proved very wheelchair-friendly, with little modification. While we were grateful to be in a real home and pleased with the location and design, Maggie and I never would have guessed that we would continue to rent Flossie's Charmian Road house for nearly nine years — until April 1984.

My mother-in-law purchased a used golf cart for us to drive around the neighborhood, and it provided wonderful freedom for me and a way to meet and stay in touch with our neighbors. I coordinated with Dr. William Higgins to form the Hillcrest Association, and through that group we successfully organized some collective action on behalf of our neighborhood. I continued walking with my braces and crutches around the quiet Hillcrest streets. While there was always the possibility of a fall, it was great exercise and allowed me to gain strength and agility. In an odd twist, someone stole my wheelchair one day while I was walking down Charmian Road. Enraged at the injustice of such a thing, Maggie's mother ran a reward ad in the newspaper, and surprisingly, it was returned.

Our second son, Henry Chase Hager, was born on May 9, 1978, and quickly took his place as an exciting addition to our family. Maggie's pregnancy was difficult, and at one point her Richmond obstetrician, Hudnall Ware, recommended that she be seen by a specialist at the University of Virginia. In September 1977, Maggie underwent an amniocentesis at the University Hospital, at which time the attending physician assured her he would call if any problems were identified. Hearing nothing, we assumed that all was well until five days before Christmas when we received a call saying we needed to schedule an appointment to discuss the negative test results that could warrant an abortion. The pall of that impending appointment hung over our Christmas holiday, and on January third, Maggie and I drove to Charlottesville together, where the doctor informed us of abnormalities with the amniotic fluid. His recommendation was that Maggie should abort the pregnancy. Of course we were stunned but insisted that we be shown the records. We needed to see all the specifics, and as I studied them, I realized that something was amiss. A careful review with the doctor soon revealed that Maggie's samples had been confused with those of another patient. We could relax with the knowledge that all was progressing normally with her pregnancy. What an experience!

Again as with Jack's birth, Maggie experienced difficulties with the delivery. I remember our entering the hospital around 1:30 p.m., and since those were the days before fathers were allowed to be present for the birth, I was directed to a waiting room as Maggie was wheeled into delivery. Worried and alone, I shuffled through papers in my briefcase for a very long time. There was no news until nearly dawn when a nurse came and said, "You have a beautiful baby boy."

"What about my wife?" was the anxious question.

There was a sort of silence. Maggie was still in the operating room where they had been working on her for hours after a difficult caesarean. I resumed my solitary vigil in the waiting room and hoped for further updates. The one solace was an occasional walk to the nursery where our newborn son slept peacefully. Hours passed before news finally came that Maggie was being transferred to recovery. She had made it though! Her stay at St. Mary's Hospital was long, and even when she finally was released, Maggie faced a tough period of recuperation at home. Fortunately, we had engaged a baby nurse to help us.

Following Henry's birth, Maggie began experiencing eye infections and stomach problems. In the second week of June, she went back to St. Mary's Hospital for a round of x-rays to evaluate the success of bladder surgery which had been performed by Dr. William Atwell at the time of Henry's birth. In each x-ray was a white line which Dr. Atwell correctly diagnosed as a needle. The obstetric doctors were called in, and they also concluded that a needle had rolled into Maggie's abdomen during the post-birth surgery. Nervously, the whole team of doctors gathered together and told me the news. Emergency surgery would need to be performed, and there was no time to waste. In fact, they wanted to operate within twenty-four hours.

At that point, plans shifted into high gear. We were allowed to select our surgeons and hospital but were urged to waste no time in taking action. We chose Dr. Armistead Talman and Dr. Tom Daniel to perform Maggie's operation at Chippenham Hospital. Risks were high, and prior to the surgery, we were warned that because her body had been so excessively traumatized by the bladder operation and caesarean, there was a fifty percent chance that Maggie might not survive the impending surgery. There also was the unsettling possibility that the surgeons would not be able to find the needle. Amidst all the turmoil and emotion, the most difficult part for Maggie was finding nursing care for our boys and then saying good-bye to Jack and Henry. Thanks to the skills of Armistead Talman and Tom Daniel, the surgery went smoothly, the needle was extracted and Maggie began the slow process of recovery, first with a ten-day hospitalization and then a period of restricted activity at home.

As Maggie and I resumed the new normal of our lives, people in Richmond reached out and were supportive and friendly. The wheelchair was an impediment but didn't stop us. Gradually, we took on more of a social life and became involved in the community. Friends graciously invited us to their homes, and in turn, we began reciprocating. Maggie and I joined the Richmond Assembly, a dance group which we enjoyed. I remember attending a function at the Commonwealth Club and thinking that maybe membership there would be a possibility some day. In these early stages of recovery, I would have been surprised to know that I would not only join that distinguished club in January 1979, but later I would serve on its board. Active involvement has continued now for nearly four decades.

We attended First Presbyterian Church, which I had joined during my first move to Richmond, and Henry was baptized there in October. Pursuing an active role, I served as a Deacon at First Presbyterian from 1977-1980 and then as Chairman of the Board of Deacons. I chaired the New Church Committee for the formation of Gayton Kirk in Henrico County, and I led our Every Member Canvas. After completing these responsibilities, I continued a leadership role as a Ruling Elder, learning to serve communion and collect offering, making my way up and down the tight rows of the sanctuary. It involved rolling my wheelchair with one hand, while with my other hand, holding communion juice or balancing the collection plate in my lap. It may have been divine intervention, but I never dropped a plate. The years have found us continuing active membership there, and presently we have an electrifying new interim minister, Steve Eason.

Each of our sons in turn went to First Presbyterian Nursery School and kindergarten, then on to St. Christopher's School. One advantage of my reduced work pressure was that I had time to enjoy their growing-up years. When Henry was about three years old, Maggie and the boys began going to the West Chop community in Martha's Vineyard and spending several enjoyable weeks each summer at her mother's home there. I

John meeting Rowan and Martin at airport.

usually limited my stay to about a week, as I found the travel to and from West Chop to be difficult and the family home hard to navigate. We still go back every summer, and I especially enjoy the opportunities to go fishing with Charlie Ashmun. I presently am a member of the Board of Directors of the West Chop Club, an active place with a storied history. As a family, we have spent many successful vacations there, and thankfully we continue to do so and can pass it on to Jack and Henry for their families.

Up until this readjustment period, the only volunteer responsibilities I had assumed were with the National Tobacco Festival, for which I was a director for many years and President in 1973. We used to enjoy the many activities associated with the festival and stayed in touch with the queens from each year. I fondly remember the 1970 National Tobacco Festival, when American Tobacco sponsored as Grand Marshals the Rowan and Martin comedian team, whose television show at the time was top-rated. We booked their accommodations at the now-defunct Executive Motel on Broad Street, and when Dick Martin's girlfriend stayed in his room instead of the one reserved for her, I spent the night at the motel in the room she left vacant. It was a lucky change of plans because the entertainers kept late nights, and I had to be sure they were in attendance when they were on the schedule, sometimes early in the mornings. After all the festivities were over Saturday night, we breathed a sigh of relief that they had gone smoothly, and we delivered our celebrities to their private jet at Byrd Field for the return trip to California. In a final gesture, Dan Rowan pulled out his red handkerchief and threw it to me. I have kept it all these years and still use it for black tie functions – a humorous reminder of the comedian. In the early years, the National Tobacco Festival included a college football game played at City Stadium, but over time the universities realized they were missing a significant economic potential by not holding games on their own campuses. Eventually, larger stadiums and economics, more than political correctness, led to the demise of the festival a few years later.

Because the University of Virginia's basketball team was enjoying great success in the late seventies and early eighties, I began to take an interest in the Cavaliers' games. This was the Ralph Sampson era, and amid all the excitement, I decided it would be fun to start attending the games. My good friends Vinny Giles and Johnny Siewers, both of whom had been great athletes at the University of Virginia, helped me secure first one and then two season tickets. Beginning in 1980, It was a treat to attend nearly all the Charlottesville games with the Siewers, and we shared the thrill of the ACC tournaments, including 1981's when UVA won the ACC Regular Season Championship. At one time, Jack was with me for the tournament in Atlanta and other years the entire family went to to tournaments held in Landover, Maryland, and to Greensboro, North Carolina. I thoroughly enjoyed the games and the success the Cavaliers earned and stayed involved with Virginia basketball for several years — until my schedule grew so busy in the late eighties that we dropped the tickets.

I took advantage of any opportunity within local civic groups, nonprofits and other organizations to assume leadership roles, through which I could make a positive impact. One of my first significant charitable ventures began when I was called and asked to be a director of Crippled Children's Hospital -- a name several of us set out to change. During my tenure on the board, we removed the adjective "crippled," which led to the present name, Children's Hospital. In the early eighties, I served as President and we were early with the push to consolidate pediatric facilities in the Richmond area. Around the same time, I became a director of Maymont Foundation and also served as the group's president. My service at Maymont was particularly satisfying because our boys participated in many activities there.

Career-wise, it was painfully obvi-

Children's Hospital Ball.

ous that I was in the midst of reinvention. Polio had left its mark, and as it would have been for anyone, it was hard for me to get used to being in a wheelchair. The goal from the beginning was to act professionally enough in a normal manner to make the wheelchair disappear. Gradually familiarity gains acceptance.

For a while, Maggie and I continued to hold out hope of eventually returning to New York, but as it became clear that I would never be the great powerhouse in New York City that we had once envisioned, we realized the futility of hanging onto our house in Greenwich. During most of the three years since the purchase, we had managed to keep it rented, but finally we sold it to the renters. Unfortunately, the sale came during the severe real estate recession of the early eighties, and our sale price came just short of the purchase price. Actually considering the real estate bust of the time, we were fortunate to suffer only minimal loss, but you should see the house today! Goodness knows the value, as it has increased by several times. I joke that I am the only person who has ever lost money on Greenwich, Connecticut real estate.

As our lives stabilized, we started having contact with Dr. Jonas Salk. He urged me to sue Lederle Laboratories, part of the American Cyanamid Company and the pharmaceutical company that manufactured the live Sabin polio vaccine. Salk promised to be a witness, and he assured me that winning a suit would be a lock, particularly as we learned that the lot of vaccine from which Jack's dose was drawn contained excessive neuro-virulence. The idea of a huge trial was repugnant to me, so I kept dragging my feet. I didn't like the concept of suing, and I was anxious to live my life without further disruptions and distractions. Furthermore, I was reluctant to be thrown in the limelight and unsure how American Tobacco would respond to such litigation, especially since the company itself was involved so often in lawsuits at this time. More than anything, I just wanted to get my life back.

For legal advice, I consulted good friends, including Rosewell Page at McGuire-Woods, and hired his associate, Jim Sanderling, to pursue the case. Jim became very interested in the ramifications and consulted regularly with Jonas Salk, who flew to Richmond once to work directly with him. Salk was vigorous in his involvement and eager to defend what was, after all, his life's work. He saw me as his ticket to redemption and urged me to pursue the lawsuit. While I had no desire to be embroiled in the publicity or newspaper coverage that would surely accompany litigation, I did strike a compromise and agreed to allow the lawyers to prepare a suit and

John with Jonas Salk and Francoise Gilot.

make inquiries to measure the drug company's response to threatened legal action. We eventually convinced Lederle Laboratories that our primary motive was to effect changes in the way they marketed their vaccine and directed its use. With a more cooperative tone than Salk had hoped to see, we warned Lederle that any refusal to change the company's approach and practices would most likely result in a lawsuit.

After our lawyers had amassed almost two years of elaborate research and inquiry and were prepared for a lawsuit, Judge Robert R. Merhrige, Jr. allowed us to meet in his private chambers prior to public notice of our filing. At that time, Lederle Laboratories agreed to pay my medical, legal and other expenses and to change their informational insert to delineate the potential dangers inherent in the live polio vaccine. Even without protracted legal action, we successfully forced positive change. The settlement amounted to a fraction of what a suit would have brought, less than a half million dollars total, but it was sufficient to pay the lawyers at McGuire Woods, to cover most medical expenses American Tobacco had not paid, to send a contribution to the Salk Institute and to provide a bit of security for my family. Everyone left happy except Jonas Salk, who continued to harbor the belief that if we didn't hit Lederle hard, they would never really change their practices. Later, Maggie and I enjoyed a memorable visit with Salk in La Jolla, California, where he lived with his wife, Francoise Gilot, formerly Pablo Picasso's mistress. Jonas Salk was a true giant of a man, and it was a privilege to have personally known him.

My father encouraged me to become a member of the Juniper Club in Florida, a hunting and fishing club which originally had been formed by a group of businessmen from Louisville. My grandfather was one of the original members, and then later, my father and uncle became members, so mine was a third generation membership. I took Jack and Henry to Juniper a couple of times to "family camp" when they were old enough, and they loved it. The club is located on a beautiful site along Juniper Creek, which flows into Lake George, and continues to thrive even today, with an influx of younger members mostly from Louisville. I began to go to the club regularly for a week in 1975 and 1976, sharing the vacations with my father. He seemed to enjoy seeing that despite being in a wheelchair, his son was up to the travel and could participate in the club's activities. Later, the Juniper Club made me an honorary member, and for a time, I hardly used the membership, but I did return in 2011 and 2012 and was made the "Captain of the Hunt" in 2012. On the occasion of my induction as Captain, I had Beam, an American Brands company, prepare special Knob Creek bourbon bottles with members' names on the labels of each fifth. In keeping with the club's tradition, as "Captain of the Hunt," my name was inscribed on one of the bricks that comprised the clubhouse's brick chimney. Looming above the huge fireplace, the chimney now has four Hager names painted on individual bricks as previous "Captains" – grandfather, father, uncle and mine. The book, Juniper-That's Me, covers the history of the club.

My first civic membership was with the Metro Richmond Chamber of Commerce, where I served as company representative for American Tobacco and went on to join the board in 1978. In conjunction with my participation with the Chamber, I was invited to the White House by President Jimmy Carter, the only time I received an invitation

John and Maggie at the White House.

via Western Union. This fascinating opportunity involved a briefing with the Secretary of Defense on Strategic Arms Limitation Talks (SALT). On October 4, 1979, I drove to Washington, parked on the front lawn as instructed, and entered the White House, proceeding to the East Room to join a relatively small group that had been assembled. The presentation was interesting, and then President Carter, who proved to be more impressive in person than on television, spoke to the assembled attendees.

Little did I imagine that in the ensuing years I would return to the White House numerous times for a variety of meetings and special occasions. Each White House memory is distinct in its own way. During Ronald Reagan's administration in the eighties, Susan Magill, Senator John Warner's chief of staff, invited my family to watch Fourth of July fireworks from the White House lawn. When George H. W. Bush signed the Americans with Disabilities Act on July 15, 1990, Maggie, our son Henry and I had the privilege of sitting up front and witnessing the legislation become law. During the years 1998-2001 as I served as Virginia's Lieutenant Governor, there were meetings and receptions at the White House. As a response to 9/11, an extraordinary meeting to discuss Homeland Security with state representatives and Tom Ridge took place in March 2001, and later more meetings followed. During my service at the Department of Education, numerous sessions convened in the White House complex.

While Henry worked in the White House, first as a volunteer in late 2001 and then full-time in Karl Rove's office, Maggie and I had opportunities to visit. We were there on occasions after Henry and Jenna Bush, daughter of Laura and George W. Bush, became engaged and were married. During the summer of 2008 after the wedding, the Bushes included us as hosts at the White House for a large reception that proved to be a joyous and memorable occasion. We also were invited to attend a notable dinner for President Sarkozy of France and an evening celebration of Ben Franklin. One particularly memorable reception at the White House occurred when Maggie and I were honored to host a reception for the Richmond Symphony. We attended several Christmas Open House events, a festive and light-hearted gathering. There is no doubt that it was a sad day when the Republicans lost the November 2008 election (also ending our White House days for the foreseeable future).

On the home-front in Richmond, an invitation came in 1978 to join the Forum Club, a distinguished Richmond group which formed from the old Douglas Southall Freeman Debating Society. For several years I served as assistant to the secretary-treasurer, Hoke Palmer, who was a magnificent person and taught me a great deal. My year as program chairman was highlighted by having Jacques Cousteau as the speaker in front of a huge crowd on February 17, 1986. The next year I became president and in later years, was a speaker on at least two occasions. Over the years, the Forum Club has expanded its membership and presently hosts a dinner and speaker on the third Monday night of every month except in the summer. When joining, I was the youngest member; today, I am among the oldest, and throughout the nearly forty years of my membership I have found the Forum Club to be a great vehicle through which to meet and work with a broad range of community leaders. Plans are underway for the 100th Anniversary in 2018.

I started becoming involved with several other organizations that were affiliated with the Greater Richmond Chamber of Commerce. In late 1979 Tom Bliley, who was Richmond's mayor at the time, called together a group of Chamber directors and we founded Leadership Metro Richmond. This group seeks to nurture an understanding of local needs and to build bridges of communication among various segments of the community. I was a director of this group, starting in 1980 and then chairman for two years, beginning in 1982 — a somewhat rocky time to head the fledgling group. In those early years, it seemed uncertain whether or not Leadership Metro Richmond could survive, but survive it did, and its influence continues to permeate issues in the greater metro area. Presently, some thirty-five years after its inception, I remain the only person who has ever held that chairmanship for more than one year.

In 1984-85, I served as chairman of the Metropolitan Foundation, now named the Greater Richmond Chamber Foundation. Also in 1984, I became involved with a group called CONTOUR. This group later became the Metropolitan Richmond Convention and Visitors Bureau and presently calls itself Richmond Region Tourism. I joined them for their first meeting, and as of this year I have served on their board for thirty-three years, currently Honored Past Chairman. A great relationship has formed with Jack Berry, President and CEO of Richmond Region Tourism, and the very capable staff.

In late 1984, after my significant involvement with the Richmond Chamber of Commerce, I was asked to accept a place as fifth in line for succession to the chairmanship,

John's parents with him at Greater Richmond Chamber of Commerce dinner to honor John's chairmanship.

which meant assuming the top leadership role in five years. On that basis, American Tobacco approved my progressive involvement. Then the unexpected happened. Over the next twelve months, all four directors who preceded me in succession resigned, each with a valid reason: Bill Berry became chairman of Dominion Power; Gene James of Southern States became president of their national trade association; George Yowell became president of a bank in Tennessee, and Dick Wright moved his insurance business to North Carolina.

There I was, as unlikely as it had seemed, the next chairman of the Chamber. I relished the challenge to take the reins and make a positive impact. When I assumed the chairmanship, the headquarters building on Franklin Street was in the midst of renovations, and the staff was working in temporary quarters with no date in sight for returning to their offices. In fact, the building project had stalled and seemed to be floundering. I realized that our first priority should be the completion of office upgrades so that the staff could work in respectable conditions. We set Labor Day as the deadline for concluding the renovations and avowed that we were going to get rolling whether or not the building was ready. Happily, we didn't have to test our resolve – work was finished in time for the move by our deadline, and the program year commenced without further disruption. The Executive Director, Paul Ellsworth, and I hit it off from the start, and we enjoyed a full and involved time together. Elizabeth Dole came for the annual dinner and capped

Richmond Marathon

off the huge year. Interestingly, American Tobacco had begun by this time to see the value of civic engagement, which became one of the paths by which I proved my value.

In the early nineties, I also joined the boards of the Virginia Chamber of Commerce and the Urban Partnership. The Urban Partnership was an organization which grew out of the state Chamber and worked actively to promote cooperative city-county relations throughout Virginia. My varied experiences in these groups, including travel around the state, would later serve me well as I stepped into the political arena.

Despite my involvement in these many activities, my life continued to be somewhat restless. I had been exercising by walking with crutches, but around 1988 I became attracted to the Richmond Marathon. I decided to enter the wheelchair division, and with an old modified wheelchair, I completed five miles my first year. This first race began in downtown Richmond and set off on an uphill climb - from Shockoe Bottom up Cary Street to Ninth Street and then up Main. It was sheer determination that got me to the summit.

From then on, I concentrated on wheelchair racing most of the year rather than exercising with my crutches. Not long after that first race, I bought a true racing wheelchair, and ultimately I completed thirteen Richmond Marathons over that many years, three Marine Corps Marathons in Washington D.C. and an untold number of shorter races. The toughest wheelchair racing I ever completed was the Marine Corps Marathon's last half mile, a straight uphill climb that ends at the Iwo Jima Monument, a real endurance test at the end of a 26.3 miles. Over the course of my marathoning, I had three or four different racing wheelchairs, and I found that like racecars, a new improved model comes on the market every year.

My good friend Jim Moncure trained with me on a regular basis. We began meeting in the late 1980s at First Presbyterian Church's parking lot, and he would run while I did the course in my wheelchair. With my first and only slightly modified wheelchair, Jim was always in the lead. Then I bought a better race model, and I caught up with him. He started riding a bike, and once again, I was left behind until I gradually gained speed and managed to catch up with him again. Pushing each other to excel, we participated in the Olympic Torch Run through Richmond and many specialty races. We enjoyed several good years of training together before Jim passed away in 1998. So many people had noted his attachment and dedication to my effort, and his death was a real tragedy for me.

Getting my feet wet through the array of nonprofit, volunteer and civic activities, I gained experience and confidence and assumed leadership positions in many of them. I joined the board of the Virginia Institute of Political Leadership, now known as the Sorenson Institute at the University of Virginia. Upon returning from Washington in 2008, I rejoined the board of that group and was elected chairman, an office still held today. Involvement with the Westhampton Citizens Association resulted in my becoming a director and later president of that group. In the early eighties, I began my first round on the board at the Country Club of Virginia. I could no longer play golf, but back in the 1970s I had joined the Knockers, a golf group that holds outings and dinners that are interesting and enjoyable. We "graduated" from the Richmond Assembly and began attending the Richmond Hundred's dances and also joined the Richmond German. Both groups have fine events.

In many ways, since my political ambitions grew as I participated in various committees and boards and recognized that they could be effective mediums for action and change, these civic and volunteer groups were the genesis of my reinvention and political involvement. In the late 1970s, several influential Republicans — including Dick Short, Bill Royall, and others — met with me at the Downtown Club in Richmond to urge me to run for the General Assembly. Basically, the prospect of running for political office scared me, but I agreed to become involved. After seeing how politicians had manipulated the truth about the Sabin polio vaccine, I was drawn to the possibility of helping to shape responsibility and honesty in the political arena.

I had long been a Republican, as were my parents before me. We thought in terms of freedom and free enterprise and considered Republicans the more supportive Party for business. The Party's tendency to favor less government and more regulation through the marketplace corresponded to my own business interests. I always had the feeling that we are responsible for our own fate and that government should not be expected to financially safeguard individuals. Self reliance and self determination came to the forefront in my life during my struggles with polio and I saw the Republican Party aligned with those values. In fact, since I supported all the basic tenants that the Party espoused - lower taxes, budgetary restraints, faith in God, support of the Second Amendment, a pro life agenda, and backing of the right to work - I had no problem supporting Republican candidates. I recalled Ronald Reagan's quote, "If you support me 90% of the time, you are 90% my friend, not 10% my enemy!"

I called the chairman of the Richmond Republican City Committee, Bo Moore, and asked if I could join the organization. I'll never forget his less than encouraging response, "Well, we're full right now. I'll call you when we have an opening." Can you imagine such a response today?

That might have daunted my enthusiasm, but it wasn't long before he called, and I began attending Richmond Republican City Committee meetings. I volunteered to be a precinct captain, an alternate to the District Committee and proxy to the State Central Committee, which is the governing body of the Republican Party in Virginia. One thing leads to another, especially in politics, and as I met people and attended more events and conventions, my colleagues gained confidence in my abilities and several opportunities developed. In 1978, I attended the Republican Third District Committee meetings, serving as vice-chairman. Next it was a run for the State Central Committee, which was successful. In 1980, I boldly ran to be an alternate delegate to my first Republican National Convention and was elected.

In July, I flew by chartered flight with the other Republican delegates from Virginia to the National Convention in Detroit, where we stayed in a hotel quite a long way outside the city. Governor John Dalton and his wife Eddy had arranged for their car to be brought up for the stay, and as they were fond of me and aware of the complications a bus ride would entail, they invited me to join them in their car for the drive each night to the Joe Louis Arena. That was a real convenience because it saved me the twenty-five-or-so-mile bus commute from our hotel.

This was the electrifying convention when Ronald Reagan was nominated as the Republican candidate for President. No one knew who would be nominated for Vice President, but all the delegates thought they would have something to do with the choice. In truth, they probably had no say in the final selection of George H. W. Bush, but it all made for a rousing week. It was especially exciting to meet Ronald Reagan, an opportunity that stemmed from his daughter Maureen, whom I had come to know in Richmond at our state convention activities earlier in the year.

Every night when we adjourned, the Virginia delegation returned to the hotel and gathered for a large buffet dinner. The nightly gatherings were all very convivial, so different from today's political animosity. One of the delegates was Senator John Warner, who was married at the time to Elizabeth Taylor, though their marriage was beginning a downward slide that eventually would lead to a divorce. John chose to stay downtown to attend to "official business," while Elizabeth Taylor returned to dine and schmooze with the rest of the delegation. She enjoyed cocktail hour, replete with mixed drinks and wine, and when it came time for her to call it a night, the job always fell to me. She wouldn't ignore final call from a man in a wheelchair, so I would have to remind her that the bar was closed and be sure she found her way back to her room. It was always a bit of a relief when I had successfully herded her "home" and heard the lock latch on her closed door. It was pretty rare in those days to be a normal, active convention participant in a wheelchair, but one other delegate, John East, who was a rising star and soon to become a U.S. Senator from North Carolina, was also wheelchair bound. Everywhere I went, people thought I was John East, not John Hager, so I became popular with the media and accessed several special events. Why not? It was a chance to live and learn and be a real part of something big.

I observed a great deal about wheeling and dealing from my roommate, Bob Patterson. Conventions were old hat to him, and he knew how to take the pain out of the lengthy sessions. "I have a plan," he told me. "Meet me outside the arena when you arrive."

Once I had pulled up to the arena in the Daltons' car, I would search him out, and Bob would proceed with his scheme. He would stealthily tape a bottle of Scotch under my wheelchair and roll me onto the convention floor. Security was pretty lax in those days and no one suspected me of any shenanigans, so thanks to his smuggled Scotch, Bob managed to provide libations for the Virginia delegation and anyone else he was courting.

After returning from the National Convention, I wrote a guest column for *The Richmond News Leader* on October 24, 1980, in which I attempted to give what I termed an "Insider's View of a National Political Convention." I explained that I saw the convention as a way to help make things happen, rather than to be just a spectator watching events unfold. I also described the process of forming a platform, selecting candidates to run for President and Vice President, and offering a forum for diverse views. I tried to describe the variety of participants and the interplay of those in attendance. Whether "a governor, an alternate, or a guest in the balcony," each person was able to contribute, and an atmosphere of respect dominated the proceedings. Finally, I described the tradition of the convention process and changes that emerge from a national convention. My participation there had been very special, and the political maneuverings that unfolded there were instructive. It has been my honor to attend every Republican National Convention that has been held since 1980 with the single exception of New Orleans in 1988. Of course, politics has changed, and in the 2016 State Convention, several of us "establishment" types were left off the delegate slate.

One interesting tidbit from my early political involvement occurred in December of 1981, when I was attending the Advance, the Republican Party of Virginia's annual "retreat" in Staunton. The major decision at hand was how the nominee for U.S. Senator would be determined the next year when Virginia's long-time Senator, Harry F. Byrd, Jr. was resigning. We were working for Paul Trible, who was aiming for the nomination, and during the Advance, I received a phone call in the middle of the night and was told that I had been chosen to present a proposal that the candidate should be selected by a primary vote rather than a convention nomination. Thrust into the political limelight, I felt redoubled pressure when I was told the proposal needed to be made as part of a plan at the State Central meeting early the next morning.

I prepared the presentation, and it was exciting to see a positive reception. Our side carried the day and won the vote that year, but interestingly, Virginia's politicians are still arguing the same question as to whether candidates should be chosen by a primary or a convention. It is a thorny issue since primaries can involve so many citizens – those who have strong feelings and opinions and those who casually exercise their right to vote. Conventions, on the other hand, require a willingness to travel to the site, which at least for some of the delegates can be considerable distance, as well as a willingness to participate for however long the convention convenes. Consequently, the only individuals who agree to be delegates are those with strong commitments to a cause or candidate.

All too often, conventions are dominated by activists and special-interest groups, especially diehards who are willing to show up with their own agendas, disrupt the status quo and drag out the proceedings. Then when election time rolls around, they don't follow through and advance their candidate to a win. Later, I would personally feel the sting of such maneuvers.

But here in 1981, I was just beginning to test political waters. Through participation in the national, district and state conventions, the Advance, countless fundraisers and committee meetings, I had caught the bug and become immersed in politics. In 1982, the chairman of the Richmond City Committee, Dave Johnson, asked my permission to enter my name as one of three candidates for the Richmond City Electoral Board, a group that runs elections in the city. He warned me, however, that though he was required to submit three names, I would most likely not be selected because there was someone else whom the city leaders supported. On that basis, I agreed to have my name submitted to help him, but since the odd offer didn't hold much chance for coming to fruition, I didn't think about it again until weeks later when I received a call from the City of Richmond Registrar, Alice Lynch.

"You were named by the judges to the Electoral Board, but they are taking back your selection," Alice fumed.

"Who are *they*?" I asked.

"The bureaucrats," she told me. "The 'in' crowd at City Hall wants the position. You were rightfully selected, but they're taking away your appointment. We're upset in the office because we believe you would be a great member, and it is just not fair what they're doing. It's downright wrong."

I didn't know how to react to such a situation, but I called Rosewell Page, my lawyer friend, and asked him to delve into the proceedings. When he got back to me, he corroborated Alice Lynch's version of events. "You were selected. No amount of politics can change that. Your name was one of three submitted on a list, and you were chosen by merit. You should call the judges and inform them of the turn of events."

The situation had turned into a real curiosity because being a member of the Electoral Board was a position I did not seek, did not expect to have, and did not anticipate ever doing. But once they took it away from me, I bristled. "Hey, wait a minute," I thought, "not so fast. Maybe I will serve on the Electoral Board, and that will be another great learning experience."

As it turned out, after some fits and starts I did assume my rightful position on the board. I replaced a good friend, Clarence Townes, who had decided to resign after serving for two terms.

Clarence and I had met years earlier, in April of 1968, shortly after Martin Luther

King was shot. At the time, I was Assistant to the Director of Manufacturing at American Tobacco with my office at Virginia Branch. The company feared that in response to King's assassination, riots would break out around Richmond that Saturday night, and as a precaution, extra security, which I oversaw, was put into place. We felt that we were ready for whatever might happen, and we remained vigilant during the night, but thankfully, the factory vicinity was without incident. Apparently, the action in Richmond was up on Broad Street and more pronounced in other cities, like Washington, D.C.

On Sunday, I was scheduled to begin a special, week-long vacation, an unusual respite for me. I flew to Atlanta to stay until Tuesday when I planned to go to Augusta and attend the Masters Golf Tournament with Uncle Jack, who knew some of the crowd there. I arrived in Atlanta on Sunday afternoon and went to my hotel only to find the lobby engulfed in total bedlam because of the throngs of people in town for Martin Luther King's funeral the next morning. I made my way through the crowd and entered the hotel bar, where I shook hands with a man who introduced himself as Clarence Townes from Richmond. He added that he worked for the Republican National Committee in Washington. I told him I was from Richmond and a loyal Republican. He offered to introduce me to a lot of new people. We chatted for quite a while, and eventually Clarence asked me, "Where are you sitting for the funeral?" He assumed the company must have sent me down for Martin Luther King's service.

"I'm not sure," I confessed.

"I'll take care of you," he promised. "I'll make sure you get a good spot."

Sure enough, I attended Martin Luther King's funeral from a prime vantage point because I just happened to be in Atlanta and just happened to meet Clarence Townes.

From the funeral I went to the Masters, which was an unforgettable vacation experience. I had a great time with my uncle amid the whole lush scene of the Augusta National Golf Club. This was the year of the scorecard incident with Roberto DeVicenzo, and it all took place behind the Butler Cabin, where we were staying. Years later in 2008 I had the pleasure of returning for a long weekend at the Masters, this time with our son Jack. We both enjoyed the experience immensely and still watch with avid interest the event on TV every April.

When the Electoral Board convened for its first meeting since my appointment to fill the spot previously held by Clarence Townes, I was promptly elected chairman. I didn't realize at the time that the board had only three positions: chairman, vice chairman and secretary. Whichever party happened to be in power had the right to pick the preferred office, and the Democrats, who held sway, chose to be secretary. It was only later that I learned that the position of secretary paid twice as much as the other two offices. Actually, I was fortunate that Michael Cummings had selected that office because it entailed a great deal of work, which he performed admirably. Michael and I enjoyed serving together on the Electoral Board and became good friends. When I received my first state paycheck as chairman, I had no idea why the payment had been sent. The amount of compensation was not significant, well under $100, and it took some delving into the paystub for me to confirm that the check was actually my remittance for accepting the chairmanship.

As though my appointment to the Electoral Board had not already been convoluted enough, the very next day after my first meeting, we were hauled into court because one of the candidates in the Ninth District City Council race sued the board over alleged issues with the election. Ironically, I went from not holding a seat on the Electoral Board to being a member, then to being chairman of the board and then to being sued as part of alleged improprieties that occurred before my tenure even began. That was the ragged start of my nine-year career in electoral board politics. What a way to begin!

Eventually, we worked our way out of the lawsuit, and I learned a great deal about the job and about elections. In those days, Richmond had nearly a hundred precincts, and at each election, police drivers took the members of the Electoral Board to oversee precinct voting stations. On election days, I would take a vacation day from work since we began early in the morning as soon as the polls opened, and continued late into the night.

I remained chairman of the Electoral Board for all nine years of my participation, and I was eventually elected president of the Virginia Electoral Board Association. With this latter group, I particularly enjoyed their annual gatherings for a weekend each March at the Homestead Resort during which we attended meetings and socialized with other members. Even after I resigned my membership, the association invited me back a couple of times to speak at their annual meetings, and most recently in 2015 and 2016, I was invited to report as co-chairman of a new workgroup of the State Board of Elections named General Registrar and Electoral Board (GREB).

In the course of the long days that I spent overseeing city elections for the Electoral Board, I became very close to my police driver Bob Walker, a fine man whom I found to be very knowledgeable about Richmond. Eventually, my family formed a personal relationship with Bob, and in subsequent years after he retired, he worked for us as well as for Maggie's mother. We are still very close friends with his widow, Carol.

Meanwhile, back at American Tobacco, I continued to work steadily in my position as Leaf Services Director. My office was located on Jeff Davis Highway until American Tobacco converted the Process Development Laboratory at Bermuda Hundred into administrative headquarters, and I relocated there. The headquarters expanded further in 1987, when several New York office departments moved into the Bermuda Hundred complex.

My comprehensive responsibilities included supplying quality, aged tobaccos to the company's manufacturing locations. The seasonal stemmery operations in Richmond, Reidsville and Lexington, Kentucky, culminated in the storage of over 200 million pounds of tobaccos worth then nearly $500 million. I also was charged with coordinating various parts of the operations and overseeing the continuing expansion of outside business through contract services that served the tobacco trade. At Bermuda Hundred, the Hamner Division, which contained three large paper mills producing reconstituted tobacco, was my responsibility along with communications with our Oriental operations.

The company held regular planning meetings, usually in New York, and by the late eighties, I was again included in these operational discussions, a substantive reflection of the enhanced role. My position at the company had once again evolved to one of

John in Mexico for American Tobacco.

prominence and responsibility, and my expertise, born of experience in many areas, was actively sought.

There was increasingly a need for me to travel, usually within the United States, but internationally as well. My first overseas trip since returning after polio coincided with the timing of my promotion, and during the years to follow, as Leaf Services Director I traveled to Canada, Brazil, Chile, Argentina, Guatemala and Mexico, where the company was buying a fair amount of burley and flue cured tobacco of high quality with competitive prices. I also visited Turkey and Greece for Oriental Tobacco and flew on occasion to London to coordinate with Gallaher's leaf people. Airports were not particularly friendly to handicapped passengers in those days, and I was rolled up and down many aircraft steps. Most everyone was quite accommodating, and that allowed me to carry on.

The July 1985, *Newsleaf*, the American Tobacco Company's newsletter, highlighted my work. The article described my return to American Tobacco:

It is a tribute to John Hager and a measure of his resiliency that, in facing and recovering from a severe illness in February 1974, he returned to work and has learned to surmount the handicap resulting from his illness that might have retired a lesser person permanently...He has not missed a day since returning to work!

Chapter 11

Reinvention

In 1982, we had a great opportunity for our family, one that required lots of my attention and came about in an unusual way. It all began in March 1982, we received a call from First and Merchants Bank asking for the family of "Jackie Hager." The bank was handling the estate of Mrs. Hamilton Baskerville, and this call proved very important.

Mrs. Baskerville had been a close friend of Maggie's through their memberships in the James River Garden Club. Maggie had visited at her house on Nottingham Road and helped with much of the horticultural work in her massive gardens. Many times, Maggie took Jack to visit the elderly friend, whom he called Miss Ethel. When Miss Ethel realized that she and "Jackie," as she called him, had the same birthday, May twenty-first, she insisted on having a little birthday party together, which she organized. In May 1981, she arranged for her cook to prepare a birthday cake, and the two of them – elderly lady and young boy – celebrated their special day. The next year, January 1982, Mrs. Baskerville passed away, and as her house was being emptied, it was found that Miss Ethel had left notes beside her bed and round about, saying that she wanted "Jackie Hager to be raised on her property." In other words, when she died, she wanted our family to be given first right of refusal on a piece of her land. The bank was attempting to heed her wishes when they called us.

By this time, Maggie and I had come to terms with the fact that American Tobacco would not be moving us back to New York, and we might as well consider Richmond our permanent home. Ever since our return from the Rusk Institute, we had been looking for a suitable house that we could make wheelchair-friendly, but we had found nothing really workable for our family and for me. It was a frustrating process. We, and especially Maggie, made a truly exhaustive search all over the city and surrounding areas, but the potential houses were too narrow or too small to redesign for wheelchair compatibility, and it seemed nearly every house in Richmond had four front steps. When we did find a house without entry steps, its interior space couldn't accommodate a wheelchair.

One house in the West End on Stockton Lane was quite attractive, but it was at the top of a big hill. In my optimism and determination to make the house work for us, I assured Maggie and our agent that the steep driveway would present no problem. Then I promptly tried to maneuver my wheelchair down the drive, lost control, and careened to the bottom where I broke my collarbone in the final crash. So much for that house!

Discouraged by our futile search, we were delighted by the prospect of choosing a building site from the lots that Mrs. Baskerville owned, and after careful deliberation and consideration, we put a contract on two joint lots. Meanwhile, the bank put the other lots on the market, and one by one, they all sold for the asking price. We were about to go to closing when a man named Nelson Saunders approached the bank and offered to buy all of Mrs. Baskerville's property, including her house, which had not sold, as one block sale, for a price that would exceed the sum prices which the bank had negotiated through separate deals. The bank tore up all the existing contracts, including ours, and accepted Mr. Saunders' offer. Maggie and I were bitterly disappointed, as I'm sure the other potential buyers must have been. The dream of finally building a perfect house of our own seemed to disappear before our eyes.

At the time, I wasn't acquainted with Nelson Saunders, but I found someone who did know him, and we arranged a meeting. Hearing our predicament, Mr. Saunders agreed to try to work with us. He suggested that what we really needed was a single lot, smaller than our original two-lot selection across the street. We were unsure that the corner lot was large enough to accommodate the sort of house we wanted, but at Mr. Saunders' suggestion we consulted an architect.

Next came contact with the architect, Jim Glave, whom we knew from Maymont days. Unlike so many architects, Jim was really tuned in to disability issues, and he assured Maggie and me that we could make the lot work for our preferred house design. After that conversation, we agreed to the purchase, despite the inflated price that Mr. Saunders charged — not far from the same price that I had previously agreed to pay the bank for the two lots. Maggie, Jim and I formed a team to design and build a house that

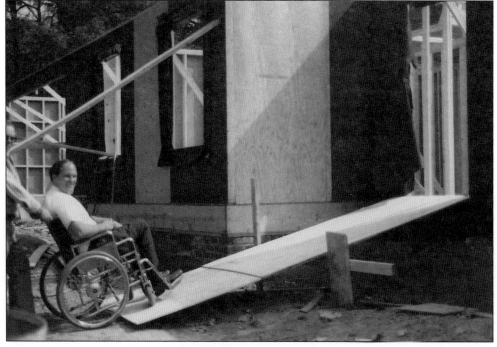

Checking new house construction

could accommodate my wheelchair but have no visible "disabled" appearance: no ramps, flow-through design and no obvious markers. Mr. Saunders' construction company submitted the most competitive bid for building our home, and we contracted with them to do our work.

Shortly before our new home was completed, Maggie and I hosted a large party on the deck and in the yard at the Charmian Road house we were continuing to rent. The cocktail party was in full swing when the deck, with guests bunched in conversation, started to sag. I remember watching our friend Kay Williams, who was pregnant at the time, swaying down on the deck. There was no dramatic collapse, just a slow sinking all the way to the ground so that Kay and others were thrown off balance, but no one was injured. We picked up the bar, moved it to the yard and let the party continue. The next day, we found that much of the deck and underpinnings had rotted, and we told Flossie Bryan, the owner, that the deck would need to be rebuilt. This incident confirmed our resolve that it was time to leave Charmian Road.

Construction of our new home took more than a year, and we moved to on April 14, 1984. For the first time since we had lived on Tuckahoe Avenue in 1973, we had nothing in storage, a true milestone. On the night we moved, our boys — Jack, who was eleven years old and Henry, six — excitedly ran across the street and down to the canal. Mrs. Richard Reynolds lived in the house across Sulgrave from ours, and when she saw Jack and Henry run towards the canal, she telephoned us in a frenzy. "Your children are gone forever! You'll never see them again. There are snakes and alligators down there."

Her over-zealous reaction to our boys' romp might have been attributable to the fact that she enjoyed her toddy in the afternoons. At any rate, the boys came back about an hour later, and Maggie and I duly warned them to be careful of snakes and alligators when they traipsed around the canal. For a brief time, Mrs. Reynolds continued to live across from us, and when she moved, our good friends, Peter and Judy Brown, bought her house. The Browns have been great neighbors, and Peter, a godsend when any medical problems have arisen.

Our home on Sulgrave Road provided a great deal of stability for the family. It was a good move that we would not regret. The house is roomy, functional and welcoming. Its carefully planned details helped establish Maggie as one of the country's most knowledgeable experts on disability design. Our conveniently located neighborhood was and continues to be terrific, as Windsor Farms is popular, well planned and meticulously maintained. I did my service for five years on the board and as president of Windsor Farms,

Hager family – 1986

Inc., and through the years, oversight of the area has continued to be strong. There are several gatherings each year that provide an opportunity to mingle with our neighbors, and two outstanding manor houses located within Windsor Farms, the Virginia House and Agecroft Hall, hold special events as well.

On July 27, 1990, an article appeared in the *Richmond News Leader* entitled, "Couple Turn Challenge into Victory." With accompanying pictures, the feature article detailed our home and the accommodations we had made. In glowing terms, it described the house:

> ... *spacious as a Southwestern plateau, stretching for distances and widths rooms rarely attempt. The ceilings were raised high, the lighting made indirect yet full. The front steps were erased from the design, replaced by a smooth, even walkway.*

The success of the design of our home is a testament to Maggie's careful research and vision as well as Jim Glave's expert skills.

At about the time we moved into Windsor Farms, there was a big brouhaha about the Reynolds property down the street off Lock Lane, where the grandmother of the Richard Reynolds family lived in an old, elegant farmhouse, surrounded by expansive acreage. I was familiar with the property because I had often ridden there from Charmian Road in my hand-controlled golf cart. The boys and I roamed the Reynolds estate, sometimes seeing one of the Australian nurses rolling Mrs. Reynolds in her wheelchair down the driveway. When Mrs. Reynolds died at 102 years old, there was instant interest from potential developers of her property. After much excitement and many hearings, the plan of the current Lockgreen development was approved, and construction began. All came out fine, and we have many good friends who live in this former farm, now estate development.

By the mid-eighties, I had become even more involved with the Republican Party and continued to get my feet wet politically through a multitude of volunteer jobs. I was serving on both the local committee and the State Central Committee of the Republican Party of Virginia along with the Richmond Electoral Board. In the early eighties, some influential Richmonders formed the Public Affairs Group, which was composed of about twenty-five "young guns" from the city who were determined to make a difference. I joined shortly after the group's inception. They were very involved with several political campaigns and would eventually play a major role in funding my own efforts. Early on, we supported Paul Trible in his quest for a seat in the Senate and later would back Senator Walter Stosch and numerous Republican statewide candidates. Just about all the members have served as president of the group. I actually served two terms and enjoyed arranging the programs and introducing various key individuals from business, politics and the community. It is a tribute to these individuals that the group has grown and still meets monthly for breakfast. From the early eighties to the present day, it has continued as a very effective organization. In April, spouses are invited to a big annual dinner with a featured speaker. In 2015, Maggie's friend from New York, Stephanie Stokes, spoke about her field of interior design, and in 2016, the editor of the Cook Report enthralled us with stories of wild political developments.

During 1986, the main focus of the group involved work with Roy West, who was running for the office of mayor of Richmond. We believed he could be an effective leader, and a couple of us in the Public Affairs Group set out to enhance West's chances for election. Bill Royall and I regularly met downtown on Saturday mornings with leaders from West's entirely African-American campaign committee and other representatives from the community. Involved in this effort were George Martin, a partner with Mc-GuireWoods LLP, who was Rector of the University of Virginia, and Leroy Hassell, who became Chief Justice of the Supreme Court of Virginia. Our efforts paid off when West won the election, and though he did become embroiled later with several problems, as all Richmond mayors seem to do, he served his first two terms very well. During the process of helping West's political runs, I formed what has proved to be long friendships, which continue today. For instance, Bill Royall, with whom I worked so closely, currently is chairman of the Virginia Museum of Fine Arts' Board of Trustees, where I served on the executive and other committees -- again working closely with him.

Our involvement in civic activities continued almost non-stop. I fondly remember just before Christmas of 1985, Maggie and I hosted the Children's Miracle Network Telethon event, to which popular singer Andy Williams lent his celebrity status. Also that Thanksgiving, Maggie, who served on the board of the Richmond Ballet for several years, invited all the dancers and staff to a rip-roaring dinner at our house.

In 1986, the organizers of the Henrico Autumn Harvest Parade, successor to the National Tobacco Festival, named me as the Civic Honoree. Purdue University honored me with their Alumni Citizenship Award, and when Maggie and I returned to Indiana for a fascinating weekend on campus, we were humbled by an enthusiastic welcome and special ceremony.

By 1987, American Tobacco had moved its headquarters from New York City to Stanford, Connecticut, though many administrative offices were located in Bermuda Hundred. My responsibilities continued to expand, especially in response to the company's emphasis on building our contract work, through which the company was paid for performing services for other companies. I also stayed abreast of new developments and technology in the industry, and in conjunction with this area of interest, I set out on an extensive overseas trip in early '87. I flew commercially to London and then traveled to Winchester, England, where I met with Dickinson Company, producers of large cylinders that were part of a breakthrough for processing tobacco. Returning to London, I flew to Austria and met some good friends who toured Vienna with me on the weekend. Joining Dickinson representatives, we drove into the countryside and observed Dickinson's applications in tobacco factories there. Finally, I continued on to Germany for more exposure and the return home from Frankfurt.

My responsibilities also began requiring more meetings with the company's legal counsel in Washington, D.C., legal sessions to which Bob Walker usually drove me. By 1987, this exposure on the D.C. front led to my being named the company's representative to the Tobacco Institute's State Activities Policy Committee, a responsibility that quickly became a significant part of my schedule. I began attending committee meetings at least monthly in Washington and worked with them on special projects, all of which involved a lot of time but also put me in a position to meet some outstanding individuals. A major focus of the institute involved an effort to block hikes in state excise taxes on tobacco, with California being a key state in this endeavor. I flew several times to San Francisco over the course of a couple of years as we fought hard against the tax increases. Despite our efforts, California finally managed to eke out the votes to pass tax hikes. During this time, I learned a great deal about the legislative process and policy, all of which was a wonderful grounding for the future. In the late eighties, Maggie and I enjoyed convention trips out West that, as company representative, I attended once or twice a year.

I also continued to be heavily involved with American Tobacco's labor negotiations, so much so that in 1988, negotiations at the Hamner Division, the reconstituted tobacco factory, forced me to cancel my plans to attend that year's Republican National Convention in New Orleans, which remains the only national convention I have failed to attend in all the years since my first, in 1980. Company negotiations were too important to neglect in any way, and though we took a tough stand, I believe it says something about the professionalism of our process that my opposite in the negotiations, Lee Busic, who was Vice President of the United Papermakers and Paperworkers Union, still calls me annually to catch up.

By 1988, one of my many, miscellaneous company jobs involved responding to declines in sales and the aftermath of enhanced automation and the consolidation of our manufacturing and leaf facilities. When Richmond Branch, the smoking tobacco factory located at Twenty-first and Grace Streets was designated to be closed, I brokered the sale to Pinkerton Tobacco Company and negotiated with the labor union about the shutdown of the plant. Not long afterwards, I became involved in the sale of the series of unused buildings that American Tobacco owned in downtown Richmond, including Virginia Branch. One of the major developers in the area was Bill Abeloff, with whom I negotiated a deal that stipulated the payment of a balloon premium in the event the development, known as Tobacco Row, truly succeeded after a period of time. In 2006, long after The American Tobacco Company had ceased to exist, I was working in Washington when I received a phone call saying the goals had been met and there was a $3 million royalty check waiting for me. I was the only person they had managed to locate to receive the payment. I put the developer's lawyers in touch with the company's former lawyers, and Tobacco Row paid the royalty check to Brown and Williamson — part of British American Tobacco, which had bought American Tobacco.

Charles Mullen, Vice President of Sales and a long-time friend was named President and Chief Executive Officer of The American Tobacco Company in 1987, and in February 1989, my work was more formally recognized, as I was promoted to Vice President of Leaf. Mr. Mullen had a great deal of faith in my abilities and readily entrusted me with increased responsibilities. I had been attending the company's planning meetings for years, but under Mullen's leadership I was asked to be a member of the Operating Com-

American Tobacco executives honoring Charles Mullen

mittee, which met quarterly, usually in Connecticut. In this capacity, it fell to me to make presentations at numerous board meetings. I also was named President of The American Tobacco Company in the Orient, a small subsidiary company. In conjunction with those responsibilities came more frequent travel to Greece and Turkey.

In December 1989, *Tobacco Reporter Magazine*, the top industry publication, ran a profile article that described me as "differently-abled." Profiling my background and past service with the company, the article detailed my struggle with polio and subsequent come-back, personally and professionally.

John Hager's office at American Tobacco Company is spacious and distinguished, yet – like the man – not extravagant...The atmosphere surrounding the vice president of Leaf is layered with optimism, good humor and southern hospitality...A self-described team player and eternal optimist, Hager is modest about his accomplishments and generous in his praise for his colleagues and other company employees...Strolling in his wheelchair through the aqua halls of the American Tobacco Company facility in Chester, Virginia, Hager speaks to each and every employee he encounters. He is relaxed, yet cordial and interested. He espouses a management phi-

Tobacco inspection in Greece

losophy of coordination and consensus...His personality, diverse interests, willingness to drop things at a moment's notice to switch gears on important projects – constantly balancing and negotiating priorities – provide a sterling portrait of a dedicated individual who gracefully overcomes all obstacles in his path.

It was an article that reinforced my regained position within the company.

In April 1989, I wrote an article entitled "Differently Abled" for Children's Hospital's newsletter, *Bear In Mind*. By this time, I had served on Children's Hospital's Board of Trustees for some ten years, had been President from 1985 to 1987 and was serving as chairman of the Corporate Planning Committee. I wrote the following:

If I am different from so many others who serve the Hospital in various capacities, it is in appearance only. For while I am confined to a wheelchair and have been for 16 years, due to vaccine-caused polio, I really don't feel any different and others certainly accept me on an equal footing. I say this quite frankly because our young patients and their families need to know that they too can lead very normal, productive lives today, in spite of problems incurred or dark days along the way...

It will not be long before we will all begin using "differently abled" to describe our children and adults with physical mobility problems. The cycle will be complete because "abled" is the key and so many are recognizing that fact.

For sure, for those affected there are adjustments needed when problems occur. We all have to make adjustments all the time though, and everyone else has to make adjustments as well. Our challenges may be greater, but the biggest adjustment required is "will" – the will to live, the will to do, the will to succeed. It is a necessity for everybody; certain of us just have to go about it a bit differently.

On the home front, our sons, Jack and Henry, were growing up. Our family joined the Philadelphia Quarry Club, where the boys enjoyed swimming for hours on end. Both boys, in turn, participated in Indian Guides. At one time during an outing at Berkeley Plantation, we participated in an Indian Guides presentation, a tribal performance that was judged. One of the other dads, Freddie Reed, brought a horse, and I brought lots of hands of cured tobacco. It was quite a show and good enough for our group to win the top award!

Both Jack and Henry went to Camp Hanover, and after becoming Boy Scouts, each attended Scout camp in Goochland County. Henry's years with Boy Scouts culminated with his achieving Eagle Scout. The boys also attended Woodberry Forest School's sports camps in the summers, and Henry went to other sports camps, including one at Wake Forest. As they advanced through St. Christopher's, they were involved in numerous programs, pageants and sporting events.

In 1987, Jack went for his first summer at Camp Morehead; two years later, Henry went for his first year at Camp Seagull in North Carolina. Every summer, they went with Maggie to Martha's Vineyard. Those were good, carefree years of their growing up.

John, Henry and Jack with (2nd row) Joe Grimes, Jack Hager, and Virgil Hager.

In September 1988, Jack transferred from Saint Christopher's School to Salisbury School in Salisbury, Connecticut, where he completed his last three years of upper school. When Jack graduated from Salisbury School in 1991, I was invited to give the graduation address, my first of what later would prove to be many graduation talks. I was pretty nervous about this initial address, where I would speak before my son's peers, and it was a bit intimidating to receive the auspicious list of those who had spoken in prior years. I talked of the importance of "being involved," telling the seniors that it is better to be part of the action than to sit back and watch it unfold.

I can think of no instance in my life, particularly having gone through the crucible of polio at age thirty-six, where this philosophy has not worked – in business, in civic work, in the church, in sports, in politics and with family – all this for a guy in a wheelchair. The involvement of one's whole self – TO BE – is the essential ingredient of success.

I compared life to a marathon and pointed out the five things I believed to be requirements for success in the "marathon of life." They were dedication (commitment both when faced with adversity and tempted by ease), hardiness (the strength of spirit, soul, and body), intelligence (the ability to keep learning), integrity (a clear mind, confidence and pride) and hard work ("You must grind it out in this world; there really aren't any simple alternatives; the road to any place worth going rarely is easy.") Ross Mackenzie, a good friend who headed the editorial pages of the *Richmond News Leader*, helped me polish this important graduation address as I carefully prepared.

After spending three years boarding at prep school, Jack decided to attend college close to home, and he chose Hampden-Sydney College in Farmville, Virginia for his undergraduate work.

Henry continued at Saint Christopher's, thrived in that atmosphere and graduated in 1996. He ventured farther afield to attend Wake Forest University for his college years. We had many memorable trips to Farmville and Winston-Salem and served on both institutions' Parents Councils. Jack and Henry later completed their education at Darden School of Business at the University of Virginia, graduating in 2006 and 2008 respectively.

Maggie and I were eager for the boys to enjoy active vacations, and after Christmas one year, we went to Beaver Creek, Colorado, for a skiing vacation, during which I tried sit-skiing. We enjoyed ski vacations at various slopes in Colorado, Virginia, and West Virginia, and while not very accomplished, I found sit-skiing exhilarating. Throughout Henry's and Jack's school years, we took family spring and summer vacation trips to interesting destinations, including the Cayman Islands, the Abacos, Antigua, destinations in Virginia like Sandbridge and Chincoteague, and beaches in North Carolina — Nags Head, Southern Shores, Duck and Figure Eight Island.

As the boys grew older, I joined Jack and Henry in active, outdoor sports such as hunting. In the late eighties and nineties, we enjoyed dove hunting together at Newtown Hunt Club and other places, and I can vouch for the fact that both of them are good shots. Randy Gibbs and Peter Brown were exceptionally good and generous organizers of various hunts, and with them we ventured off to a variety of sites. Tom Capps invited a group to go goose hunting in Maryland, and for three or four years, I enjoyed being included in those very enjoyable expeditions. Peter Brown often tells the story of a long

John sit-skiing

hunt on the Eastern Shore when I snagged the last goose of the day in front of everyone. Peter continued to organize goose hunts at Upper Brandon and now Willow Hill, but my shooting prowess has definitely declined!

The boys and I spent memorable days at Custis Hunting and Fishing Club in King William County, which in recent years has become an even more significant part of my life. Jim Moncure and I went together to buy an eighteen-foot runabout boat, which we took on the James and other rivers, with our two families alternating use. Lots of experiences came from these ventures.

In 1989, after serving two terms on the board, I became President of the Country Club of Virginia, and my good friend Robert F. Norfleet, Jr. became Vice President. Our major thrust involved working with the club's new manager, John Hightower. In the Country Club of Virginia's one hundredth year history book, there is the following quote:

John Hager spent most of his presidency integrating the new manager into the club and putting into place a more comprehensive long-term plan and implementing a more effective financial structure. It was, upon reflection, the beginning of a five-year period of earth-shaking social and directional change.

These were indeed exciting times, and I found that CCV's presidency was a job that demanded a great deal of time.

Reflection from Robert F. Norfleet, Jr., former Vice President and President of the Country Club of Virginia, retired executive with Crestar Bank, now SunTrust Bank

John called me out of the blue and said, "I want you to be Vice President of the Country Club of Virginia and follow me as President. I've gotten to know you from your time as Chairman of the Board at St. Christopher's and your chairmanship of the Chamber of Commerce, and I believe you can serve the Country Club of Virginia well."

We didn't discuss his motives for asking me, but I believe John wanted someone in the office who had proven that he could command respect and was involved in the community. He probably also wanted someone who would carry on whatever it was he planned to do as president. Up until this time, I had known John for the most part through the Chamber and the Convention Center discussions, and I had seen him occasionally for banking business during his employment at American Tobacco. I can't say, however, that I really knew John very well.

I was happy to agree to his suggestion, but I said to him, "What makes you think I'll be elected?"

He assured me that wouldn't be a problem, and so John put my name on the ballot as vice president with him as president, and sure enough, we were elected in 1989.

Shortly after the election, John pulled me aside and said, "We need to make some changes in the club."

I remember thinking, "Wait a minute. I didn't plan on this." As we talked, he explained, "We have a new club manager, John Hightower, and he is a ball of fire. You and I need to transform this club into more of a family club."

"I subscribe to that," I assured him.

"My job," he continued, "is to get this club into strong financial shape and set it on a positive course. Then hopefully, you will know where to take it after that."

So we began our new positions. I had supposed that being vice president of the Country Club would be a position that would involve more glory than toil, but the next two years with John Hager and John Hightower proved to be somewhat contentious with the membership and a whole lot of work.

What really surprised me from the get-go was John's level of energy. I wasn't prepared for it. I am a fairly hard working guy and was used to being around people who worked diligently, but all of a sudden, I found myself sweating it out at the Country Club until midnight or one o'clock in the morning on a fairly regular basis. We poured over numbers, studied spreadsheets, met with staff people, reviewed how things had been done in the past and planned how we should prepare for the future. It was not unusual for us to leave the club at midnight or later, with John Hightower and me walking beside John Hager, who rolled himself out to the parking lot.

I distinctly remember the first few times we tried to assist John, but we quickly learned that he needed and wanted no help whatsoever. It always amazed me that he maneuvered himself into the passenger side of the car, folded his wheelchair and threw it into the backseat, and then slid himself behind the wheel – all with no assistance. We would have a few final words, and then off he would drive and be ready the next morning, with no trouble, to begin another day at his real job in a demanding executive position at American Tobacco. He never, ever was sick. His handicap was something that he refused to allow to get in the way of anything.

I came to spend a lot of time with John, and until I knew him, I had never before understood how difficult it is for people with handicaps to move around, the Country Club being one location that was hard to navigate, but other places as well. I never once heard him complain, but John regularly took me in doors that I didn't know about, into places I had never seen, on elevators I never knew existed, and he didn't want assistance unless it was absolutely necessary. There are many ways to enter a building that most people do not know, but John knew them all. His strength and perseverance were nothing short of inspirational. He was a very powerful guy from the waist up, and he used his strength to steer his way over treacherous ground. It was never in his psyche to admit anything more than that something might be a little difficult.

The Country Club of Virginia was and is a way of life for many people in Richmond. There was a whole contingent of members who didn't want to see any changes whatsoever, but many clubs were facing challenges during this time period, and though the Country Club was in fairly good financial shape, with John Hager at the helm, we began adopting policies that would secure its future. I learned from John that the strength of any club comes in having a membership that represents the community, not just the upper strata of society. Against the backdrop of a resistant membership, we took steps to stabilize the club's finances, we adopted a more family oriented attitude, and we sought to become more diversified. This latter issue was one that definitely raised hackles among a segment of the club members, and we had to navigate some irate sentiment.

One day at the club, John turned to me and said, "There's something I need to do, and I want you with me."

"Fine," I said.

"I need you to go with me to see our newly elected governor, Doug Wilder."

I said, "John, I'm not a political guy, and I don't know Doug Wilder. Why do I need to go see him?"

"We're going to ask him to be an honorary member of the Club," John replied.

I said, "John, let's think about this for a minute now. You want me to go down with you to talk to Doug Wilder, who hasn't been inaugurated yet."

"You got it," he assured me. "Consistently, in the past, the Country Club has offered honorary membership to governors. This is an opportunity we do not want to miss."

I said, "John, I don't want to get in the middle of this stuff! I thought this was going to be an easy job."

"Rob," he said, "if you do what's right, nothing is easy. You've got to go with me because I need you."

I almost said I wouldn't do it. I'm not a political person, and the whole idea seemed over the top and unnecessary, but John was convincing as usual. We drove down together, and Doug Wilder was in an office building near the Capitol since it was still two or three weeks before his inauguration. Once again, John and I went through some side door most people have never seen, on an elevator that I would never be able to find again, and we entered a not very spacious office. Mr. Wilder's secretary said, "The Governor will be with you shortly."

When went into Doug Wilder's office, John introduced me, and he and the governor-elect started yakking about politics and how Mr. Wilder had come to win the election. They talked for a half hour or so. I was fascinated because it was clear that they were friends and enjoyed each other. I don't know that they agreed politically on a lot of things, but they were relaxed and comfortable together. They obviously liked each other. They respected each other. I was a bystander who was privy to an unusual meeting.

Finally, the governor-elect said, "Now, John, you can appreciate that I have a bunch of things to do, and I know you aren't here to chew the fat about the good old times."

"I'm here to extend an invitation to you," John said.

"Fine, what is it?" Mr. Wilder asked.

"I'm the President of the Country Club of Virginia," John answered. "Rob's the Vice President, and we're here to extend to you an invitation to become an honorary member of the Country Club of Virginia."

Doug Wilder leaned back in his chair. "Let me get this straight," he said. "You and Mr. Norfleet here are running this Country Club of Virginia place, which is a pretty fancy club, and you are down here to ask me to be a member? And bring Patricia in with me?"

He took a deep breath. "John," he said, "I am speechless for the first time in my life. Just speechless."

"Well, Doug, we've done this before. We've offered an honorary membership to other governors in the past," John answered. "Some of them have taken it. Some of them haven't."

"Let's think about this," Doug Wilder continued. "John, I won this election on a platform that said I would represent the breadth and length of the state, mainly middle class people. I would be the people's governor. How do you think it would appear if I showed up at the Country Club of Virginia having run on that platform and having become governor on that kind of base?"

"I think people would understand," John reflected.

"I don't think so," Mr. Wilder answered. "I can see it right now. Patricia and I would come in the front door, and reporters would be there. They would raise hell about it. John, you are a good friend, and I am flattered. Mr. Norfleet, I appreciate your being here too, but I wouldn't take that membership if you forced me. I appreciate your invitation and your thoughts, and I'm sure I would be well received if I did go to the Country Club of Virginia, but I can't accept the invitation."

They talked a bit longer, and then John and I left, making our way through some labyrinth *of seldom used elevators and hallways.*

I said to John, "Did you know what was going to happen?"

"I was pretty sure," he answered. "But to me, I think that was the right thing to do."

I learned then and there, and I saw more than once, that John, though he is a political animal and is good at politics, wanted to do the right thing and set out to do it, even if it might prove difficult. Though Doug Wilder was the first African-American governor of Virginia and a Democrat, John felt it was right to extend the invitation. Yes, he liked the governor-elect, but even if he hadn't, I believe he would have offered the membership. He felt it was a good precedent to set, not just because of the man, but because of the office.

Socially, John was extremely well equipped to be a President of the Country Club of Virginia. For one thing, he knew how to circulate in a crowded room quickly and effectively. He had learned the art of giving a lot of people attention for a short time, to make eye contact with them and listen to them, but in a unique and polite way to extricate himself when they became too involved in the conversation. Maggie was helpful to him in keeping her husband moving without diminishing the graciousness they conveyed.

At parties in their home, John planted himself at the front door and greeted every person who entered, then said good-bye when they left. He mentioned to me one time, "To tell the truth, I get in people's way. If I start whirling around, I'll run over some lady's foot and knock over drinks. It's better for me to stay in one place."

"With your strategy, you always know who leaves the party early," I remarked.

In typical John Hager style, he saw the positive side of the situation. "It's a good thing for some people to leave early," he explained. "We love when our guests come in, and we appreciate that when some of them leave, I have more room to move in the crowd."

For the record, I am the only person who has served as President whose golf handicap did not soar during the term of office!

In 1990, American Tobacco celebrated its one hundredth anniversary. While the parent company, American Brands, had moved its headquarters to Old Greenwich, Connecticut, the annual meeting continued to be at the Waldorf Astoria Hotel in New York City. I was asked to participate in the annual meeting in 1990, the first time since 1969 that my presence was requested – resounding proof that I had successfully attained, for a second time, real power and influence in the company. In December 1990, *Tobacco International* named me Man of the Year. The article that accompanied the award detailed my history with the company as well as my civic activities:

"Confined" to a wheelchair is hardly how one would describe Hager, who was back on the job three months after an illness in 1973 which left him without the use of his legs...There isn't much "time off" in Hager's life, but that doesn't seem to bother him.

"I'm a people person," said Hager, explaining how he has always enjoyed spending his free time involved in a multitude of civil, church, neighborhood, club and political activities.

John's Richmond Office 1989

The article concluded with the statement, *Hager is a person everyone in the industry can cite with pride as an exemplary tobacco man.* This was the pinnacle of my comeback at American Tobacco. It had been a long road, but life was good.

Work and travel kept me busy, particularly related to overseas procurement of leaf tobacco. Since I was involved in labor negotiations and multiple other activities, time constraints usually forced me to schedule no more than one or two international trips each year. Fortunately, I had qualified people who could handle most of the other overseas travel.

My position entailed involvement in a great variety of industry related activities. We became active with the Tobacco Association of the United States, which held a gathering each year over Memorial Day weekend at the Greenbrier Resort. Maggie and I enjoyed attending these part-business and part-social events, and we made good friends and associates there from all over the industry and the world.

In December 1990, we organized what became an annual American Tobacco Leaf Conference, during which key people in the company and some from outside gathered to formulate our strategic plans, to review our policies and activities and to coordinate planning for the subsequent year.

The company had an outstanding team of individuals in the leaf organization – Bob Bouse and R. H. Ligon in leaf buying, John Tucker in manufacturing and processing, Bill Kramer at Hamner Division and George Cummings in Oriental tobacco. These talented colleagues were instrumental in making my job successful and enabling me to expand my horizons.

Maggie and I traveled to London in late November 1991 and 1992, leaving the day after Thanksgiving for the Gallaher Leaf Conference. Those were wonderful trips, and I was able to help significantly in Gallaher's planning and coordination with American Tobacco.

All through these years, Maggie was the glue that held us all together. She was a great mother and took her responsibilities seriously. She participated in a variety of activities, but her focus was always on the family. Her first-hand knowledge about disabilities made her especially qualified to serve in several significant capacities. Locally, she chaired the Richmond mayor's Committee

John in London with Gallaher Inspection

for People with Disabilities. In 1988, President Ronald Reagan nominated Maggie to be a member of the fifteen-member National Council on Disabilities, a Senate-confirmed appointment. Service on this council was the culmination of years of work that she conducted on behalf of disabled citizens, and it highlighted Maggie's recognition as a leader in the field. Fortunately, her appointment, which demanded a great deal of time, came during a period when she was freer to travel and participate. Her first meeting was in San Francisco in January 1989, and in the years of her involvement, we attended many events where we met people who were involved nationally with disability initiatives.

During her time on the National Council, Maggie helped compose the landmark Americans with Disabilities Act. When the ADA was signed into law in the summer of 1990, Henry and I accompanied Maggie to the memorable event on the White House lawn. In 1992, Maggie participated in a fascinating trip to Prague with the National Council for Disabilities. As often happens when one works in the nation's capital or in government, Maggie eventually tired of frustration that seemed inherent in every assignment, though she continued to learn and apply much in this field. As her National Council term expired, President George H. W. Bush named her to the Access Board for a five-year term. The Access Board is a federal agency that promotes equality for people with disabilities through accessible design and the development of accessibility standards. Little did I imagine that later, when working in Washington, I would be called both to address and serve on the same Access Board. In 1994, George Allen selected Maggie to serve as director of the Department for the Rights of Virginians with Disabilities, a state agency. Her service to the disability community was one of true distinction and dedication.

We added an important addition to our family in 1991, with the arrival of a black Labrador retriever. Jack wanted to name the puppy "Casey," while Henry chose the name "Midnight." Jack won out on the name selection, but Maggie, Henry and I nixed his idea of his carting Casey to college, especially since the puppy quickly became a vital part of our household. I would often wheel myself to what was then the new development of

Lockgreen, and Casey would run with me down the hill, all around and back. A loyal companion, Casey endeared herself to all of us, and when she passed away in 2000, it was a sad loss for the family. We never replaced our beloved Lab, in part because the city's leash laws had taken effect by that time, and it was too cumbersome for me to manage a leashed and running dog. By that time too, Maggie's life was rather busy, and the idea of training a new puppy seemed daunting.

My career responsibilities had evolved and expanded so that by the early nineties, I was working with American Brands' subsidiary companies as well as with American Tobacco. I chaired the Operating Committee at Golden Belt Manufacturing Company, which produced a variety of packaging materials and necessitated my making many trips to Durham, where I worked with Jim Galioto, Golden Belt's president.

On one occasion, my friend Bill Goodwin, who owned Ben Hogan Company, flew with me to New Bedford, Massachusetts, to visit the Acushnet Company, an American Brands subsidiary and manufacturer of Titleist golf balls. We were hoping to attract Bill's interest in using the company's production facilities, which did not come to be, but it cemented a strong relationship between the two of us.

I enjoyed my colleagues at American Tobacco and cultivated, as I always had attempted to do, a personal connection with our employees. People around me responded positively, as one letter demonstrates:

We all have hectic schedules and lead busy lifestyles which leads us at times to forget to thank the people responsible for the good things that happen to make our lives more enjoyable. So please let me take this opportunity to say, "thank you very much," for all the things that you have made possible for me this past year, i.e. new computer equipment, training classes and seminars, the generous salary increase, new office furniture, etc. But most of all, thank you for your trust and confidence in me as a member of your team.

I still have a long way to go, but with your leadership, combined with the tools of the trade, I hope to continue to learn and improve my abilities so that I may serve you and our Company better. Again, thank you for having faith in me and for allowing me the opportunity to work with such a wonderful superior and friend.

When Durham Academy awarded me the Distinguished Alumni Award in 1992, our family had a grand gathering for that occasion. My parents, and many other relatives were in Durham for the festivities. We weren't able to gather often in those years, but it was always special when we could reunite.

During the award ceremony, Josiah Murray, who was a classmate and General Council for Liggett & Myers Tobacco Company, introduced me by giving background details of my education and professional career as well as my civic involvement. He closed with these reflections:

How would one describe John Hager? Colleagues of his have described him as an achiever – a gentle man – a family man – and a community man. In my mind, he happily melds 1) significant ability, 2) a willingness to work, 3) an ever-optimistic attitude, and 4) more than a small measure of courage.

John informed me that he is proud of having attended Calvert Method School. I do not think that I am presumptuous in informing him that the collective group of people who are Durham Academy is equally proud that he was and is one of theirs.

In a speech to Upper School students during the Alumni Weekend, I shared with them my personal motto: *esse quam spectare* (to be is better than to see) and my personal philosophy, often repeated in different contexts: that it is better to be part of the action than to sit back and watch the action.

Life is like a marathon, and if your course is like the Richmond Marathon, it is quite a challenge...After an easy start there is a big, long hill for three-and-a-half miles. Reaching the crest is a bit like completing your upper school education. You know clearly and positively where you have been, and for a split second you can look back and see.

It even becomes tempting to cruise for a while during the next couple of miles. But the knowledge of many monster hills and steep downhills tends to keep your mind on the race even though the temptations to deviate from the course become greater.

My interest in Virginia's politics continued to increase, and in 1992 I decided to run for Chairman of the State Republican Party. Bryce Powell provided an office in Midlothian My campaign manager was Kathy Graziano, who presently is a member of Richmond City Council. She had a great deal of energy, which was a good thing, because the campaign necessitated my attending many mass meetings and other functions all over the state before the convention in early June at Salem, Virginia. Somehow, she and I both managed to work all day and then meet in the evening to take our message from one end of the state to the other. That was my first campaign and the first time in twenty years that Virginia had seen a contested race for Republican Party Chairman. Maggie joined the effort and every Saturday campaigned with Susan Allen, whose husband George was angling for the office of governor the next year.

U. S. Senator John Warner publicly supported my efforts, but during the campaign, his influence was undermined by his defense of U. S. Senator Charles S. Robb, who was under a grand jury investigation because of unlawfully leaked conversations by his staff. While I had great support from General Assembly members and the "establishment," severe weather caused some of my supporters to stay home from the state convention in Salem. Pat Robertson, primarily known in those days as a television evangelist, supported my conservative principal opponent, Patrick M. McSweeney. Some things never change in Virginia, and the ultra-conservatives dominated the convention so that in the end, I lost by fewer than 300 votes. Still, I had come a long way in the Party. Those who backed me — the so-called regulars or establishment — still squabble today on a steady basis with the "Tea Party" and "Libertarian"- other right wing types. Several supporters who had traveled to Salem were so upset that they vowed never again to attend a conven-

Victory Campaign Bus Tour, 1992.

tion, a refrain that has become all too familiar.

After the spirited race for Chairman was over, Pat McSweeney approached me the next Sunday to say he could not be effective without my help to pull the Party together. He asked me to run for Treasurer, which was the number-two job in the Party. I agreed to do so, and subsequently was elected Treasurer at the next State Central Committee meeting. He also asked me to accept the co-Chairmanship of the 1992 Victory Campaign, a position I accepted. Ironically, as events evolved, I participated in the Party's more exciting activities while Pat McSweeney began having health problems and was seen less and less.

The 1992 Victory Campaign required travel all around the state and interaction with many people. I continued as co-Chairman of the 1993 Victory Campaign, co-Chairman of the Oliver North Campaign in 1994 and co-Chairman of the statewide bus tour in 1995. All of this activity was still as a volunteer since my work at American Tobacco remained my primary responsibility, but I was gaining political experience and meeting many worthwhile contacts.

That summer, I was elected at the Republican State Convention to be a Virginia delegate at the Republican National Convention. Jack joined me and was able to participate with the delegation through this exciting, busy week. Houston was a great place and it was a thrill to attend the nomination of George H. W. Bush. When the convention ended on Friday, we had a free day before our return flights to Richmond. Jack and I decided to drive to Galveston, and from there we chartered a boat for offshore fishing in the gulf. We caught a huge number of red snappers, which we had cleaned on the dock and packed in a cooler. Then Jack and I stopped by to see my niece Ruthie in Houston and dumped about thirty pounds of fillets on her kitchen table. She later told us that she ate red snapper for the next year! Thanks to our giveaway, we returned home without a single fish, but we had plenty of convention souvenirs and lasting memories. An array of campaign buttons from each four-year cycle are framed in the back hall of our Richmond home.

In the fall of 1992, I drove to Raleigh and met with Senator Jesse Helms, who was a personal friend of Charles Mullen and a strong supporter of American Tobacco. Jesse Helms and I sat on his porch and passed away the afternoon talking. It was a memorable day and a true pleasure to meet with this great icon. Later in the year, I went at the request of Mr. Mullen to events at the Jesse Helms Institute at Wingate College.

One of my notable political experiences occurred in October, when President George H. W. Bush, the Republican nominee for President, came to Richmond to debate Bill Clinton at the University of Richmond. I was chosen to be part of a small group to meet him that morning at the airport. I was honored to do so, but I left the airport saying to myself, "Something's wrong. He's not going to do very well."

Sure enough, that particular debate at the university's Robins Center is often cited as a factor in eventual loss of the Presidential election. Something was just out of step, and the press quickly picked up on every dubious detail, like his checking his watch several times. He had a very young grandson with him that day, George P. Bush, who just now is getting involved in Texas politics while his father, Jeb Bush, competed this year for the spot as Republican Presidential candidate. It is amazing how things evolve in politics.

In 1993, George Allen ran as the Republican nominee for governor of Virginia. He faced a long nominating battle, and there was a huge convention in Richmond in early June. One of my Party assignments was to organize a post-convention bus tour around the state that commenced the day after the Allen people had received the nod. I continued my heavy involvement in the campaign as co-Chairman of Victory '93. There were events all over the state, many of which were becoming "old hat." We participated in another weeklong bus tour just before the election and savored the hard-earned victory. My family all attended inaugural events in January and celebrated with George and Susan, who had become good friends.

During his term of office, Governor Allen named me to the boards of the Virginia Museum of Fine Arts and the Jamestown-Yorktown Foundation. More recently, Governor McDonnell appointed me to those same boards. Governor Allen also appointed me as Virginia's representative to the Southern Growth Policies Board, which functions as an arm of the Southern Governors' Conference. I attended their annual meetings for several years, up to 2004, when leaving for service in Washington.

In 1994, I co-chaired the Oliver North campaign in his bid against Chuck Robb for the Senate seat. We attended many exciting events around the state with at least one major event happening every week until the November election. A particularly memorable event was the debate at Hampden-Sydney College, at which time I visited Jack, who was a senior. I participated in all we possibly could schedule in my calendar and joined a bus tour for Oliver North that covered the state. It was disappointing when the Senate seat went to Chuck Robb, but my exposure to many people and experiences during Lieutenant Colonel North's campaign would prove valuable as my own political aspirations broadened. I stayed in Richmond the night of the election, and then left late on Bill Goodwin's jet to get to Sea Island for an American Tobacco operating committee retreat.

These were busy times in politics and at work. The fall 1993 issue of *Golden Leaf News* featured an article entitled, "Marathoner, John Hager," which highlighted my career at American Tobacco, especially through the years after 1974. "Being 'differently-able' has not soured John's outlook on life," the article stated. It went on to quote me as saying, "We work for what we get, but we live for what we give," one of my favorite mantras. The article then highlighted my years of wheelchair racing. The write-up was especially meaningful to me because it clearly indicated how dramatically American Tobacco's attitude towards my disability had changed since I first contracted polio.

Chapter 12

The Sand Shifts

By the early nineties, the over-riding goal of all of us at American Tobacco was to transform the company under the American Brands umbrella into a multifaceted, diversified enterprise. For my part, there continued to be numerous leaf-related activities and considerable travel, both domestic and international. In the fall of 1993, I went with a small company delegation on an international mission to Russia and spent a memorable week in Moscow. Upon landing, I was relieved to see that my wheelchair had arrived safely, and two burly looking men who appeared strong and able were ready to assist me. They indicated a long set of steps that we needed to descend, and I used sign language to explain how they should tilt the chair back and let the wheels do the work of rolling and bumping me down the steps. It wasn't the most comfortable means of reaching the bottom, but when we finally got there, I gave them each a generous tip, and they seemed very pleased. The next day, some other representatives were arriving at the airport, and we drove out in a rented van to meet them. We entered the terminal, and I immediately saw that right next to the stairs was an elevator! So much for helpful Russians!

Russian Business Trip, 1993.

It was exciting to be in Moscow for a week, during which we had time for some touring. The people we met were extremely kind, and I enjoyed the exhibition and the sales meetings. On return, I flew Aeroflot through Reykjavik to Dulles and then on to Charlottesville. Aeroflot's reputation for safety and reliability was somewhat suspect, which alarmed some of my associates, but I decided to take my chances. Sure enough, the Russians did the trick and got me home on schedule.

The next few months were a juggling of work-related travel, politics and civic activity. In January, I attended the Republican National Committee meeting in Washington. From there, I flew to Istanbul for a meeting with contacts for sales and then continued on to Izmir for several days with Managing Director George Cummings and The American Tobacco Company of the Orient. What great and historical countries Turkey and Greece are, with new sights to see at every turn and tobacco growing all over. We worked with several leaf dealers who were very meticulous and responsive to our needs.

There were many opportunities to attend charity and civic functions as the company's representative, and some of them were quite memorable. On one occasion, I flew on the Philip Morris plane with a group from Richmond to New York for the National Conference of Christians and Jews' elaborate black-tie dinner. The program spotlighted several tobacco industry honorees. It was a quick trip with a flight to New York and return flight the same night, but it was typical of many special gatherings that I had the pleasure of experiencing.

All of us in management were diligently working to make American Tobacco successful, and we felt confident that the company was performing better than it had in many years. It was gratifying to measure the steady progress that was being achieved. Our commitment and shared dedication made the news of April 4, 1994, especially shocking. On that day it was announced that The American Tobacco Company was being sold to the British American Tobacco Company and would merge with Brown and Williamson, its American subsidiary. Like most everyone else, I was completely blindsided.

By the time of the announced sale, I had returned nearly completely to the level of my pre-polio responsibilities. I had earned the trust and confidence of colleagues at every level, and I was involved in a variety of endeavors. It was fulfilling to know that my efforts toward effective organization and cooperative interaction had contributed to the company's rebirth. For me, life was satisfying, exciting, and full of promise, and many other talented executives and employees felt the same sense of achievement. Our loyal commitment to American Tobacco made the news of its sale all the more difficult to fathom. The last thing in the world most of us wanted was to stop and retire, but once the deal became public, we knew that the impact on our lives would be immense. We were told that we should work normally while the particulars of the sale were finalized and government approval was obtained, but we all sadly realized the handwriting was on the wall.

So started a whole new, fast-paced series of events, planning meetings and activities that led to the transition and final sale. It seemed that all my work of the last twenty-one years was futile – all the struggle from 1973 to 1994, the extreme efforts to make a major come-back and the recognition within the company a second time – it would mean nothing in the face of the sale. Thus, 1994 was a year of climbing up, up, up, only to plunge down again. The second half of the year seemed rather surreal as the situation unfolded. None of us knew exactly what the timing of the final transition would be, though initial predictions suggested six months, an assumption which would prove fairly accurate. We were assured that we would receive full retirement benefits and did not need to worry about personal finances, but there was too much uncertainty to feel complacent. None of us in the organization were happy with the situation, and none of us felt comfortable about our futures. Nor did the irony of the sale escape our notice: American Brands, which had been created by The American Tobacco Company, was now selling American Tobacco.

The final news of approval of the deal arrived early one December morning, and since I had planned to drive to Smithfield, North Carolina, to call on K. R. Edwards Co., a leaf dealer, I went ahead with the road trip. As a supplier to American Tobacco, K. R. Edwards was directly affected by the sale, and our colleagues there feared the sudden and significant disruption of their lives as much as we American Tobacco employees. We tried to make some sense of the sale, but answers were few, and all of us felt extremely discouraged.

At the end of the year, following lengthy preparation for the sale, I was named Senior Vice President, nearly the same high title that I had held before I was stricken with polio. Just before Christmas, an announcement confirmed that the transition would be completed early in January 1995. As we reached American Tobacco's end date, Brown and Williamson asked me to remain for an additional month to coordinate some community affairs and to facilitate the transition for the remaining leaf operations. I agreed to that brief, part-time extension, during which I detailed American Tobacco's civic involvement, described some of our subsidiaries' activities and helped transfer my responsibilities with the Tobacco Institute. When I finally left the building for the last time in February 1995, it took a moving van to transfer all my effects from my office to our house. Papers, books and memorabilia arrived and were unceremoniously unloaded. It was a slow process to assimilate the accumulation from thirty-four-years that – much to Maggie's dismay – filled our living room.

My career with American Tobacco had spanned my entire work-life, thirty-four years to be exact, "the sort of longevity" that was endemic to my generation but is virtually unknown in today's world. In part, it was family heritage that pointed me towards my life's work, but beyond that initial predilection, I had, from my youth, developed skills, work habits and knowledge that positioned me as a valuable asset to American Tobacco, and once I was part of the company, my all-out commitment assured a swift move upward to the highest levels. Achievement and success, in my mind and in the view of my co-workers, were intricately tied to hard work, and practically speaking, as we stayed with a single company, we earned the accumulation of generous benefits. We stayed with American Tobacco because we were loyal and because as family breadwinners, we were unwilling to risk the stability our jobs offered. Completely absent on the scene during this era was any feeling that the government would take care of us, and that attitude may also have contributed to our aversion to risk.

When I left American Tobacco, I bought the "company car" that I had been using, a two-door Oldsmobile '98 with plenty of room in the back seat that allowed me to pull in my Everest and Jennings wheelchair without assistance. As time went on, American manufacturers downsized the back seat areas of new model cars and to a great extent eliminated two-door, full-sized options entirely. I had been spoiled for years with large cars that I could manage alone – jumping in, pulling in the wheelchair, sliding over and driving with hand controls. The essence of true independence comes from needing no help, and I made a concerted effort to locate auto models that met my personal needs. Once I found a workable one, I stuck with it. In fact, for the last twenty or so years, I have cycled through a fleet of some eight or nine 1992 or 1993 Cadillac Coupe de Villes, sedans that allow ample room for me and my wheelchair. This was the last model year for this style of 2 door sedans and I still hunt for them to have a new one on the ready. Through political campaign trips of all kinds, personal travel and a lot of coming and going, I have documented driving or being driven well over a million miles, always managing to function up to the task. It never would have happened without these Caddies.

At one time, I met with Rick Wagoner, who was then Chairman of General Motors, and attempted to persuade him to produce a readily usable, handicap-friendly car. My pleas fell on deaf ears, however. He preached vans, which I hated and still do for a variety of reasons. Suitable cars have been harder and harder to find, but one individual, Art Hudgins of Holiday Cadillac in Williamsburg, continues to keep me supplied, as he has through the years. His loyalty is truly appreciated.

On January 4, 1995, the House of Representatives' Republican majority, led by Newt Gingrich, was sworn in, and I spent the day in Washington attending the ceremony. Afterwards, I joined the huge party hosted by good friend, the Richmond U.S. Representative Tom Bliley, who had been appointed chairman of the Commerce Committee. It seemed strange not to have to report to work every day during this month of transition with Brown and Williamson, but it was an appropriate way to begin what would become the political focus of my life.

As I sorted everything out, I virtually lost contact with the company for about four months. Then a Brown and Williamson executive, Ernie Pepples, called and asked me to return to work at their headquarters in Louisville. For legal reasons, company officials had been advised to wait that long before contacting me, but by then I had become involved in plans for a potential political campaign to seek the office of lieutenant governor, and my life was busy enough. Maybe I had experienced all the disruption I could handle from the tobacco industry. At any rate, I declined the offer.

Brown and Williamson then made an attractive offer for me to return as a part-time consultant, working in Richmond on government and public affairs. I accepted that position for the foreseeable future. Financially, these consulting duties provided a bridge after the takeover, but I realized that my relationship with the tobacco industry was nearly over. A new phase of my life was beginning.

In negotiating my consultant position, Brown and Williamson had assured me that I could continue to pursue my political campaign, and they proved very accommodating to that personal schedule. Most of my consulting work involved government affairs like attending the Tobacco Institute meetings and conferences around the country, and ironically my continued involvement in these sorts of activities actually fueled a growing interest in politics.

In the summer of 1995, I found myself with an uncharacteristically light work schedule and joined a group of friends for a trout fishing expedition in Montana and Wyoming on the Big Horn and Green Rivers. We had a great time, and the trip provided a new experience for me, as I had never seen that Western part of the country. As a bonus, it was a shock that I could be successful at fly-fishing from a boat floating down a river.

It was during this period that McGuire Woods offered me an office to use, which was a godsend to help keep me organized and effective. John Bates orchestrated this gracious offer, and I remain appreciative of my many friends there. While I was here, we organized leadership sessions for some of the younger associates. I learned alot about litigation in my time here.

With more time at my disposal, I intensified my involvement with several civic activities, the answer to being productively occupied during the major life change into retirement. I was very active in the Sorensen Institute, as I continue to be today. At the request of Mark Warner, I had joined the Virginia Health Care Foundation, where I became chairman. This foundation serves the state's underserved and uninsured, and I was instrumental in securing a million-dollar challenge grant from the Teresa Thomas Foundation. Many hours were spent with the Metro Richmond Convention and Visitors Bureau, a commitment that led to the Tourism Leadership Award.

In 1996, I received the Richmond First Club's Good Government Award, where my acceptance speech was summarized by one of the attendees, George Smith:

A capacity crowd was on hand for the 42nd presentation of Richmond-First Club's Good Government Award...During his speech...Hager expressed his belief in the benefits of regionalism, the need for leadership from all segments of the community and the positive impact the above activities would have on Metropolitan economic development.

Downtown revitalization is a priority of John Hager's. As a leading advocate of the Urban Partnership initiatives, John has provided visionary leadership to the proposed expansion of the Richmond Centre, lobbying politicians and businesses to move forward on this important project. The result was an increase in hospitality taxes passed by the Virginia General Assembly. John is now on the "belief" phase of this multi-million-dollar construction project, with regional jurisdiction support...John firmly believes that the $11.5 million annual operation costs will be offset easily by the economic benefits of having the largest convention facility in the state located in Richmond. The current facility is an economic liability for our region and leaves the Metro area out of the competitive convention market vital in such cities as Baltimore and Charlotte.

In conclusion, John spoke of the broad based leadership that has coalesced around the issues of the Urban Partnership and emphasized the need to continue the dialogue and teamwork as we move forward together as a region. There is a need for a proper visitors' center, attractive gateways, transportation linkages between attractions and localities and, above all, rebirth of civic pride.

The challenges await us all: thankfully we have individuals such as John Hager to provide invaluable leadership.

I also served on the board and held the vice chairmanship at Westminster Canterbury in Richmond, a continuing care retirement community. In the nineties, the board faced the major decision whether to build "The Glebe," a cluster of detached houses that offered independent living within Westminster Canterbury's care network. The board was divided as to whether or not this project was feasible, and we batted about the pros and cons for hours on end. I felt strongly about the advantages and finally presented an ultimatum: either we moved forward with construction or I would resign. With that impetus for action, the board voted to accept the proposal for "The Glebe," and construction began shortly thereafter. From the beginning, the concept was positively received, and "The Glebe" became a major success. In 1997, I received the Lettie Pate Whitehead Evans Award for outstanding service to Westminster Canterbury. Today we have many close friends at the facility who encourage Maggie and me to join them there.

Chapter 13

Plunging into Politics

Elected politics were on my agenda and in my future. I began putting out feelers and talking to people about whether or not it made sense for me to run for a political office, and if so, which one should be attempted. My state delegate, senator and congressman were all good friends, thus precluding these offices. Since I wasn't a lawyer, there would be no run for attorney general, and I knew there were not enough guts, background or organization to run for governor. The office of lieutenant governor was the only realistic spot to consider. I was determined to assume a larger role in politics, but the path had many roadblocks. It was time to get rolling.

On January 26, 1996, my fledgling campaign for lieutenant governor hosted a large fundraising luncheon at the Jefferson Hotel. There I began to offer my platform, taking a stand for "faith, family, freedom," a conviction that government needed to be managed like a business, and the belief that Virginia should promote itself to capitalize on tour-ism and export trade. Further, I stated, "If Virginia Republicans articulate their positive vision for Virginia and marshal community support, no one will be able to stop us from making the improvements needed in our schools." Does all of this sound familiar today? There was tremen-dous support from many friends and as-sociates, but the Commonwealth is a huge and diverse place, and I needed to begin working almost full-time on the venture. By July 15, 1996, the first very early finan-cial report showed that my campaign had raised more money in that cycle than any Republican candidate for Virginia's three statewide offices — governor, lieutenant governor and attorney general. Of course, the race wouldn't be until November 1997 so there was still much to be done and a long journey ahead.

National Convention 1996

Shad Planking 1997

The Republican National Convention was in August 1996 in San Diego, California, and that forum afforded me an opportunity to talk with numerous Republican leaders. There were 125 delegates and alternates from Virginia at the convention, and while the Party was nominating its candidate, Senator Bob Dole, I reported to several radio stations back home about our activities. Henry, who was still at Wake Forest, went with me to the convention, and during a great week in San Diego, we covered a lot of groundwork at the varied activities there, including a day trip into Mexico. Henry boarded the bus with a group from Virginia, and by day's end, he and George Allen were best friends. I believe this early exposure helped stimulate Henry's growing interest in politics and his understanding of political behavior.

During the week, the *San Diego Union-Tribune* published an interview with me. There were reminiscences of my relationship with Jonas Salk, who lived there, and emphasis on the fact that I considered him a "great man." Describing the Virginia political scene, the reporter noted, "Getting people to take responsibility to help themselves is a favorite theme of John H. Hager's." They included a quote of mine — "I am a work horse, not a show horse." — alluding to my future competition-to-be. The article stirred quite a buzz.

By early 1997, we finalized the staff, organized volunteers and attended an enormous array of events. As I zigzagged across the state, I shook hands with Republican leaders and ordinary folks at every stop. Coleman Andrews, who was routinely billed as "the front runner" for lieutenant governor, was a formidable opponent. The only way I could hope to outrun him was by meeting as many voters as humanly possible, selling them on my viability as a candidate and convincing them to embrace my vision for Virginia and to participate in the process by voting in the primary. Despite strong supporters like the Virginia Federation of Republican Women, many General Assembly members, the so-called business establishment and moderate stalwarts in the Party all over the state, I had massive work cut out for me to win the nomination, but since the slate would be decided by a primary, there seemed to be a good chance I could win.

Style Weekly's December 17, 1996 edition included an article entitled, "Marathon Man," with the subtitle "John Hager's taking on one of the longest and toughest battles of his life." The feature article described my "reputation of being everywhere, including the city marathon." It began with a description of how I get out of my car.

He eases into the passenger seat and opens the passenger-side door. Then he reaches into the back seat with his right hand and hauls out his folded wheelchair and snaps it open. He grabs his legs and shoves them out the door, then lifts himself into the chair.

This isn't something he makes a big deal about, although it's certainly the most obvious thing one notices when first meeting him...It seems Hager's disability and his political life are intertwined. Both brought him to long races that he intends to win...There's little doubt that Hager is a fighter. For the past 12 years, he's participated in marathons – his best time is a respectable 3:40 – and he won the most recent Times-Dispatch half-marathon wheelchair division. "I would have done the full marathon, he says now, "but I had a political event to go to that afternoon."

...Hager has injected himself into a fight that should prove as long and difficult as one of his marathons...He has a long race ahead, says political observer Robert Holsworth, a professor of political science at Virginia Commonwealth University. "He's fighting an uphill battle here... but if he is able to raise money so that he can be halfway competitive in television advertising, he might well be competitive."

The June 1997 Republican Party primary, took on special significance for my campaign because, like every potential candidate, we could not qualify to run until we had amassed 10,000 signatures on petitions with at least 400 from each of the eleven congressional districts.

Most of the winter and spring had been devoted to gathering these signatures from all over the state, and once we had accomplished that feat, we were ecstatic. Not only did we feel confident that we had fulfilled the requirements, but we were sure that we had well exceeded the stipulated numbers. My staffers loaded the boxes of signed petition pages in my lap, and we took them directly to the State Board of Elections Office for submission. At about the same time, my competitor, T. Coleman Andrews III, also successfully completed the gathering of his signatures, but a third candidate, Jay Katzen, failed to meet the deadline and was thus eliminated from the primary contest. It would be Andrews vs. Hager.

I promised that if elected, I would eschew the usual part-time role most lieutenant governors assumed and would give full-time service to Virginia. Because I could devote my energies to the office, not divide my efforts between it and a business career, which

Coleman Andrews would have to do, I could make the role of lieutenant governor a powerful one. "I'm running with integrity," was my statement. "I'm about people, not money; accomplishments, not broken promises." Somehow, my whole life had resulted in this destiny quest.

In an interesting side angle to my campaign, John Goolrick wrote in *The Amelia Bulletin Monitor*, Thursday, February 27, 1997, an article entitled, "Hager seen as getting 'the nod' in GOP race for Lt. Gov." Goolrick began with a political recollection:

In bygone days of Virginia politics, it was often the custom of the Democratic hierarchy to give "the nod" to someone it favored in a battle for a party nomination.

It was done in different ways. Perhaps it was Harry Byrd, Sr. conspicuously greeting a particular person at the Shad Planking or maybe a kind word from on high conferred the blessing. The idea was to send a message to the faithful without having to make an outright endorsement.

Mills Godwin recalls those days, since early in his political career he was a recipient of "the nod" and later a provider.

Recently, former Gov. Godwin showed up at a Richmond fund raiser for GOP lieutenant governor aspirant John Hager and said that while he wasn't taking sides in the nomination battle for that position, John Hager was a long-time friend and a fine man well qualified for high office.

Despite Gov. Godwin's professed neutrality, several who were there clearly recognized it as "the nod." Said one, "He didn't leave me with any doubt he's for John Hager. And I think everyone else there had the same idea."

By April, some six weeks before the primary and well into the campaign, we were scheduled to attend a big fundraising luncheon with national leaders of the disability movement in Arlington. Maggie and I were being driven up Interstate 95 by one of the members of my staff when I received an unexpected phone call. It was from Ross Mackenzie, longtime friend and Editorial Page Editor of the *Richmond Times-Dispatch*. "Are you firmly in your seat?" he asked. "You are going to receive a call from Coleman Andrews, who is withdrawing from the campaign!"

"Really?" I said, incredulous. "That is too wild to believe, especially since I'm supposed to be the underdog."

Unlikely as it seemed, about fifteen minutes later, Coleman Andrews called and told me that due to a family medical concern, he had decided to withdraw from the campaign. "Are you able to be in Richmond this afternoon for a press conference?" he asked.

"Yes, we will try to get there." I responded.

"I think it would be wise," he urged me.

It was quite a day. We continued on to the luncheon in the Arlington hotel where I spoke. It was emotional as I thanked the attendees for their support and raised some money. Then we hightailed it back to Richmond and to the State Capitol's third floor press briefing room.

Sure enough, Coleman Andrews officially withdrew from the primary campaign. He publically stated that his daughter was suffering from an illness and he wanted to devote his attention to her. Truth be known, there was a swirl of information and rumors, but only Coleman Andrews knows the truth about why he withdrew. Whatever his reasons, with no other qualified opponent, I was immediately declared the official Republican candidate for lieutenant governor. My campaign team and I were elated, though I went from having tough competition for the Republican primary nomination to having a tough opponent in the general election for the office. Still, Andrews' withdrawal meant that we could concentrate on my race to defeat the Democratic candidate, Lewis F. Payne.

L.F. Payne was a well known and well liked Democrat in Virginia. By the time we vied for the office of lieutenant governor, he had represented the Fifth District in Congress for ten years and had earned a position on the Ways and Means Committee. A good man, he knew people all over the state. Further, he had the ability to raise a lot of money, and he would be running as part of a strong ticket with Don Beyer, the Democratic nominee for governor. Many people questioned his decision to run for lieutenant governor, though it was obvious that the office would be a stepping-stone to his becoming governor four years later. Ominously, he started the campaign with a thirty percent lead. That was enough to keep us focused!

Also running on the Republican ticket were Jim Gilmore for governor and Mark Earley for attorney general. In Virginia each candidate runs individually so that early in the campaign, I was on my own to make my case against my Democratic opponent. As the election drew near, the team coordinated efforts and ran more and more as a single Republican choice.

It seemed essential that we make a concerted effort to reach a wide range of voters across Virginia and to appeal both to urban and rural constituents of every class. Jack and Henry took to the campaign trail as often as they could, and Maggie campaigned quite extensively, traveling to various events around the state where she made appearances and often took to the podium. She was an effective campaigner, and with her help, I was able to broaden our appeal far more than might otherwise have been possible.

Reflections of John's wife, Margaret "Maggie" Chase Hager

Polio is an involuntary illness, with an individual having no influence in contracting it, unlike an accident that follows someone's reckless actions or a disease that develops after an individual puts himself in harm's way. I have been told that people who contract polio often pursue very active lives. They become even more involved, outgoing and responsible than their peers, and that seems to be the case for John. He has been chairman or president of so many committees and programs, and it is revealing of his character that he has pursued a wide range of involvements and interests despite his disability. I believe the many activities and sheer busyness of our lives have helped us stay grounded.

He is a giver, and that really is at the root of his character and the motivation for his amazing record of involvement. It is in his nature to be understanding of other people and to help them with their problems. He believes in active involvement, not passive observation.

John also is blessed with a gift of tremendous leadership. Whether working in civic, political or family arenas, he is motivated by the same tenants: never complain; do your very best; keep going despite circumstances that make the path difficult, and strive to achieve positions of leadership and greatness as you travel through life. These are the lessons that guided him in every pursuit, and they are the tenants he taught and demonstrated for our sons. As for Henry and Jack, they are remarkable boys, and much of the depth and wisdom they demonstrate as well as their strength of character comes from their being in a family in which the father is disabled.

When John first entered politics, I had no idea what was involved. As the campaign unfolded and the reality of political life came into focus, I was inspired by the realization that John was the greatest gift I could give to the people of Virginia. What a true gift to have him in a leadership role and working with and for the citizens of the Commonwealth. I became very involved in the campaign and basically ran an office in our home as an adjunct to the campaign office. I started my own speaker's bureau, as calls would come to our home with requests for me to speak at various occasions. I was very self-reliant: writing my own speeches, scheduling my appearances, confirming the directions and driving myself to functions. Sometimes I was with John, but sometimes I was completely on my own.

There were times when I was spread pretty thin. September and October were key months before the November elections. At about two in the morning on Saturday, September 13, 1997, my mother phoned to tell me that my sister had passed away very suddenly. I had several speeches scheduled for that day. I went over to my mother's house and stayed for a couple of hours and then returned home to dress. I remember thinking, "Do I put on a black dress for my sister or a red dress for John?" I changed into a red dress and started off to Petersburg, then continued on to Virginia Beach with stops all along the way. We all paused a few days later for the funeral at St. John's Church in Washington. It was a sad time.

After John was elected lieutenant governor, I invited some of the Republican women's clubs to lunch in our home. Because they had never been recognized, I wanted them to be in the home of a lieutenant governor. I started with my own club, Tuckahoe Republican Women's Club, and branched out to Henrico, Goochland and then with a wider and wider reach until I had invited more than a thousand women to our home for lunch. I couldn't afford a caterer or to take them out, so I fixed the lunches myself. I invited them to come around 11:30, and then I planned another activity for them around 2:00, usually a tour of Agecroft Hall or the Capitol. The tricky part came when I was out at some event with John until one o'clock in the morning

One of Maggie's Luncheons

before one of these luncheons. I knew the ladies would soon be arriving, and I had to get started
steaming chicken breasts and preparing as much as I could before I fell asleep.

On July 7, 1997, we announced our "Rolling Across Virginia" tour. At the press conference, I began rolling my wheelchair a short way down the street, a move which was filmed and then later used in part of a television ad that was developed. I vowed to visit and participate in an activity in every locality in Virginia, that is in every one of Virginia's one hundred counties and thirty-four cities. That was the ambitious goal we set, and that is exactly what we managed to accomplish, touring up until a week before the campaign ended.

It was a challenge in itself, but I was determined to prevail. The idea originally came from Doug Wilder's successful effort that is detailed in his book, *When Hell Froze Over*. I have always had a close relationship with Doug, and we have talked about how important it is to involve the people of Virginia in political action.

Our campaign slogan was, "The courage to lead, the experience to care," as we relentlessly took this message to the people. A second slogan was, "Turning challenge into opportunity."

Running a statewide election campaign and turning out the numbers that are essential for winning is a tremendous job that could never be done without a competent staff, a cadre of supporters and many volunteers. We had opened an office off Staples Mill Road and assembled the key positions. Three professional consultants joined our team:

Courtesy of the Richmond Times-Dispatch

Campaigning "Rolling Across Virginia"

Tim Philips, now president of Americans for Prosperity, Phil Cox, most recently with the Republican Governors' Association, and Jim Lamb, who heads Commonwealth Consultants. Jim and Tim hired other people, including a scheduler, to fill critical spots. Beverley "Booty" Armstrong assumed the role of finance chairman, and full-time staffers set to work: Lars Wiechmann, Beth Thornton, Alicia Brittle, Paul Wieland, John Pazur, Ashley Taylor, Mike Salster and Anne Shercliff. Three additional staff members – Gretchen Moss, Laura Bell, and Sandy Canada – worked part-time with me on regional fundraising.

At no time did I attempt to make my disability an issue. There were plenty of events on picnic grounds, at riverbanks, on the backs of flatbed trucks or in spots with a high stage, where a wheelchair made for tough going, but people were always willing to lend a hand if I had to be lifted over an obstacle or up some stairs. On August 5, 1997, *The Culpeper Star Exponent* described the sentiments that many observers could have echoed:

You would be hard-pressed to find a less conventional, legitimate candidate for a major, statewide office than John Hager. Hager is believed to be the first Virginian to vie for statewide office in a wheelchair.

After the election, it was confirmed by the Lieutenant Governors Association that I was indeed the first lieutenant governor in a wheelchair – not just in Virginia but in the entire country.

There were several factors that were positive influences on our campaign, and they all contributed to a growing momentum. First, we were able to raise enough money, some $1.5 million, to manage the campaign effectively, including running television ads. Also, we were aided in some ways by the tide of history, as Jim Gilmore was seeking to succeed a popular, Republican governor, George Allen. Additionally, I fared well in a couple of debates with L. F. Payne. Finally, I was fortunate to receive editorial support from newspapers around the state.

Our dogged, face-to-face campaign across Virginia took hold, and the perception of me as a novice campaigner changed to a recognition that I was a viable candidate with a practical message: that people, not the government, know best how to solve the problems they face. Virginians responded positively to the insistence on common sense. Issues they cited as most pressing became the platform I emphasized — the reform of education by empowering local school boards to try innovative ideas and to move toward performance-based systems of education; economic development and the protection/nurturing of Virginia's mature industries; smaller, more responsive government and a moratorium on tax increases; enhancement of Virginia's transportation network; focus on tackling drug and gang threats through cooperative efforts with local law enforcement agencies; emphasis on community principles; opportunities for the broader disabled community with an emphasis on self-reliance, and protection of the environment through innovative ideas.

The real secret of politics is convincing people that you can do something for them.

Jerry Kilgore and John on the campaign trail

I drew on my experience of working with many different types of people and tried to show my fellow citizens that I could accomplish worthwhile actions that would make a difference in their lives.

Our byline, "The experience to care and the courage to lead," was one we repeated over and over. I ran on the premise that I would work hard for the citizens of Virginia, assuring our audiences that my being wheelchair-bound would not mean that I would spend more time on issues facing people with disabilities than on other issues or citizen groups. I felt that the best way to serve the disability community was to demonstrate accomplishment, whatever the endeavor. As I stated in an interview with Gary W. Melton for *Paralegal News* (October 1998):

The fact is, we live in America, and people should have great dreams. If they are willing to work hard and to focus, and if they are willing to try, there is no reason why all readers of this magazine shouldn't be able to live out their American dreams...Regardless of where people are or their status in life, they can still dream and do better. We can help them. We cannot do it for them, but we can help make sure they have a chance. That's what motivates me as an officeholder, as a politician.

The campaign dominated my life the whole year, but I remained involved in my civic activities to the extent possible and continued wheelchair jogging as time permitted. I was also involved to a limited degree in some interesting legal cases, stemming from my

Newt Gingrich campaign event

prior work with American Tobacco. For three or four years after the company was bought out, I was periodically contacted by Dan O'Neill, a partner at Chadbourne and Parke law firm in New York. He would talk about the carryover of health-related lawsuits, and in three of the cases I was deposed along with many others by plaintiffs' lawyers. Usually to prepare fully for the court proceedings, I would meet Dan in Washington the night before, and then the next day I would testify. I never really had any trouble fielding questions, and my proudest courtroom moment came when I went a full day with Peter Angelos, the renowned trial lawyer from Baltimore, who never managed to extract anything useful from me. At one time, the press tried to make something out of my testimony, but I had said nothing incriminating and it proved to be a one-day story.

Mine was a long and hard political race leading to November 1997, but around September, there was a shift in momentum as Jim Gilmore started making inroads in his own poll deficit by touting the repeal of the state's personal property tax on automobiles. Simultaneously, people began to connect me with the Gilmore ticket and "No Car Tax." The state Party printed thousands of signs depicting the Republican ticket with Gilmore, Hager and Earley so our posters seemed to show up everywhere.

Maggie and I continued attending all sorts of events, sometimes accompanied by various celebrities. Many people lent their names and status to advance my cause. Jim Nicholson, Chairman of the Republican National Committee, spent a couple of days on the campaign trail with me in the Roanoke and Lynchburg areas. On one memorable day, Newt Gingrich attended an event for me at Christy and Michael Jarvis's house. We also went to the Virginia Home, where Maggie now serves as a Director. Dan Quayle participated in an event for me in Northern Virginia. A late infusion of cash from some of my supporters in the Public Affairs Group and others in the business community enabled me to finance television ads that spread my story of overcoming polio, achieving success as a business executive, working as a community leader and excelling at wheelchair marathoning. People began to notice.

The Republican Ticket

About three weeks out from the election, I suddenly realized it could happen. The campaign had a momentum that the Democrats couldn't muster, and we were going to win! The Sunday, October 26, 1997, *Richmond Times Dispatch*, ran a particularly advantageous editorial entitled, "For John Hager:"

He's upbeat, positive, can-do – as one must be to overcome the adversity of a major handicap. He toiled long in the vineyards of Virginia's many charities and volunteer agencies. He was a top executive with one of Virginia's major corporations. For years, and with considerable success, he helped lead the state's fractious Republican Party toward precisely the consensus Virginia now needs if it is to keep on keeping on.

Of course, these developments did not translate into an eased schedule. The weekend before the election was wild with several ticket events. On Election Day after voting, my staff planned a typically packed trip to Northern Virginia with symbolic stops in the Eighth, Tenth and Eleventh Districts. While driving back down the Interstate towards home, I received a phone call in the car from my friend Larry Sabato, political author and director of the University of Virginia's Center for Politics.

Larry said, "Are you firmly in your seat?"

"Yes," I answered. "Why are you asking?"

"You're going to win! I can't believe it, but you're going to win," he said.

That was exciting. I went home, and we all dressed to go downtown and wait for election results. It took hours to tally the votes, but sometime around eleven o'clock the count was significant enough to assure that I had won the spot. We took the election with 50.2% of the votes, and because a third independent candidate had added his name to the ballot, I actually defeated L.F. Payne by more than five percentage points. We carried 88 of Virginia's 134 jurisdictions, and the final margin of victory exceeded 80,000 votes.

Today, my friend Paul Galanti describes riding on the elevator with Jack and Henry and how excited everyone was as they gathered with me and my supporters in the Marriott ballroom. I took the podium and declared victory. It was a clean sweep! The entire Republican ticket —Gilmore, Hager and Earley — won the election, an unheard of accomplishment for Republicans in Virginia politics. It was the conclusion of what many considered an unachievable goal, a win that resulted from the efforts of so many. It was a fairy tale come true.

That night's victory party continues to be remembered by many as a high point for Virginia Republicans. The spirit was infectious, with so many happy people, not the least of whom were Maggie and me.

Chapter 14

Four Glorious Years

Once the election was over, it was an unbelievably busy and exciting time. We were no longer embroiled in a campaign, but the post-campaign's schedule of appearances and activities was almost as demanding. On the Sunday after my election, I was whisked up to the Willard Hotel in Washington to attend the GOPAC Convention, which was a big deal in those days. Fresh from the Republican sweep in Virginia, I was treated like a rock star, and taking the stage as featured speaker before that supportive gathering was an unforgettable experience.

About a week later, Maggie and I flew to Miami and joined the Republican Governors' Association at Doral Golf Resort. As a winning lieutenant governor, I was given full privileges at the gathering, and it was here that as a couple we met Laura and Governor George W. Bush for the first time. Who knew they would later play such an important role in our lives? One of the highlights of the association's planned activities was an evening cruise down the Intracoastal Waterway, and at the buffet dinner onboard we

Lieutenant Governor's Office Staff

happened to sit with Laura and George at one of the small tables. It is ironic to recall how we chatted with them as we cruised, all of us admiring Christmas lights along the way and neither couple aware of the future relationship we would share.

December of 1997 should have brought a bit of a reprieve in my schedule, but there was not much time between the election and the beginning of my new responsibilities. I soon began establishing the lieutenant governor-elect's office and working on the transition team for Governor-elect Gilmore. It became apparent that quite a few of my campaign workers wanted to continue working with me in the lieutenant governor's office. My old friend, Regina Payne, joined the staff. She had originally worked for Maggie during George Allen's administration when Maggie headed the office of the Department for Rights of Virginians with Disabilities. For a brief time, David Ross came to me from the Richmond Chamber. Ashley Taylor, who had been at the Republican Party of Virginia and worked throughout the campaign, came on board, as did Lars Wiechmann, who had worked as my driver and contact person during the campaign. Katherine Waddell handled scheduling for a while and was succeeded by Alicia Brittle. They were great. Others volunteered to work and helped significantly. Together, we set up shop in a large group of offices on the top floor of the Pocahontas Building on Main Street. Since my intention was to approach my new duties as a full-time job, I was fortunate to be living in Richmond, thus avoiding the long distance travel to the capital that many elected officials face.

Meanwhile, the long-time clerk of the Virginia Senate, Susan Schaar, decided on her own that with my election as lieutenant governor, a new arrangement would need to be designed to enable me to roll my wheelchair to the podium where I would preside. With the help of an architect, she proposed an elaborate lift to serve the purpose. Shortly after the election when I went downtown to meet Susan, she described to me her extensive and expensive plan.

"Susan," I suggested, "I really don't care for lifts because they can be unreliable and they emphasize disability. I think all we need is to measure the distance from the side wall and build a simple, wooden ramp. It will have to be a bit steep to fit in the space, but the workout will be good for me. I'll ask John Siewers to donate the lumber, and it will cost the state practically nothing."

She was surprised, but together we planned a workable ramp, which she covered with a fancy rug, and though too steep to be strictly ADA compliant, it served the purpose. Susan and I would come to know each other well during the next four years. Early on, she provided materials for me so that I could train to lead the Senate's proceedings effectively. I studied the Senate's arcane rules, memorized each Senator's seating position, and reviewed videos and transcripts of past proceedings. Several realistic practice sessions enabled me to learn staff duties and provided opportunities for me to interact with Capitol personnel. The going was slow at first, and I felt somewhat overwhelmed, but my pre-session efforts paid off and enabled me to assume leadership of the Senate with confidence.

Reflections of Susan Schaar, Clerk of the Senate of Virginia

When I learned that John Hager was running in the Republican primary, I began contacting my counterparts in other states. We are very involved with the National Conference of State Legislatures and the American Society of Clerks and Secretaries, so I asked if there had ever been another presiding officer in a situation similar to John's, i.e. being in a wheelchair. There had not.

Our dais is very cramped and there is only a narrow space for approaching it. While I was in Texas for a meeting, I noticed that on one side of their dais, they had installed a lift. Thinking that a lift would be the least obtrusive solution, I had them send me all the information about its installation and use.

The whole time, people were saying, "You don't have to worry about that. Coleman Andrews is going to win the Republican primary."

"Well, you know," I answered, "I've been around here long enough to realize that anything can happen in politics. I'll just continue my research."

I contacted the Department of General Services about installing a ramp, and they informed me that in order for it to reach the height of our dais and comply with the Americans with Disabilities Act, the ramp would have to wrap all around the chamber. I knew that wouldn't work since the space required would make it impossible for Senators in the back row to get in and out of their desks.

People were still shaking their heads at me and saying, "You don't have to worry about it."

Then Coleman Andrews dropped out of the race, and I said, "See?"

"Not a problem," they assured me. "L.F. Payne is going to win."

On election night, L. F. Payne did not win. First thing the next morning, I received a call from Lieutenant Governor Hager. "I'd like to meet with you," he told me.

"Certainly," I answered.

Right away, he came down, and the first thing he wanted to do was discuss how he would get to the dais. We talked about options, and he said firmly, "Well, we are not going to install a lift because there's nothing worse than getting on one of those things and having it get stuck."

I had never thought of that, but I readily agreed that a malfunctioning lift would present a bad situation.

"We'll just put a ramp in," he concluded.

I said, "Well, here's the problem with the ramp. ADA guidelines..."

He interrupted me with an emphatic declaration, "I don't care about ADA. You just put a ramp in, and I'll get up it."

"Okay," I agreed, somewhat dubiously.

I brought in an architect. We moved a few desks two or three inches and relocated where the pages sat. With a minimum of fuss, we installed a sharply pitched ramp. Despite its very steep incline, John Hager never, in the four years he was in office, required any assistance getting up the ramp. I offered to assign a page to push him, but he emphatically refused the suggestion.

"I compete in marathons. I can get up this ramp," he insisted. And he did, every single day of the session.

Another obstacle presented itself in the House Chamber. Lieutenant Governor Hager would need to go down a center aisle and ascend to the speaker's platform for the Governor's State of the Commonwealth addresses. The problem was that the center aisle had steps, and there really was no place for a ramp. As a solution, blocks that slanted down through the center aisle were installed, so that the Lieutenant Governor could roll his wheelchair down, and to ascend to the speaker's platform, four men assisted him up the steps. With as little disruption as possible, he dealt with a problematic situation.

Lieutenant Governor Hager never complained, and I never heard him try to get out of something or ask for special favors because of his disability. He would become frustrated at the slow movement of political actions, which was so unlike the corporate world he had known, but after four years in office, he came to grasp the slow momentum, frustrating though it continued to be. Through it all, he always retained his sense of humor, and he was unfailingly considerate of staff. He loves to talk to people, to listen to people and to try to help people.

There was a fateful night when Lieutenant Governor Hager went home for dinner during a recess and on the return drive, he was hit by a teen driver. The impact of the collision was severe enough to total his car. He came into the chamber with a huge knot on his head and began describing the accident to me. "Did you see a doctor?" I asked.

"No," he answered.

"Did you stop at MCV?" I persisted.

"No, we've got business tonight. I'll take care of myself later."

He stayed through the whole session, and finally when the evening ended, he allowed himself to be examined at a hospital.

That same night, one of the Senators accused John Hager of being influenced too heavily by me, especially in regards to parliamentary procedure. John shared with me that he firmly told the Senator, "When I ask Susan a question, she gives me the answer she thinks I need to do my job. She is always professional, and I make up my own mind."

I very much appreciated his magnanimous insistence that I was professional in fulfilling my duties.

I always felt that if John Hager had become governor, his sense of responsibility and fairness would have influenced him to work with both sides of the aisle. I also never had the sense that he viewed the office as a jumping off point for other political offices. He sincerely wanted to work for the Commonwealth.

While he was in office, we usually spent about an hour each morning reviewing his calendar of events. Often when I entered his office, he was writing in what I assumed to be a journal. Finally, one day I asked if indeed he were keeping a diary.

"Yes," he answered. "I have always kept a journal, and one day I'm going to write a book. Do you keep a journal, Susan?"

"No," I said, "and there are probably a lot of people who are glad that I don't."

He laughed, but admonished me, "It's too bad you haven't been keeping one, because your journals would make great reading."

Inaugural Ball 1998

Those of us who worked with him all admire John Hager. It is always good to see him when he comes to the Capitol and always a pleasure to work with him.

As the inauguration neared, there was a flurry of activity. The Senate in Virginia always convenes on the second Wednesday in January, and inaugurations are held on the following Saturday. Thus during inauguration years, the outgoing lieutenant governor presides over the Senate for the first three days of the session. With no official duties yet at hand, Jim Gilmore, Mark Earley and I, accompanied by our families, spent the week before the inauguration traveling around the state to festive events in our honor, and we had time to come to know each other well during these busy, fun days. We started in Abington on Saturday, went to Fairfax and Alexandria on Sunday, continued to Norfolk on Tuesday and returned to Richmond on Wednesday. Mark Earley held his inaugural ball on Thursday night, and mine – with a huge, joyous turnout – was held on Friday night at the Jefferson Hotel. The culminating ceremony, the inauguration itself, was on Saturday, January seventeenth. I was sworn in by Judge Leroy Hassell, who had become a friend during the time when I worked to support Roy West with the Public Affairs Group. Maggie held the Bible, and our sons stood close by as I took the oath of office. The parade afterwards was most enjoyable, and that night the huge, gala Governor's In-augural Ball at the Richmond Convention Center crowned the festivities.

My parents attended the inauguration, though my father's health was poor at the time. They were very proud of all the happenings. About two weeks later, Dad had a heart operation in Durham, and I drove down to see him. He recovered from surgery,

Inauguration 1998

but both of my parents were becoming older and frailer by this time. I always regretted that I hadn't had more time to be with them during these years, but they were happy in Durham and my sister was quite attentive to their needs. She made a big difference.

Maggie and I were just ready to leave the Inaugural Ball when Gerald Massengill, Superintendent of Virginia State Police, entered the ballroom and said, "There's a trooper down!"

In the world of the state police, who feel strong kinship with one another, there is no more distressing news than that a fellow officer has been shot. While it was in no way connected to the inauguration, the tragic news slowly brought the evening's festivities to an end. The state police had played a big role the entire week by driving us, protecting us and being a big part of the ceremonies. Their loss was felt by all of us.

When I assumed office, there were twenty Republican Senators and twenty Democratic Senators in Virginia, an interesting situation to say the least, but soon after taking office, Governor Gilmore convinced one of the Democrats, Charlie Waddell, to accept the position of Deputy Secretary of Transportation, a move which resulted in a vacancy. In a special election, Republican Bill Mims won the seat and tipped the balance to the GOP, with their twenty-one votes versus nineteen Democratic votes. For the full four years that I was lieutenant governor, the Republicans maintained this control.

By the time the Senate convened, I felt well prepared to preside over the sessions, and throughout the long first year all proceeded quite smoothly. It was heartening to have Senators from both sides of the aisle commend the fairness and effectiveness of my leadership; the decorum and tenor of our sessions reflected the respectful tolerance that was encouraged and modeled during my four years leading the Senate. I also was pleased with the overall efficiency of our efforts. Given the huge volume of legislation and the number of issues that must be considered, it was impossible to slow down and we conscientiously tackled mountains of paperwork.

It was a very interesting time in Virginia, and lots of politics prevailed in the General Assembly's lengthy 1998 session. Since I was not a member of the Senate, I had to depend on cooperation and coordination to advance any initiatives. I met with the Republican Senate caucus during breaks and before session every day. I also lobbied and worked behind the scenes with the governor and others to promote legislation that would benefit our state. One of my responsibilities as lieutenant governor was to cast the decisive vote whenever a tie occurred, though with the Republican majority of twenty-one, this seldom happened. The most important tie vote involved directing lottery funds to education, a decision that seemed very logical but became bogged down in a political quagmire before final passage.

Considerable tension came to the forefront in the Chamber over issues of germaneness, and I sometimes had to be the final decision-maker on such questions. It is not unusual in Washington for lawmakers to tack unpopular initiatives onto popular legislation, but in Virginia such maneuvers are prohibited. Everything within a proposed bill must, by law, pertain to the legislation at hand, though occasionally state lawmakers still attempt slipping pet initiatives onto unrelated bills. It is up to the lieutenant governor to rule on the legitimacy of such amendments. There were several significant times during my four years when such decisions were necessary, none more contentious than in 2001 when Governor Gilmore tacked an amendment raising salaries for state employees onto a bill concerning the state's retirement system. The governor had, in fact, submitted a host of amendments to nearly a hundred bills, many of which called into question the validity of their relevance to the original legislation, but this particular amendment forced a heated showdown.

Official State picture

Knowing that a decision against the amendment would alienate the governor and anger some of my fellow Republicans, I was in the difficult position of having to make a final ruling that could jeopardize any potential future political aspirations I might entertain. In the end, the choice was not so difficult after all. The laws of Virginia were clear, and I had no choice but to follow them and rule against the governor's amendment. I stated at the time, "I don't shy away from my responsibility...I'm willing to do what's right. Certainly the expedient thing for me to have done would be to rule this constitutional, get it out of the way and be done with it. But I cannot come to the podium this afternoon...and do something that I consider to be unconstitutional. To me, it's about integrity. It's about the integrity of the process, it's about the integrity of the General Assembly."

With Jack Berry

My own initiatives that first year primarily concerned military tax cuts and the tightening of regulations concerning teen driving. I also worked with Emily Couric to pass the Commonwealth Neuro-trauma Initiative, through which Virginia established a trust that was devoted to research into the prevention and treatment of spinal cord and brain injuries and to rehabilitative and other assistance for individuals with those injuries. The trust was primarily funded through fees incurred by convicted drunk and reckless drivers seeking to have their licenses reinstated. I successfully obtained a budget amendment that authorized the Secretary of Transportation to negotiate a loan for the building of a two-mile test track "Smart Road" in Blacksburg and to test the feasibility and commercial potential for Mag-Lev trains in Virginia. I had already worked for years on the $178 million project to quadruple the size of the Richmond Convention Center, and I continued the quest to finish that goal.

Reflections of Jack Berry, President and CEO of Richmond Region Tourism

I have had three mentors in my life, and John is one of the three. I have learned so much from him, personally and business-wise, and I have also been in a unique position to see his contributions to Richmond and the metropolitan area through his successful efforts to spearhead the building of the present day convention center.

When I first came to Richmond in 1988 as the Sales and Marketing Representative for Richmond's convention center, the facility was a $19 million, cinderblock structure at Fifth and Marshall Streets that was only two years old but was already being used to capacity.

The next year, the Convention and Visitors Bureau, in conjunction with regional representatives from the city and surrounding counties – Henrico, Chesterfield, and later Hanover – prepared a white paper, studying the feasibility of expanding and upgrading the old building. By the time the study was complete in 1990, I had become the general manager of the building, and I strongly supported the study's conclusion that the structure needed to be expanded. Problem was that no funds were available, so the study was shelved.

In 1992, I became president of the Convention and Visitors Bureau, and in July 1994, John Hager became chairman. John was one of the founding members of the organization, which had begun as a spin-off of the Chamber of Commerce in 1983. The mission of the bureau was to work in a spirit of regional cooperation to bring tourists and conventions to the Richmond region. Up until the time that he became chairman, I had not known John, but I soon had firsthand exposure to his leadership skills.

John, as the new chairman, realized immediately that we needed to formalize our priorities. He asked me early on, "What is the mission of the bureau? What is the vision?"

"I don't think we have any mission or vision, at least nothing in writing," I answered him.

"Well, we need to set a mission, set a vision and define our priorities," he informed me.

In my position as president, I had been focused on the bureau rather than the building, but as we formalized our mission and vision, I saw that the building and bureau were intricately intertwined. After a Strategic Board retreat, the board concluded that the 1990 study should be resurrected and updated. There was no doubt about it: we needed a bigger building. Right away, John started to put wheels in motion, working behind the scenes to make this goal a reality.

For a couple of years, the Chamber of Commerce, joined by regional representatives from Chesterfield, Henrico, Hanover and the city of Richmond conducted inner-city visits to Cincinnati and Minneapolis. With momentum generated from these visits and with John as chairman of the Convention and Visitors Bureau, the same consultant who had compiled the earlier study, KPMG, was asked in April of 1995 to update it with a cost-benefit analysis. This analysis outlined how we should go about securing funds for the building and it also revised upwards its prior recommendations for expansion. (Interestingly, the completed convention center, with a cost of $178,000,000 and a 35,000-square-foot ballroom was very close to the predictions.) It was this cost-benefit analysis that provided a springboard for what became a four-year struggle to provide funding for the new Convention and Visitors Bureau building.

The analysis recommended that financial responsibility for the building should be divided among jurisdictions, with Richmond responsible for fifty percent, Henrico, thirty-five percent, Chesterfield, thirteen percent and Hanover for two percent. With the focus on a new building, John managed to convene a monthly meeting of the busy chief administrative officers of all four jurisdictions. They then devised a master team of four task forces, composed of the CAOs of each jurisdiction.

John and I made many presentations about the convention center, and at the time, which was before Power Point, we compiled carousels of 35-millimeter slides for our sales presentation. After three weeks of putting one of our presentations together, those of us in my office had just put the last slide in its place when John came in and we showed it to him. "That's a great first draft," he told us. "I can't wait to see the final product."

My jaw hit the table. We had worked so hard on what we thought was a great presentation. But as it happened, a new software product called Persuasion had just come on the market, and one of our staff people knew of it. The computer necessary for making the slides for Persuasion and the overhead projector that was necessary for viewing were both the size of a large suitcase and extremely heavy, but we bought them and got back to work. The final presentation we showed John, and that he in turn showed to untold numbers of groups, looked creative, professional and slick, far beyond what 35-millimeter slideshows could offer.

Virginia's law, as outlined in the Dillon Rule, requires legislative approval before any county can raise admissions, hotel or meals taxes. Thus, in 1996, the legislative team went to the General Assembly, and based on the cost-benefit analysis study, requested permission for Henrico, Chesterfield and Hanover Counties to enact four percent increases in their hotel taxes, increases that would finance the counties' backing of the convention center.

In preparation for the meeting with the Senate's Finance Committee, many, many time consuming meetings were held. We tried to assemble every possible document and projection that could possibly be requested, and John, who was not yet an elected official, went before the Senators as project chairman. As the hearing on the tax increase proceeded, one of the Senators asked John, "You have presented us with a huge potential project. Is the mayor of Richmond on board with this?"

John answered, "I don't know, but I'll find out."

John turned to me and said, "Come on!"

It was a messy January day in Richmond, with Broad Street covered in slush and snow falling. John and I left the Finance Committee's meeting, neither of us wearing an overcoat, and we made our way across the street to the mayor's office in City Hall, with me scurrying along to keep up with John, who was definitely on a mission. We took the elevator to the second floor. Now, at the time, there was a four-week lead-time to get an appointment with Mayor Leonidas Young, but John barely paused at the mayor's secretary's desk. "Where's Young?" he asked her.

"He's in his office, but he is in a meeting," she answered.

"I have to see him right now!" John barked.

"But he can't be disturbed," she said.

"I'm going in now!" John insisted.

And with that, in he barged. The mayor was on the phone, but John went right up to his desk. While Mayor Young looked quite unsettled, John was undeterred. "I need to know one thing," he stated emphatically. "Are you for the convention center expansion or not?"

The mayor hesitated a bit but stammered out, "Yes!"

"That's all we wanted to know!" John replied. He turned and rolled right back out into the snow and to the Senate committee. "Yes, he's onboard!" he announced.

The hotel tax increase passed the General Assembly, and in the final analysis, the greatest beneficiary of the convention center's expansion would be the state because of revenue that eventually was generated by sales tax on purchases made by attendees. In light of this benefit to the state's coffers, we went again to the General Assembly in 1997, this time asking the state to contribute $60 million to the convention center's expansion. Our request was denied.

We had two-thirds of the funding but needed to fill that last third. In 1998, the chief financial officers of the jurisdictions proposed that the state raise the hotel tax by two cents in order to finance the building's expansion. We managed to squeak through passage of a hotel tax bill, and thanks to that revenue, local citizens would not have to shoulder one cent of the burden of financing the convention center. Every year, it costs $14 million dollars to run the convention center, and hotel taxes continue to pay for all of this expense.

Even with all this funding in place, we were still $10 million short. John and the four *jurisdiction chief administrative officers approached Governor George Allen and convinced him that the state should contribute this final portion. It was the last piece of the financial puzzle that ensured the building would, indeed, be built. Groundbreaking came in November of 1999, and the final opening and ribbon cutting, February 28, 2003.*

John's leadership was vital to the construction of the convention center, and the benefits to the region are immense. It remains the largest cooperative project ever achieved in Virginia. As is true with other cities like Baltimore, Philadelphia and San Diego, the capital investment around the Convention Center has exploded. Property values have risen ten times. The Federal Court Building and the $150 million development of a hotel and apartments in the Miller & Rhoads building are examples of improvements that would not have taken place without the expansion of the convention center. All told, over $1 billion in improvements are connected to the convention center, and the whole fabric of downtown Richmond changed because of it.

John is such a brilliant, smart person, and I consider it a privilege to have worked with him. I have watched in awe as John manages to gets things done, far beyond what most people would achieve. I also know that he has taught me valuable lessons along the way.

Early in my career as president with the Convention and Visitors Bureau, I realized that my position was very much entangled in politics, and this was not a situation with which I was familiar. I remember that at one time, there was an incident in which I became involved, and I went to see John, who was Chairman of the Convention and Visitors Bureau but also an extremely busy executive with American Tobacco. I explained my dilemma, and he patiently listened to me describe the entire scenario.

"Well, Jack," he said when I had finished. "That is very interesting. And I just can't wait to find out how you solve this."

I was shocked! It was a huge lesson for me to learn that I had to solve my own problems.

Wherever our board meetings are held, John participates. One year the board retreat involved whitewater rafting on class IV rapids on the James River, and John never blinked. He was there with the rest of us. We went to Kings Dominion, and John was there. One year we had a board meeting at Richmond International Raceway. After the meeting, we were told that we could take our own cars on the racetrack. John jumped at the chance. He turned to me and said, "Come on. Let's go!"

We got into his Cadillac, and he revved it up to seventy-five miles an hour, keeping up with the pace car around the track and the steep banks at the turns. My fingernails were cutting into the armrest, but he was having the time of his life and remained as casual and calm as could be.

Once the 1998 General Assembly adjourned, I began to reconnect with my civic responsibilities, though because I was committed to being a full-time lieutenant governor, the time available was limited. Even after the legislative session adjourned, my political schedule remained nearly as busy as ever because I participated in all sorts of functions. During spring especially, we were invited to attend an array of outdoor gatherings and activities: the King William Fish Fry, the Shad Planking, the Chicken, Pork, Beef, Oyster,

Cantaloupe and Tomato Festivals, associations, conventions, meetings, etc. The list went on and on, and Virginia is a big state, so the possibilities were endless. There is nothing like an election win to enhance the popularity of a politician, and we attempted to accommodate as many requests as feasible. Furthermore, during the nine months following the session, my aides and I drove all over the state as we attended bill signings and talked to citizens about potential legislation and attended endless General Assembly committees and commission meetings.

The *Richmond Times-Dispatch* ran an article on July 5, 1998, "Hager Setting Frenetic Pace," in which Tyler Whitley described my many appearances around the Commonwealth.

Where one or more Republicans gather, he seems to be there, winning favors and making himself visible...Hager estimates he and aides have driven his wife's 1992 emerald green Cadillac 20,000 miles around the state since the General Assembly session ended in March.

In 10 recent days, Hager, despite using a wheelchair because he had polio, appeared at 25 events. July 4 was particularly busy. Hager flew to the Fairfax City Independence Day parade; stopped over at a Republican picnic at nearby Fort Hunt Park; flew to Virginia Beach to attend a traditional Independence Day gathering for Filipinos; and then trekked over to a picnic at Mount Trashmore given by a local GOP activist.

In November 1998, Maggie and I flew to San Francisco to attend the National Easter Seal Convention, where I received the Johana Cooke Plaut Award for Community Leadership, the highest honor bestowed by the Easter Seal Society. This proved to be an exciting trip, and during the ceremony before a large, black-tie audience, I presented a speech on involvement, which was well received. Other awards in 1998 came when the Virginia Council of Indians presented me with their Citizenship Award and AAA Mid-Atlantic and the Virginia Cable Telecommunications Association named me Legislator of the Year.

As Christmas season approached, Maggie and I decided to expand our traditional holiday party, which we had hosted for several years, to encompass three large parties, each with some hundred-plus guests, given on three consecutive nights in early December. The first night included neighbors, the second drew social and Richmond friends, and the third gathered political friends and acquaintances from all over the state. I've always loved the Christmas season, and our house lends itself well to functions, so these gatherings were a pleasure. They gave Maggie and me an opportunity to celebrate and thank our friends, supporters and political co-workers, and they gave our sons the opportunity to meet and reconnect with many people who were important to us. In addition to hosting the parties, we sent Christmas cards featuring family pictures to a long list of friends and supporters. Thankfully, many Republican women's club members volunteered to help with the mailings.

Each January brought a new General Assembly session and an array of activities connected with the legislative work, and January 1999 was no different. As lawmakers reconvened, the calendar seemed to fill with press conferences, special events, and diverse activities. Again, I had a legislative agenda, which required garnering support of delegates and senators. After the regular session, there are long bill-signing sessions and a period when staff is reorganized for the balance of the year. The veto session, six weeks later, usually closes the Assembly.

1999 also initiated my active involvement in the National Association of Lieutenant Governors and during the next three years, I attended many of their meetings. That summer, the National Association adopted a massive community service project to promote the safe handling and storage of firearms by the distribution of gun safety locks. Financed by grants from the U.S. Department of Justice, the gun safety locks' distribution project was part of a nationwide initiative entitled HomeSafe. In Virginia, state police distributed 60,000 locks, and nationwide some 650,000 were distributed without any charge to gun owners. This project was just one of the wide sweeping and yet practical issues that the lieutenant governors tackled.

It was during this time that the association investigated and certified that I was the first lieutenant governor in a wheelchair ever to have served from any state. I assumed leadership roles within this group, serving as chairman of the Southern Sector and as a member of the Executive Committee. Each January, the Association gathered in Washington D.C., during the same time our General Assembly convened, so I sometimes drove up to attend the meeting in the evenings and the next morning, returned to Richmond in order to preside over the Senate. In July 2000, Maggie, Jack and Henry joined me for the annual meeting of the National Association of Lieutenant Governors in Puerto Rico, an event that mingled business and pleasure.

There were board memberships in two national organizations that enabled me to foster Virginia's interaction with other states. The Aerospace States Association, where I was vice chairman, and the Southern Growth Policies Board were both significant venues for promoting Virginia's interests in a broad audience.

Within the state, my duties on boards and commissions were extensive and diverse. Membership in several panels of elected officials and citizen appointees assured my participation in active, vibrant groups that recommended solutions and formulated policy to combat some of the Commonwealth's most complex issues. I formed and served as chairman of the faith-based Community Services Task Force, which promoted volunteerism and community service among people from all over the state. I assumed the vice presidency of the Virginia Public Safety Foundation, an organization that serves Virginia's first responders and their families by providing public recognition for sacrifice and crisis financial support. The Senate appointed me co-chairman of the Commission on Educational Infrastructure and Technology, a group that worked to obtain funding for local schools. In addition, I was a member of the State Board of Education's Leadership Council. By statute, the lieutenant governor chaired the Disability Commission, a bi-monthly commitment to a group that championed the state's response to the needs of its physically and mentally disabled citizens. I also served on and was co-chairman of the Specialized Transportation Council, which grappled with issues concerning transporta-

With Maggie and Margaret Thatcher, October 1998

tion for the disabled. I was a member of the Commission on Family Violence Prevention, which worked not only to propose legislation relating to family violence but also sought to train professionals to combat this problem. I was appointed representative to the State Crime Commission and served on the Drug Task Force.

Probably the most significant and time-consuming service of this kind came during my last year in office, when I joined the governor's Commission on Transportation Policy, for which I shared the responsibility of chairmanship with Kenny Klinge. This commission attempted to break the logjam that stymied agreement on solutions to Virginia's transportation challenges and sought to generate sound legislative proposals in the contentious area of transportation policy. We met often, worked diligently and compiled a list of recommendations as a blueprint for action by the next administration Unfortunately, the incoming Democrats back-burnered our report, but even today, the proposals we advocated would work well.

The staggering number of meetings these memberships required assured a full schedule, and when these responsibilities combined with the many other demands on my time, the resulting mix was far more than a full-time job. There was no such thing as an eight-hour day as each one was filled to the brim.

Since my entire calendar each year could be filled with conferences and gatherings, it was necessary to limit attendance to those that were deemed most significant to the state. Meetings and conventions like those for the commonwealth attorneys, the sheriffs, and the Virginia Chamber of Commerce, the auto dealers, etc. gave me an opportunity to mingle with the movers and shakers within the state. Because they often met in pleasant

Fiddlers' Convention in Galax, Virginia

places like the Homestead or Virginia Beach, they also provided a relaxed setting for and meeting people and tackling the work at hand. During this time, my interest was more policy-oriented than political. For both focuses, however, it was invaluable to meet and interact with a broad range of leaders who were involved in various segments of Virginia life.

During 1999, I delivered a number of graduation addresses around the state, speaking at Old Dominion University, Radford University, Richard Bland College, Averett University, the University of Mary Washington and the University of Northern Virginia. and I received honorary degrees from the latter three. There were also numerous speeches at dinners like the Alexandria Olympic Boys and Girls Club Annual Banquet, celebrating receipt of the 1999 Americanism Award. I often referred to my wheelchair marathoning experiences as I addressed young people: *I haven't finished first in every marathon, I assure you, but in finishing, I feel like I have won all of them...Remember, the alternative to last place is no place.*

As lieutenant governor, I participated in many activities that were such fun that they retained a lasting appeal long after the term of office ended. One such case was NASCAR, to which I was introduced during this period. I tried to attend all six Virginia races — two in Richmond, two in Martinsville and two in Bristol each year. (Virginia claims Bristol for the Commonwealth, even though the race track actually is just across the border in Tennessee.) I usually participated in some way during NASCAR's opening ceremonies, which made for a really exciting appearance, especially in Bristol where some 135,000 spectators gathered for the races. It was quite a thrill to helicopter onto the racetrack, meet the drivers and enjoy at close range the excitement of the races. In truth, few race fans actually listened to my opening remarks, but the overall enthusiasm of the crowd was hard to beat. NASCAR continues to be an exciting sport to watch, even without the helicopter entrance and VIP treatment, and I have enjoyed a continuing relationship with track officials in Richmond.

On the same weekend that the summer NASCAR race is held in Bristol, Virginia/ Tennessee, leaders in Southwest Virginia hosted the Governors' Cup, a good-humored golf tournament between the two states, Tennessee and Virginia. The governors of the two states put on an elaborate show, and the race provided a grand Saturday night backdrop. In 1999 when I attended, Jack played and I rode in the golf cart around the course. The next year, Henry played as Maggie drove the cart. Other activities in that part of the state included the Fiddlers' Convention in Galax, the Virginia Highlands Festival in Abingdon and the autumn Kilgore family picnic in Gate City.

Recalling the Fiddler's Convention brings back fond memories. Bruce Wingo, Vice President of Government Relations for Norfolk Southern Corporation, would organize a large group of legislators and their families for a busy weekend of activity, including a float on the New River. One year I was in a raft with John Paul Woodley and his wife Priscilla. We had hung back to do a little fishing when a huge thunderstorm appeared, and we hunkered down next to the bank. It passed, thankfully, and there was a frantic search for us until we floated down to the take-out.

Another favorite opportunity came when we attended football games, most notably the annual Commonwealth Cup game between Virginia Tech and the University of Virginia, a showdown that alternates between Blacksburg and Charlottesville. I made a point of saving time in my schedule for that game, usually the Saturday after Thanksgiving, when we could immerse ourselves in the whole, colorful scene and share the good-natured rivalry with friends and associates. The tradition has continued to the present, and it is exciting to be a part of the enthusiastic football crowd. It is telling of the times that talk in the president's boxes these days seems to have been overshadowed by the busy and challenging political world.

In my four years as lieutenant governor, I missed only two hours of legislative sessions, a tally that probably set an attendance record. My two brief absences were both due to funerals. During my first week in office, I was about forty-five minutes late reaching the Senate Chamber after I attended the service for the state trooper who was killed the night of the inauguration. Then in 2000, when my great friend Jim Moncure passed away, I delivered the eulogy. His funeral was held at St. Stephen's Episcopal Church in Richmond, and by the time I made my way downtown to the Senate, I had missed about an hour and a quarter of the session. In both cases, John Chichester, who was president pro tempore, presided in my absence, and he always seemed relieved to see me when I entered the chamber.

Some people thought I should have missed a bit of time when I was involved in an automobile accident on March 4, 1998 — an event which Susan Schaar briefly described and one that was particularly ironic because at the time, I was championing stricter regulations for teenage drivers! I was returning to a late-night session of the Senate when a speeding, stolen Jeep Cherokee, driven by a teen driver, slammed into the rear of my car, which was stopped at a stoplight at Ninth and Canal Street, not far from the Capitol. According to police reports, the Jeep was moving at more than ninety miles an hour, and the impact spun my car around twice before it came to a stop in the geranium bed at the James Center. The collision was strong enough to total my black Cadillac Coupe de Ville, a sedan I had managed to acquire from industrialist, Nello Teer's widow in Durham. Some-

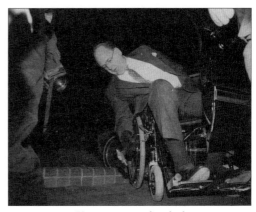

Hammering out the wheel

how, I escaped any serious injury beyond a bumped head, and I managed to extricate myself from the wreck. My first concern was that I needed to get back to the Capitol for the Senate session. I was able to borrow a hammer from firefighters on the scene and repair my partially mangled wheelchair so that it was workable. Despite feeling a bit shaken and bruised, I checked in with the Richmond police at the scene, caught a ride with the Capitol police, and wobbled on bent wheels into the Senate Chamber. As I entered, I was greeted like a ghost returning from the dead.

News of the accident, including television footage of the wreck, had raced ahead of me, and everyone expected me to be at the hospital. Susan Schaar was especially upset that I presided for several hours at a contentious session without first having my injuries

Apple Blossom Festival in Winchester, Virginia

checked. She even called Maggie to carry me to the hospital. However, I wasn't about to leave the Senate until it adjourned, so it was fairly late when the Capitol police took me for a thorough check at St. Mary's. After the emergency room visit, Maggie and I arrived home around 2:30 a.m.

The *Purdue Alumnus Magazine* featured an article entitled, "On a Roll," which described the accident and my hammering the wheelchair's frame into shape: *Vintage Hager. Things just seem to happen to this resilient Purdue graduate, but he always manages to put his life back together.*

Prior to my lieutenant governorship, I had joined the Advisory Board of the Thomas C. Sorensen Institute for Political Leadership at the University of Virginia. During this era, I remained in close contact with William H. "Bill" Wood, who headed the institute. I also enjoyed attending several of their events and speaking to classes. The Sorensen Institute's political leadership program boasts an impressive number of alumni who have assumed state and local political positions. Their courses, which are offered in Charlottesville and at other locations around the state of Virginia, include ethics training and leadership instruction aimed at promoting bipartisan cooperation and effective political leadership. The study of ethics is not a textbook presentation but involves case studies and prompts participants to think about the roles of all individuals involved. After serving my term as lieutenant governor, I was elected to my first term as chairman of Sorensen, which was interrupted by service in Washington. Later, I resumed the chairmanship which continued until December of 2016.

My involvement with the Center for Politics, spearheaded by Larry Sabato, involved annual conferences and service on the Advisory Board. Larry has always been one of my strong boosters, and I enjoyed having these opportunities to interact on a personal as well as professional level.

Gary Melton's October 1998, *Paralegal News'* lead article was entitled "Live the American Dream" with a subhead, "Encouraging people to hope and believe motivates Virginia's lieutenant governor." The lengthy article began by describing inauguration day:

With Larry Sabato

Inauguration Day – January 17, 1998 – was unique and inspirational for all of Virginia's citizens, but especially for those with mobility impairments. I can't imagine anyone not being moved while watching John H. Hager push his wheelchair up the ramp to the stage in front of the State Capitol Building. There he was sworn in as Virginia's thirty-fourth lieutenant governor.

The article included a quote from me that highlighted my relationship with the disability community:

We made a great effort to develop a unique disability coalition and try to offer a message of opportunity and hope for everyone, including the disabled...I believe a lot of disabled people in Virginia said, "Gosh if he can do it, I can do it."

I think they now feel they have been rewarded. They have learned that we can be a potent force for the disabled but at the same time do it in a consistent fashion that affects all people... We rose to a higher level than worrying about a dumb wheelchair. We rose to the level of what is really important to people.

I think a lot about the American dream and the fact that I am not a special person. I have just been fortunate that I had a good education and reasonable financial means so that when I took a big blow I was able to survive it.

On October 4, 1998, *The Virginian-Pilot's* Alexandria Berger wrote an article entitled, "John H. Hager: A profile of heroism." She recounted my background – my professional successes, my struggle with polio, the subsequent demotion and eventual rise back to the top in the company — and highlighted my political position.

From his handicapped accessible office to the Senate's podium (with ramped access), Hager presides, promoting the governor's agenda. He acknowledges, "I'm a focus-oriented, driven guy. Working full time for and with the people of Virginia, we can empower them. If you do a good job, people will push you."

Virginia Indians' Award 1998

Meeting with Scouts at the Shenandoah Scout Park

Now, at age 62, Hager needs no pushing. He's a champion wheelchair marathon racer who thinks that's nothing special.

"There are many people who suffer worse disabilities, have fewer resources, and less education," Hager says. "They, like me, have fought adversity and won."

Yet as the only visibly impaired lieutenant governor in the United States, Hager is an inspiring public example of the meaning behind the children's classic "The Little Engine That Could." He's always thought he "could."

As Hager puts it, "You already inherit what came before. We're here to do better, and we can."

Richmond's public television stations decided to follow and tape me one day to emphasize the story and ran the show, *A Day in the Life of the Lieutenant Governor*. It received lots of coverage as it portrayed a typical day – jam-packed from early morning to late night. The reporters and crew were somewhat aghast at the pace.

Politics of one sort or another came to permeate all my activities. Because it is a people business, contacts and relationships become increasingly important and being a people-person myself, I was enjoying every minute. Of course politics has a dark side, but one thing for sure — it is never at a standstill. There is always a push towards the next possibility, even if the individual is happy where he is. So it was that in 1999, we began to mold efforts towards a possible run for governor.

Our first step was to hire Dick Leggitt, who was well known in political circles and a former consultant to Jim Gilmore. In essence, this commitment to engage Dick initiated my tenure-long battle against Attorney General Mark Earley to become the Republican candidate for governor in 2001, and our team was further strengthened when Dick brought in Jim Dornan to succeed David Ross as chief in the office.

As one of his first efforts, Dick tried to strengthen my speaking skills by suggesting that we should focus on popular issues and a prioritized list of points. I tried hard and did improve in his eyes, but some habits never die, and even today my speeches practically drive him crazy. My style is my own: too folksy for the professionals. I tend to appreciate the crowd and to respond to the moment – prefer speaking off the cuff rather than memorizing or reading, and though I usually prepared for every speaking engagement, I didn't hesitate to meander beyond the script. However good or bad they were, speeches played a part in the extensive fundraising network we built all over the state.

By early 1999, George W. Bush was beginning his run for the Presidency, and Jim Gilmore and I went to his first appearance in the Commonwealth, a luncheon held in Roanoke. Referring to this appearance at the beginning of his campaign and my commitment, I like to say that I was the first person in the state publicly to endorse George W. Bush for President. At the time, Bush, was a strong contender but not a shoe-in. Through the next year, 2000, he faced primary and convention challenges all over the country. The outcome was far from certain. Virginia's Republicans were relieved when Bush's popularity soared and were especially pleased that it was in the Virginia primary that the tide finally swung in his favor. By late spring when we attended a George Bush rally near Willow Lawn Shopping Center in Richmond, it had become obvious that he would receive the Republican endorsement. I had endorsed him very early and never regretted it.

In April 1999, Maggie and I flew from San Francisco to Taiwan with Delegate Bob McDonnell, who later would become Virginia's governor, and his wife Maureen. Also with us were Virginia State Senator Randy Forbes, who later served as Congressman, and his wife Shirley. The six of us spent a week touring Taiwan and learning a tremendous amount about that country's history, productivity and politics. We delved into the tactics Taiwan employed to maintain independence from its huge neighbor, China. When our week was over, the McDonnells continued traveling in the Far East and invited us to join them, but we declined because of other commitments.

In the fall of 1999, Bill Latham, a good friend who had flown me in his private airplane to several campaign stops, invited our son Jack and me to join him for pheasant hunting in South Dakota. Initially, I was reluctant and protested to Bill that pheasant hunting was not a sport to be undertaken in a wheelchair, but he had devised a solution. I was able to go along with the hunters on the back of a four-wheel Gator, and it proved to be a great trip. The Lathams have done so much to support us over many years.

As 1999, the end of the millennium, drew near, there was a great deal of hype about what would happen to all the computers, clocks, grid systems and digital functions of businesses and governments around the world with the arrival of 2000. Speculation ranged from total disruption of services, utilities and government agencies, including

Radio interview with Oliver North

the military, to a nonchalant attitude that all would be well. On that night, which was so full of hopes for the future and apprehension about possible disorder, Maggie and I attended a big New Year's Eve party at the Governor's Mansion; afterwards, I remained at the Capitol to be on hand if any problems arose. As it happened, the night passed peacefully, but it was an interesting experience to be in the midst of Virginia's response team for the new millennium.

My mother passed away on March 23, 2000, at the age of ninety-three. She had fought a valiant fight, and I had tried hard to visit in Durham as often as possible. It was a real blow, and we all traveled there for the visitation and service, where I spoke for the family. She had been very proud of me and was much loved. Though Mother's passing left my dad alone, my sister was nearby, and lots of good help allowed him to remain in his own home.

We began campaigning during 2000 for the Republicans who were up for re-election to Congress in Virginia, and in June we attended the Virginia Republican Convention in Virginia Beach. It was at this time that a new chairman was selected and delegates were chosen for the National Convention to be held in Philadelphia, and I secured my spot.

When Maggie and I left the convention, we flew directly to New York and then on to Tel Aviv, Israel. Mel Chaskin, who headed the Virginia-Israeli Partnership, had arranged the trip so that we could participate in a three-day technology-trade summit in Tel Aviv. We found that there were many capable Israeli companies at the summit, all of them involved in what was, at the time, the emerging technological revolution. So much was changing so fast, and the summit was a real eye-opener to the diversity of possibilities for Virginia. For instance, I remember being surprised to find that there were more cell phones in Israel than landlines, which was indicative of the ways technology was beginning to affect the world. Even the ways we campaigned would be transformed by technology in the years ahead.

Once the summit ended, Maggie and I had an opportunity to tour Israel for about three days, and we literally traveled all over the country. It was so exciting to go to places we had heard about all our lives. When we reached Jerusalem, we asked, "How far is Bethlehem?"

We were assured that it was situated close by, but because it was in Palestinian held territory, we wouldn't want to visit.

"I can't be this close and not see Bethlehem," I insisted. We had no intention of missing such a sight because of Palestinian-Israeli political tensions. Sure enough, we braved the checkpoints and proceeded to Bethlehem. We had an exceptional tour there, including a stop at the Church of the Redeemer, though I would say that everyone was relieved when we passed back through the checkpoints and returned to the Israeli side.

Not long after that memorable trip, we packed our bags to attend the Republican National Convention in Philadelphia, during which George W. Bush was officially nominated as the Republican candidate for President. All day, every day, we were involved in activities, and the excitement was palpable. Maggie and Henry went with me, and Jack joined us there. Dick Cheney was staying in our hotel, and his presence hyped up the excitement. With an eye on the 2001 election for Virginia governor, Jack Rohrer, from my team, made sure we optimized the week, and the result was that every minute was busy as we met as many people as possible and sought every available bit of publicity. Republicans were very upbeat coming out of the convention, and everyone seemed united to help elect George Bush as President.

Chapter 15

The Big Loss

By the time we returned home from Philadelphia, we were moving into real campaign mode. I fully supported the Bush-Cheney election effort and participated in events for them as much as possible, but my own effort to win the Republican nomination for governor in 2001 became more and more dominant in my life. In September, we held an important informal kick-off at the Commonwealth Club, where the featured speakers were Paul Galanti and former Governor Mills Godwin. That was exciting because both men commanded great respect. Paul, who is a popular Vietnam War hero, is an excellent speaker as well as a good friend. Mills, who was well respected but aging, participated in few events by that time. He had been a friend and mentor to me for some time, and he represented traditional Virginia values.

Announcing run for Governor

Our son Henry returned to Richmond to work full time on my campaign. Henry had graduated from Wake Forest in the spring of 2000 and traveled to Australia to accept a position, credentialing the press for the Summer Olympic Games in Sydney. Once his duties ended in September 2000, he turned his attention to my run for governor, and during the campaign months, his efforts meant a great deal.

We were very excited by the Bush-Cheney victory in November and by Virginia's endorsement of the winning ticket. In Virginia, there was little need to push hard for the candidates, since there was never much of a question that Bush and Cheney had the lead. Republicans were pleased to regain the White House — to say the least.

A couple of weeks after the national election, my campaign hosted a big party at Tredegar Ironworks, where guests included political leaders: Walter Stosch, Patricia and John O'Bannon, Tom Bliley, Morton Blackwell, Clarence Townes and Bob Goodlatte, as well as many friends like Ted Mortensen, Paul Galanti, Ray Spence, etc. Jack spoke and introduced me, and the excitement was frenetic. We were off and running.

During that Christmas season, Maggie and I again held large Christmas parties at our home and covered the state with Christmas greetings. Then we turned our attention to the Presidential inauguration and festivities in Washington, all of which were exciting and enjoyable. We spent the third weekend in January participating in several inaugural events, seeing many friends and politicians and celebrating the new leadership in D.C. The state police helped get us around, which made a tremendous difference.

My last General Assembly session convened in mid-January 2001. Our priorities during this legislative session were familiar areas that I had championed the other years of my term as lieutenant governor: tax relief, support for education, efficient transportation, expanded and improved technology, criminal justice, highway safety, a commitment to our veterans, "informed consent" for women's personal decisions, affordable health care, refinement of faith-based efforts and volunteers, expanded services for disabled citizens and the cessation of imports of trash into Virginia. I had gained valuable experience in getting my initiatives accomplished so the fresh list included variants of winning issues.

Another benefit from working with the General Assembly was the formation of lasting friendships with so many individual legislators. The Richmond contingent, Bill Howell and Kirk Cox in the House and in the Senate, Tommy Norment, Ken Stolle, Bo Trumbo and Walter Stosch stand out in my mind. We shared a conservative philosophy with a desire to get things done. Virginia has benefited from strong representation over the years.

During Session, we stayed active at night and on the weekends. The Emporia-Greensville Chamber of Commerce presented me their Leadership Award for work in Southside Virginia. The Virginia Chapter of the March of Dimes honored me as Volunteer Extraordinary and enrolled me in the Volunteers' Hall of Fame. The Virginia Board for People with Disabilities gave me The James C. Wheat, Jr. Award, their highest honor and one that is named for a good friend and personal idol.

There are always show-stopper stories to recall. On January 19, 2001, a cold and dreary afternoon after session, I was due to make an appearance at the downtown Rich-

Signing bills as pages observe

mond Marriott Hotel. Lars Wiechmann and I started rolling up Ninth Street to Broad Street and the Marriott Hotel. We had gone about half way, when we were interrupted by an African-American lady who was running across the street, gesturing at us as she went. Her name, as I would come to know, was Doris E. Winford, and Doris was shouting, "Stop! Stop! I must see you!"

Somewhat taken aback, we said we were late for an appointment.

"You don't know who I am, but I know you, Mr. Hager," she replied. "I saw you on TV, and I listened to you. I was down and out, but I said to myself, *If he can do it, I can do it!* That's what I did. I got myself straightened up and now have a job at Criminal Justice Services. I'm working here on Broad Street, all because of you."

We were stunned. Such a story! Such a compliment! We heard her out and then vaulted the rest of the way to the Marriott. The VACCO gathering was big, but my talk was conventional. It was hard to get Doris Winford out of my head, and this anecdote was one I used many times in the campaign ahead.

We were organized and ready as the General Assembly adjourned, and we turned our attention to full-time campaigning for governor. Virginia law prohibits the raising of campaign funds during the legislative session, so as soon as we could, on the Monday after the session ended, we held a gala fundraising luncheon at the Jefferson Hotel — this time with John Warner speaking and endorsing my effort to run for governor. From the day of that luncheon in March 2001, I began a nearly non-stop campaign

Campaign brochure

JOHN HAGER

When I could walk, my journey through life seemed pretty uncomplicated. I had a wonderful life, and "adversity" was not a word with which I was particularly familiar. Then my life changed forever. I was stricken with polio.

In facing the challenge of a paralyzing disease, I discovered an inner spirit. I discovered the true meaning of faith. And I learned what perseverance is all about.

For me, perseverance does not mean just existing. Perseverance means facing life head on, no matter what adversity is thrown your way, and moving toward tomorrow knowing you are even stronger for the experience.

In fact, I've always seen our fight for control of the General Assembly as a matter of perseverance. In spite of a century of Democratic rule and decades of obstacles, together we held fast to our principles and faced adversity head on. And now, with Republicans in control of both the House and Senate for the first time in Virginia history, we can truly say that we as a Party are even stronger for the experience.

I was deeply honored when the people of Virginia put their trust in me to be their Lt. Governor. Now, the people have placed their trust in our Republican Party to lead the entire General Assembly. The people's trust is a sacred trust, and we must never allow it to be betrayed. All that we have fought for and all that we have achieved will be meaningless unless we hold fast to our values, our beliefs and our principles as we strive to govern the Commonwealth with wisdom and vision.

We have persevered. The people of Virginia have handed us the reins of their government. Together, let us meet the future of our beloved Virginia head on.

John Hager

Campaign Letter

for the nomination. We had tried for a primary, but the State Central Committee would have none of it and voted for a convention to be held in early June. A primary would have put the vote to Republican citizens of the state, but with a convention the slate of offices would be determined by only the selected delegates who showed up.

In an effort to remain active in programs that would move Virginia forward while at the same time meeting people and getting my name "out there," I continued my involvement in diverse activities like the Global Internet Summit at George Mason University. Many groups that support a candidate anticipate that the individual will, at least to some extent, participate in their events, and I considered it important enough to garner support that I tried to accommodate most requests, even though some of them, like the Elks, were rather uncharacteristic for me. At an Elk function in Winchester, I found the members so eager for me to join, that I had little choice. Similarly, I became a Moose, and then when you add my membership in Ruritan, Rotary and Kiwanis Clubs, you get an idea of the involvement necessary.

We once again assembled a campaign staff of paid workers and volunteers, a wide range of people, including some of my staff who left the lieutenant governor's office and began working for the campaign. I had two podiums, both specially designed to be lowered or raised as necessary, which Jack Cousins of Virginia Beach generously commissioned to be made and donated for my use. Tom Swope, who worked for the state, hauled the adaptable podiums all over Virginia for me. We had a close relationship with the Executive Protection Unit (EPU), and often I would attend state sponsored events in a state police car, driven by either Trooper Johnson or Trooper Dziedzic.

Shad Planking in Wakefield, Virginia

Numerous Republican leaders across the state threw their support to me. Typical of the many letters that circulated on my behalf was one sent by several leaders to Fairfax County Republicans that made strong arguments for my election. It reiterated that I am a fighter.

In facing the challenge of polio, John showed an inner spirit and discovered the true meaning of faith. He overcame that "adversity." John Hager never lets up, never gives up, and is determined to see every cause through. His persistence is infectious...John Hager is an effective spokesman for our Party's conservative principles...Whether cutting taxes, fighting for anti-crime initiatives, or protecting the Right to Life, the Right to Work, or the Right to Keep and Bear Arms, John Hager has effectively fought for and defended our principles...He has earned it [the nomination...He has the experience to lead...John's record of civic leadership is unmatched. John's personal triumph is a wonderful inspiration.

In April 2001, I spoke for the second time at Virginia's venerable political gathering, the Shad Planking. I had been attending the annual event since John Dalton's election as governor, the same year the Tri-Cities Republican Women's Club began holding a pre-Shad Planking luncheon, and I had previously been invited to speak in 1999 as lieutenant governor. The Shad Planking in 2001 was the first time that multiple candidates for governor made a joint appearance, and all three of us – John Hager, Mark Earley and Mark Warner – took advantage of the opportunity. Our various campaign workers had been busy for days posting signs in preparation for the event, and so on the big day, there were thousands of political placards lining the access roads and site. It was quite a scene, with our signs battling for attention and a real battle royal unfolding among the three of us candidates. Henry was in the thick of it with our staff and volunteers, and we felt that we outshined the other candidates!

Mark Warner was in the enviable position of being the uncontested Democratic nominee, but on the Republican side, Mark Earley and I both were running hard for the Republican nomination for governor, and at the same time the Republican attorney general's nomination was also hotly contested, with four candidates vying for that spot. We pitched our positions and made the rounds among attendees, shaking hands and exchanging pleasantries as we went. It was a rite of passage for Virginia politics.

I have returned to the pre-Shad Planking luncheon and the Shad Planking almost every year since this 2001 appearance and have formed good relationships with the groups' leaders. Several years after my run for governor, I began introducing the speaker for both occasions, the luncheon and the planking. I have helped them from time to time in lining up their speakers, a responsibility that has become somewhat more challenging and contentious in recent years.

In 2014, when Mark Warner spoke, we both received the "Plank Award," which was a real rarity since it has seldom been awarded. Then for 2015, I was again selected to be the speaker, a high honor for someone out of office and out of the spotlight for so long. In recommending me as a speaker, Robert Bain, on behalf of the committee, said, "John is a true conservative, respected by both sides and just the type of person who exemplifies Virginia."

As spring unfolded, political mass meetings ratcheted up around the state. We had our share of victories in electing delegates to the planned June convention. However, Mark Earley also enjoyed good success. One Friday afternoon in the middle of May, Mark Earley stopped by the lieutenant governor's office and wanted to chat. I was all ears. He stated that he felt he had the upper hand in the race, and he asked if I would consider dropping back to the slot of lieutenant governor. He would take the Republican nod for governor and would endorse me for re-election to the number-two spot.

We both had been fighting for delegates, but with Virginia's Republican Convention only two weeks away, I realized that, much as I hated to admit it, Earley was probably correct in his assessment that he was in the

The Plank Award

lead. I had thoroughly enjoyed being the state's lieutenant governor, and I believed I could make a positive impact on the office during another four-year term, so I agreed to his proposal. Earley suggested that we hold a press conference on Monday morning and make the decision public. Key people were informed, including my staff, all of whom incredulous but went along and we had a meeting to strategize our next moves.

After this abrupt change of plans, it was nothing short of shocking when over the weekend, Earley decided that the arrangement was not to his advantage. He reneged on the deal. We had scheduled the press conference for Monday, but on Sunday night, Earley called to say he wouldn't proceed with the proposal. Evidently his campaign manager, Anne Kincaid, convinced him that his proposal would upset the ultra-conservative Jay Katzen crowd, since Jay was running for lieutenant governor. I was definitely taken aback, and in hopes that he would intercede, I went to see Governor Jim Gilmore, though by this time, his endorsement, which never materialized, would have had little effect. There was never much doubt that the governor leaned toward Earley. We had no real choice but to stay the course. Approaching the Republican Convention in Richmond with inner apprehension, but drawing on all the strength we could muster, we projected faith that the vote would go our way. We went in with wonderful support, but for a variety of the usual reasons, many of our backers did not show up, and several of the conservative single-issue groups had blocks of delegates who attended to support Mark Earley.

Henry delivered a rousing address at the Republican Convention, one that was so giving in spirit and so clearly delivered that some people avowed it was the best speech they had ever heard. He had been a true boon to our efforts. Maggie — whose "Maggie for First Lady" buttons were a real success — wrote a heart-felt letter to the Republican Convention delegates:

Over the years, I have watched John become a "hero" to our boys, and they reflect their admiration of him (and me as their mother!) continually during their daily lives. He has instilled in them the strong foundations of integrity and honesty and faith and respectfulness with which they go forward with their own productive lives. We love them with all our hearts. We are blessed to be a strongly bound family of four.

John is loving, compassionate and caring, and he has matured into a great leader. He is a consensus builder capable of bringing people of differing views together to solve difficult problems.

As our Virginia Lieutenant Governor, John has studied and reviewed every piece of legislation strictly abiding to the code of law and has presided over the Senate with a standard of fairness and justice which the Senators and citizens have told me is admirable.

As a Captain in the Army, as an executive at the CEO level in his 35-year corporate career and as a chairman of over thirty community and charity boards and commissions, he speaks often from his experiences of "bringing in an era of personal responsibility and accountability." I am proud that he has had the exemplary business training and background to "run government like a business" responsive to the customer, the citizens of Virginia.

And as a lifelong Republican volunteer actively serving the Party at all levels, he is the "consistent conservative candidate for Governor" who stands up for the right to life, right to work, right to bear arms and private property rights. That's why so many of the national conservative leaders have endorsed his campaign.

And as the man who has traveled continually throughout the Commonwealth, to visit with you in order to listen and learn, I can share with you this great man who truly works closely with people to solve problems in order to bring about solutions. We know him and see him as the man who has certainly taken adversity in hand and turned it into accomplishment.

My convention speech was well received, but Mark Earley had packed several delegations, and the nomination went to him. We were reminded that conventions can be weird and unpredictable phenomena and not necessarily representative of the broader Republican constituencies or the electorate. It was painful for Maggie and me to watch Earley's acceptance speech. So many staff and supporters were devastated, but we tried to leave united.

Despite our disappointment, I participated during the subsequent months in several events to support the Republican ticket and Earley's campaign. Many of my supporters decided that they could not support Earley, and they threw their vote to the Democratic nominee, Mark Warner. Earley had a lackluster campaign, and come November, the Democrats enjoyed a win.

Could I have claimed a victory over Mark Warner? Many people voiced the opinion that I could have won, but we will never know. As for Mark Earley, he more or less disappeared from public life and devoted himself to prison ministries. Even today people come to me lamenting that they supported Earley. But that is politics!

For the balance of 2001, I continued the duties of my office. Pete Giesen, who had health problems, resigned as chief-of-staff and Robin Williams assumed that post. Maggie and I attended several events, but knowing that my bid for office was over and my term as lieutenant governor was winding down, I couldn't muster the same enthusiasm for these functions. Life settled into a more normal pace. Maggie and the boys went to Martha's Vineyard that summer, and I joined them for a spell. I enjoyed another fishing trip to Bozeman, Montana. My membership with the National Council of Lieutenant Governors involved meetings in Minnesota and Kentucky. It was a rewarding time, but much quieter and less hectic than the months prior to the convention.

The political staff moved on. It was Henry who settled the campaign books, sold the furniture and computers we had used and finalized the closure of our political office. We had accepted a long lease on our office space, the terms of which made for a formidable liability, but Henry convinced Jerry Kilgore's manager that with the successful nomination of state Attorney General candidate Kilgore, they would need bigger offices. The Kilgore staff assumed our lease, moved into the space and freed us from that unnecessary expense. We held a couple of events to help eliminate campaign debts, and by the end of June, we closed the books for good.

By this time, Henry was beginning to consider options for employment, and it was after a chance meeting with a friend, Tony Gius, that he applied for an internship at the White House. We had just completed our late summer, family vacation in Martha's Vineyard when Henry, stepping off the ferry, received a phone call asking him to go to Washington the next week for an interview, and in late August, he accepted an offer to intern in Karl Rove's office, a position he held from September until Christmas 2001. While Henry was working from his West Wing office at the White House, Maggie, Jack and I took opportunities to visit. On one occasion, we enjoyed a tour, and we have a picture of us from that day: Maggie, Jack, Henry and me, with President George W. Bush in the Oval Office. The picture is dated the week before September 11, 2001, with all the craziness that surrounded that fateful day.

It happened that on 9/11, I was en route to Washington for a meeting of the Aerospace States Association, an organization for which I served as a board member. As I was driving, I received a call on my car phone from Maggie. "Jack just said something big is happening. He saw it on television," she told me.

About the same time my cell phone — a second phone that I had with me — began to ring, and someone from my office said, "We aren't sure what exactly is happening, but you had better turn around and come back."

At the next interchange, I started back to Richmond and returned to the Capitol. I arrived at the third floor of the Capitol building before Governor Jim Gilmore and stayed all the rest of that ill-fated day and into the night at the Capitol where we had meeting after meeting and press conference after press conference. At one point, we were asked to pinpoint the most vulnerable spots in the state, and we sat there, listing them without ever considering that we, ourselves, might be at risk in the Capitol. It was a surreal situation. And it kept getting worse and worse, particularly after the news came that the Pentagon, located in Virginia, had been hit. With one development after another, we were more and more shocked, but things finally calmed down.

In the early afternoon, I received a cell phone call from Henry, describing the pandemonium he had experienced in Washington. Karl Rove was with the President visiting in a Florida public school, where President Bush, at the time of attack on the World Trade Center, was reading to a group of kindergartners as part of the "No Child Left Behind" initiative. Henry, from his second floor office in the West Wing, had actually held the phone up to the television so that news reports of the attack could be conveyed to Karl Rove. Streams of phone calls began to pour into the office — New York's Governor Rudy Giuliani, Washington's Mayor Vincent Gray and many others, trying to reach Karl Rove, and Henry patched their calls through to Florida. As concern rose for the safety of those in the While House, staffers gathered in the Navy Mess, and then at the direction of the Secret Service, they left the building by way of West Executive Drive. Amid the mayhem of reporters filming the evacuation of the White House, traffic confusion and blockages, the drone of fighter pilots overhead and the loss of cell phone service due to jammed lines, Henry set out to walk home. When he was unable to reach his own place in Virginia, he went to a friend's apartment in Georgetown and watched the events of the afternoon continue to play out in tragic news reports, one after the other. It would not be until later that he could return to his Arlington apartment.

As the day wore on, Governor Gilmore left Richmond to go to the Pentagon, but I remained at the Capitol until events clarified somewhat. It was late when I finally decided I could head home. I went to get my car, and one of the Capitol police said, "I'm going with you."

It was in that moment that I realized everything had changed. Starting the next morning, I concentrated on homeland security for Virginia. It was important to oversee the state's response, and since I was available, part of the job fell in my lap. Governor Gilmore hurriedly initiated the Virginia Preparedness and Security Panel, and I was named co-chairman. For the first weeks, everything was somewhat disordered, but we began to plow our way forward and focus on what Virginia needed to do to protect its citizenry from outside threats. Our commission met and discussed many ideas, and in time we began to work cooperatively with federal authorities. While I continued to be involved with numerous organizations, at least half my time became consumed with our emerging but still ill-defined homeland security efforts.

With the November election and Mark Warner's decisive win over my nomination opponent Mark Earley, the Democrats prepared to assume control of the governor's office. By tradition, the winning ticket goes to New York two days after the election for an annual Virginia Chamber of Commerce luncheon. Because of my previous involvement with the state Chamber, I decided that I would join them in New York. It was haunting to visit the twin tower site as our first stop. We were at the luncheon when Mark Warner

Ground Zero in lower Manhattan

turned to me and asked, "Would you consider being in my Cabinet? I have a job in mind for you."

I hadn't thought that the new Democratic governor would want me in his administration. In fact, I had been actively inquiring about the possibility of going to Washington and working in the Bush administration. When he approached me with this initial proposal, I assumed that Governor-elect Warner wanted me to become Secretary of Commerce and Trade or something like that, but when we returned to Richmond and had an opportunity to discuss the job, I learned that the governor-elect had an entirely different idea in mind. He wanted me to become Virginia's Homeland Security Director, a position every state was required to create in response to 9/11. The department would be called The Office of Commonwealth Preparedness, but in effect, it was the state's mandated homeland security office, and I agreed to consider the possibility of heading it.

Reflections of Paul Galanti, Commissioner of the Department of Veterans Services and Former Prisoner of War

Long before he was heavily involved in politics, I met John through Ross Mackenzie, and I was the opening speaker at his first fundraiser when he decided to run for the Republican

With Claiborne Gregory

nomination for governor. At that luncheon, I said that I had agreed to speak because John is one of my heroes.

He demonstrates intestinal fortitude, and I really admire that quality. Over the years, I have never once heard John whine or complain. I've never heard a "Poor me." John is the motion-challenged version of Jim Wheat, the blind business leader in Richmond who ran his own brokerage firm that bore his name. I would run into Jim Wheat, and he would say, "Hey, Paul, good to see you!" And this was after he had been blind for forty years or so. John demonstrates the same sort of attitude.

A big, strapping guy, he was on the path to become CEO of a huge company, American Tobacco, when polio struck and he lost the use of his legs. After that sort of misfortune, people can retreat into a morass of self-pity or they can react as he does and make positives out of the situation. He was thrown a massive curve ball by life, but John just swallowed hard and pressed on. As he tells it, "I get a lot of good seats now. I can roll my chair right up to the front."

There may have been momentary lapses and at first it was slow going, but he persisted and rebuilt his formidable business career. He and Maggie are involved in every sort of activity. They have used their intelligence to break down the barriers for those with disabilities, both in law and in practice.

His stamina is legendary. On the night John won the election for lieutenant governor, I was with the Hagers. His sons, who are the salt of the earth, had worked hard on the campaign, and both young men were dragging as the late night returns came in. Their eyes were glazed over from exhaustion. On the other hand, their father, who probably hadn't slept in the last twenty-four hours, was wide-awake and in party mode.

John really got the shaft at the 2001 Republican Convention. At the time, Jim Gilmore was both governor and head of the Republican National Committee, and he and political strategist Boyd Marcus decided to ease Hager out of contention and put in Mark Earley. I hate to say that anyone was owed an election, but John had paid all the dues known to man, and he should have been the candidate.

I sometimes say that John Hager got Mark Warner elected governor. No one knew who Mark Warner was, but after the Republicans blocked John's candidacy, many of us veterans gathered at the newly built Virginia War Memorial and endorsed Warner for governor. Mark Warner's Chief of Staff later told me that endorsement swayed the election and made all the difference in the Democratic candidate's winning the governorship. The classiest thing Warner did during his tenure was to appoint John as Secretary of Homeland Security, an office John created and made effective.

But the bottom line remains: John Hager should have been governor.

A real highlight and one of my fondest memories from my time as lieutenant governor occurred on my last day of presiding over the Senate in January 2002, when several Senators spoke eloquently and gave testimony about my service – an humbling and tearful end to four great years.

Later in January, there was a special ceremony during which my portrait was dedicated and hung in the Senate chamber. The artist and good friend, Claiborne Gregory, portrayed me seated, as are many of the other lieutenant governors in their portraits, and in mine, no wheelchair is visible. The portrait was well received by our many friends and family on hand for the dedication ceremony. It receives positive comments to this day and retains a prominent spot in the Virginia Senate Chamber.

Chapter 16

9/11 Strikes Home

I discussed with many people the pros and cons of accepting the appointment as assistant to the governor for Virginia's homeland security. In Washington, I met with Republican Senators John Warner and George Allen. I spoke with financial supporters like Bill Goodwin and Booty Armstrong and talked to numerous political figures in the state. Everyone said the same thing. Virginia and America faced a crisis; they were sure I could do a good job, and this was a role that must be accepted, whatever the political affiliations. Since serving on the Virginia Preparedness and Security panel, I was already involved in discussions, preparations and responses to the whole new situation that had formed since 9/11. On December 19, 2001, I met with Governor-elect Mark Warner and agreed to accept the position, which was to be officially called Assistant to the Governor for Commonwealth Preparedness, a Virginia title for Homeland Security Director, He also asked me to be on the transition committee for his new administration. With these new duties came several meetings in December 2001.

Our future seemed very confused. After Christmas we flew with the Lathams to the Gator Bowl in Jacksonville, Florida. The New Year's Day game pitted Virginia Tech and Florida State, and although Tech lost that day, it was an exciting contest. Many loyal Virginia Tech fans were also Hager fans, and it was always great to be with them.

When the General Assembly session began, I continued to preside over the Senate until the new administration's inauguration and participated in festivities. The day after the inauguration, on January 13, 2002, I was sworn into my new position. The first Cabinet meeting was held on January fourteenth, and we were off and running again. Interestingly, being a member of the governor's Cabinet was a new experience for me, since I had not been a part of Governor Gilmore's Cabinet during the previous administration. In hindsight, that is a telling statement about the previous four years and the relationship between the governor and lieutenant governor.

Homeland security was an entirely new concept, and while the panel, which I continued to co-chair, remained open, we were dealing with many issues that previously had not been considered: the idea of being threatened by terrorism, the balance of protecting and empowering individual freedoms, the necessity of bringing officials together and strengthening our defenses against threats, the reinforcement of the state's ability to withstand aggression in whatever form it might take and most important, the development of a cohesive response that would transcend traditional barriers. It was a

165

brand new world, and we faced a daunting task.

Since homeland security had never before been undertaken in such an organized fashion, we had few resources at our disposal to help chart our way. No one really knew the "right" way to proceed, and in the early months we were grasping at straws. We did have good support from many quarters. The state was beginning to receive substantial monetary funding from the federal government to finance improvements in communications and to strengthen infrastructures. That was important to our efforts. Expectations and concerns ran high so we wasted no time in organizing the office and working with other agencies on Capitol Hill and around the state to forge sensible, effective policies. Governor Warner was supportive, and the office was able to function as an independent agency.

My credentials matched the demands of the position. I had proven my worth in a bipartisan manner and chose to rise above the fray. Legislators had a certain comfort level with my leadership because they felt as though they knew me and recognized some political savvy. We were provided good connections in Washington and nurtured relationships with the new administration. I also had military experience that facilitated my discussions with officials from the armed services. Finally, my successful private sector career instilled confidence among business connections and made contacts easy.

In the small office in the Ninth Street Office Building, there was a staff of five, which included Regina Paine, who had worked with me in the lieutenant governor's office; Constance McGeorge, whom we hired from emergency management; George Foresman, who would assume the leadership role when I left; and Craig Suro, a newcomer to government. We were an unusual agency in that we were so small and accomplished most of our goals by working with and through other officials and leaders. Indeed, much of what we implemented was achieved through help from other departments, local governments and businesses. Being new, there was no playbook, and as an independent entity, we pretty much had free reign as we focused on the immediate job at hand.

For the first year starting from scratch, we had little legislative agenda, but it wasn't long before we began to implement policies and to push various agencies to work cooperatively. Prior to 9/11, there was a great deal of dysfunction as agencies within jurisdictions, like the police and emergency management teams, did not always work cooperatively with each other or with others. The counties didn't work with the cities, nor did they work with the state. States didn't work together, even when they bordered each other. There were petty jealousies and distrust, most of which stemmed from pride for one's agency, tradition and the focus on diverse, narrow missions. Our first priority was to convince various localities and organizations to transcend past divisions and to work together. We put the Cs to good use: cooperation, communication, coordination, collaboration and consolidation. Sometimes it also took coercion, persuasion and the bully pulpit.

My most important visit to Washington in conjunction with the new position was on March 11, 2002, when the homeland security directors from each state met for a full-day session in the White House with Tom Ridge, who was then the advisor to President Bush. I remember that the early focus was on individual states, and at this meeting I asked for guidance on what should be done for urban localities that transcend borders — a concern that directly affects Virginia. The Greater Washington area includes Maryland, Virginia, and Washington, and more people who work in Washington live in Northern Virginia than in Washington D.C. As a result, Virginia's most vulnerable area, in many regards, was and continues to be the Northern Virginia portion of the National Capital Region. We received lots of attention as we focused on urban areas.

Although Henry had left his White House internship at the end of 2001 and was working at the Salt Lake City Winter Olympics, we retained a warm connection with Karl Rove. While we were in Washington for the meeting of state homeland security directors, Maggie delivered a tin of her famous lace cookies to Karl.

That week, on March 14, my ninety-seven-year-old father died. His health had deteriorated in recent months, during which time, I had tried to visit him as often as possible and my sister, living close by, continued to be very supportive. His death was a real blow to us both, and the family gathered during this sad time. I didn't know what to say or do, but somehow persevered in speaking at the funeral, after which we remained in Durham for a couple of days to be with the rest of the family.

Back at work, we began to develop outlines for action, goals to be achieved and effective use of federal money in homeland security. Eventually the state would receive almost $3 billion in federal funding to use for various purposes in strengthening our preparedness.

One of our early steps was to name the Secure Virginia Panel, a very distinguished group comprised of twenty-two members with representation from around the state and from many specialties such as ports, transportation and communication. The Secure Virginia Panel met monthly and became the vehicle through which we surveyed ideas and came to a consensus on making recommendations — first to the governor, and subsequently to the General Assembly or other appropriate agencies. Legislative recommendations, regulatory considerations, policy specifics and budget allocations were all subjects of our scrutiny. The panel was the successor to the group first created by Governor Gilmore in response to 9/11.

Especially notable was our success in 2002 in obtaining General Assembly approval for the reestablishment of critical links between state government and federal military installations across Virginia. After this approval, the Virginia Military Advisory Council, which I co-chaired, was created and charged with coordinating and cooperating with active duty and reserve military components in the state. This council met quarterly at different military facilities, and during my term in homeland security, it provided Governor Warner with more than seventy-five major recommendations, including legislative changes, which were approved and implemented.

We also continued the Commonwealth Preparedness Working Group, a cross-agency team composed of key representatives of state agencies involved with preparedness and security related operations. This organization coupled with the Secure Virginia Panel made for a plethora of meetings and responsibilities. The two groups worked closely together in any threat situation, incident or challenge facing Virginia. They also proposed projects for funding and sought ways to by-pass the old "stovepipe" structure of state government.

Looking to Washington, we began with our counterparts to form a group of four representatives called the Senior Policy Group of the National Capitol Region. I served as Virginia's representative alongside a key member from the federal government, one from the mayor's office in the District of Columbia, and the Homeland Security Director from Maryland. We each had a deputy, mine being George Foresman, so there were eight members at each meeting. We met often, bonded well and covered a whole host of activities and perceived threats. The Senior Policy Group was very effective in having a major impact on Washington area coordination, and we were soon working with other agencies all over the region.

All these groups, which met regularly, became the dominant focus of my activities. Meanwhile, I was attending Cabinet meetings every week, writing progress reports, holding weekly meetings with vendors who were trying to sell all sorts of security-related products and participating in conference calls with Washington. These were the days of color-coding perceived threat levels — green, blue, yellow, orange and red, with red being a severe threat level — and we spent many hours talking with the developing Homeland Security organization when threats or perceived threats occurred.

Integral to our progress was the vulnerability and threat assessments carried out by local governments in the state. In simplistic terms, our methodology provided a template for cities and counties that identified risks and threats and then balanced these against existing capabilities. In this way, local needs could be specifically identified. Each individual city and county assessment was then aggregated regionally into a statewide analysis to support the establishment of overall funding and program priorities.

We had a good year, especially since there were no further terrorism attacks, though we had reason to believe that some were prevented. The state's defenses were strengthened. The United States had always been strong in recovery and response, for instance after natural disasters, but the focus of homeland security was to uncover and stop threats before they happened. That was the real distinction between our charge and what had gone before.

In the November/December 2001 issue of the *Virginia Review*, Robert W. Woltz, Jr., President and CEO of Verizon Virginia Inc., highlighted my efforts as Virginia's Homeland Security Director:

First, John is tireless. He is likely to show up anywhere, always with energy and always upbeat. He is determined to get beyond debate and discussion and focus as quickly as possible on actions which can contribute to the goal of the panel, the security of Virginia. He still manages to employ a business approach which requires that the cost and benefits of a particular action be enumerated, not just the concepts. And finally, once the panel has adopted a recommendation, it becomes his. He accepts the responsibility to get it approved by the governor and implemented. He is an advocate for quick action, not for pages of recommendations awaiting action. He leads by example, and it is hard to match his dedication or his energy.

By January 2003, the three panels had developed solid ideas and recommendations, and we had a significant legislative agenda to get through the General Assembly. I expended a great deal of effort working on approval of our legislative agenda. Simultaneously, we continued to extend our activity in the Washington area and to participate with the Senior Policy Group in D.C. It seemed George Foresman and I were driving north every week.

We felt encouraged that we had significantly heightened public awareness of threats and that we were reaching out to all parts of society with activities and information that educated citizens about possible disasters. Our goal was to engage academia and businesses as well as government in the process of research, development and standards. We were concerned about many possible scenarios like threats to nuclear power plants, but in many ways the power plants were better prepared for possible terrorism than most other operations. They had always been acutely alert to security problems and were designed to withstand even direct attacks. A great deal of time was spent in Hampton Roads talking with the port authorities, though we soon realized that they had previously formed a Port Security Committee, and the idea of everyone working together was not foreign to them. In fact, the Port Security Committee routinely engaged ports, localities, shipping interests and federal, state and local governments in coordinated policies and activities. They had learned that teamwork needed to be a way of life because the alternative wouldn't work. Compared to other seaports in the country, Hampton Roads was far superior in its preparedness, and it was a pleasure to deal with them.

The nation's capital and surrounding areas, particularly Northern Virginia, where there are so many government contractors and so much defense activity from the Pentagon down to Fort Belvoir, were vital focal points. Working on this facet of security was probably the most exciting and rewarding part of my job, and over time we received more and more federal funds to facilitate our interfacing with Maryland and the District.

I made good friends during this time. As federal Homeland Security emerged with Tom Ridge acting as the first Secretary, we forged close ties. Because of Virginia's geographic proximity, there were extensive exercises with the federal government to test various systems and levels of preparedness.

As homeland security's reach expanded, continuity became a priority as we considered what sorts of repercussions would emanate from various incidents. We considered all that would need to be done to keep the government running, to keep officials safe and to maintain essential services in the event of a true disaster. As in previous years, there was an extensive 2004 legislative agenda to present to the General Assembly. It focused on planning, continuity and some practical contingencies — such as the proper response if top government officials were lost and where government would relocate if a move were necessary. Because many federal back-up sites are also in Virginia, we dealt not only with the state but also with the federal government's continuity planning. It was at this time that threats from natural disasters began to be more seriously considered. These various points of focus would eventually morph together in subsequent years.

Demands on my time definitely had geared back up, but I was determined to continue some civic commitments and to stay in contact with various groups. I participated as much as possible in many of the activities that I had always enjoyed like the Sorenson Institute, the Virginia Public Safety Foundation and the Greater Richmond Convention Center Authority.

In the early part of 2003, Karl selected Henry to work with Ken Mehlman on the campaign to re-elect George Bush as President in 2004, so Henry was one of the first employees of the Bush re-election campaign. He left the White House after nearly a year, and with the title Staff Secretary to the Campaign he went to the Republican National Committee, where he kept an office until opening the campaign headquarters in Arlington.

Meanwhile, Jack had been working in Charlotte, North Carolina, where he had lived since graduating from Hampden-Sydney College in 1995. We visited him there from time to time, especially during the Wachovia Golf Tournament held every spring. It was fortunate that he was close enough to return home for holidays so we could all get together. Jack remained in Charlotte until he entered the Darden School of Business at the University of Virginia in August 2004. It was at Darden that Jack met his future wife, Katharine Thayer Bigelow, who was taking an advanced program in nutrition at UVA.

There were some interesting recognitions during 2004. The Interreligious and International Peace Council presented me with a Crown of Peace Award for my work on the Faith Based Task Force. As a member of the local Red Cross Board, I was asked to be a featured speaker at the American Red Cross' National Convention in St. Louis. Virginia Military Institute honored me with a Board of Visitors Resolution and special parade. Sam Witt and several other good friends were on the VMI Board and engineered the special ceremony and honor that spring. A short time later, VMI hosted a large conference to debate ideas surrounding homeland security issues. They have continued a similar conference on an annual basis.

As a result of my term as Assistant to the Governor for Commonwealth Preparedness, there was service on a number of national groups. I was a member and a vice chairman of the Emergency Preparedness Council and the Institute for Defense and Homeland Security's Center for Innovative Technology. I was also the member who represented states for the National Emergency Management Association's Board.

The more we did, the more we realized needed to be done. I was involved in politics only as it pertained to getting our legislative agenda passed, and I remained disengaged from the governor's politics. However, in the middle of 2004 Governor Warner began talking about his tax increase package, and I had no interest in being associated with increased taxes.

Somewhat wearied from state government, I resigned from my Virginia office effective April 30, 2004. By this time, I had served for two and a half years, beyond the pledge I had made to remain for at least two years. We had achieved a great deal, and I felt good about our accomplishments, but homeland security certainly wasn't my chosen career path. The move came at a logical time and freed me for other possibilities, particularly potential opportunities in Washington. While I had enjoyed the management and administrative roles of the office, responsibilities that were my strong suit, I believed that George Foresman, who had worked for me during my entire term and who would be my successor, was quite capable of taking my place. I felt confident that I was leaving the office in a strong position. As an added bonus, I avoided being associated with the governor's call for a tax increase. A final side benefit was that by this time, I had worked for Virginia more than five years and was vested for retirement.

I noted at the time of my resignation:

I have been working full-time on Virginia's preparedness since 9/11, some thirty months. While much remains to be done, and we must be diligent in our efforts, the structure, organization, and management of Virginia's role and responsibility in a response is in place, and planning is proceeding well. I don't have any questions that Virginians are safer. We can't be totally safe.

Governor Warner's remarks at the time of my resignation underlined the respect we continued to maintain for one another. We continue even today to be political opposites but good friends.

John Hager has shown a long-standing commitment to the citizens of Virginia, and my administration was fortunate to have him serve. During a time of great uncertainty following the attacks of September 11, 2001, John brought continuity, steady leadership, and solid business skills to Virginia's homeland security efforts.

It was without regret that I left the Ninth Street Office Building, which was in terrible disrepair. Fortunately, during the next year, many of the people who worked with me moved to the renovated Patrick Henry Building. Now the older building has been completely renovated as part of an extensive Capitol Square renewal.

Since life goes by so fast, it seemed the right time to move on. I resigned from the administration with no certainty as to what might be next, but considering my options, I wondered what the possibilities would be in a second Bush administration.

Chapter 17

On To Washington

Working in Washington was not an entirely new idea, as I had considered taking just such a path and had made some inquiries after my failed attempt at winning the Republican nomination for governor in 2001. At that time, any aspirations I might have had for Washington were put on hold when I assumed the position in homeland security.

In 2004, a latent pressure arose among several individuals I had known in the national disability community to take the job in Washington as assistant secretary of the Office of Special Education and Rehabilitation Services (OSERS) at the Department of Education. "You are the man for this job, and you really ought to take it," I kept hearing. I had met some of these vocal individuals through Maggie's service on the National Council for Disabilities and had previously worked with many of them on disability coalition efforts in national Republican campaigns.

The Office of Special Education and Rehabilitation Services was a huge department, with a budget of more than $13 billion and a Washington-based office of 350 employees, serving a wide range of disabled people from toddlers to adults. Special education and rehabilitation services were grouped under the Department of Education because of the nature of the targeted groups to be served. Specifically, there were seven million special education students in the United States, and with a big part of state-based rehabilitation being education-related, one-third of the rehabilitation efforts were directed towards youth. There were about two million young people in various stages of rehabilitation at any time. Another part of the office was NIDRR, the National Institute for Disability and Rehabilitation Research.

Interestingly, at the same time I was considering the position with OSERS, I also was weighing another opportunity with then Secretary of Labor Elaine Chao, whom I had come to know through politics. She had offered a position with her department as assistant secretary. While there are disability operations within the Labor Department, I felt that the bigger job was in the Office of Special Education and Rehabilitation Services.

I realized that after so many years of being disabled, I had never really done much in the disability community except to function by example. My attitude had always been that I can do the most possible good for people in disability communities when I demonstrate that a person can successfully be proficient, normal and competent even with a disability. However, I became swayed by the idea that accepting the position as assistant secretary with OSERS was an opportunity to give back and to instill a business-like approach in this arena. And so, my attention turned to that possible new challenge. I filled out massive paperwork and went to Washington for an interview, which soon led to my being nominated for the office.

The position, however, was a Senate-confirmed job, and it was necessary to prepare even more papers and laborious reports in preparation for Senate approval. It took two or three days to get the paperwork together, and as soon as it was complete, I sent the packet to Washington. In theory, the confirmation process should be simple, but Congress at the time was gridlocked, and though the President's official nomination came in the middle of June, I was not confirmed until after the 2004 election. The delay had nothing to do with me nor with the job, but was strictly a matter of Congressional gridlock. Maggie and I watched CSPAN until early morning on November 21, 2004, to view the confirmation proceedings in the reconvened Senate, at which time I officially became the assistant secretary of OSERS.

Fortunately, I was able to initiate work with the department before Congressional approval. Prior to my confirmation but after the nomination, I was named as a consultant to U. S. Secretary of Education, Rod Paige and at that time began going to Washington and working with officials at OSERS. Several people in the department were extremely helpful in setting up an office so that I could meet and greet and learn about the duties at hand. I commuted to Washington every two weeks or so for these listen-and-learn sessions, but my schedule remained part-time. During this period, I was able to enjoy my family and to travel around Virginia. In order to comply with federal conflict-of-interest rules, I regretfully resigned from many of my civic activities.

My activities in the political arena were minimal during this period. However, I was elected as an alternate delegate to the 2004 Republican National Convention in New York City in August. I drove up and spent an exciting week with many Virginia friends and delegates, during which time we visited all over New York.

When my Senate confirmation came, just two weeks after the election, my schedule immediately changed to full-time in Washington. I was officially sworn into office on January 6, 2005, in a very impressive ceremony to which Maggie and I were able to invite many friends from the Washington area. Then I officially began my new position with its formidable set of responsibilities.

Just a few days later, Hunter Andrews, who had been chairman of the Virginia Senate Finance Committee and a singular figure on the political scene while I was lieutenant governor, passed away, and I attended his funeral on January 17. It was good to catch up with so many Senate colleagues whom I missed very much, and as I mingled with friends at the funeral, I was reminded how challenging it was to be suddenly working outside Virginia.

This was an important period for Henry as well. While Henry was working on George W. Bush's re-election campaign, one of his functions entailed the scheduling of the President and First Lady's political events.

Maggie and I were elated, of course, by the election victory and were delighted the next day as we watched the President make his televised announcement.

With George and Laura Bush

Maggie and I were eager participants in the second inauguration of George W. Bush. We stayed at the Sulgrave Club in D. C. and attended the large Texas-themed event on Friday night, complete with black tie and boots. At the inauguration ceremony, we enjoyed prime seats thanks to Henry's work on the campaign. We continued on to the parade-stand at the White House, the Inaugural Ball and all the activities associated with the inauguration.

On January 28, 2005, Maggie's mother passed away. Maggie had spent the previous four or five years caring almost full-time for her, and while Sally Todd had been able to stay in her home with helpers, Maggie was the real caregiver. The loss of her mother had a huge impact on Maggie's life. The service at St. Paul's Episcopal Church was very moving, and a large crowd gathered afterwards at the Commonwealth Club to memorialize her life. Later in the year, we attended the burial service in Charleston, West Virginia.

Three days after I assumed my new position, Secretary of Education Rod Paige was replaced by Margaret Spellings, who held the position for the remainder of the Bush Presidency. I began attending her weekly staff meetings and also held weekly meetings with my senior staff as I worked to gain control of the office, which had lost structure because the position of assistant secretary had been vacant for almost a year before my confirmation. There were many problems that fell under the responsibilities of OSERS, some of which were difficult to solve. There were daunting demands on my time because of the variety of services provided by the office, extensive involvement with the states, and interaction with the many organizations that were affected. We were associated with numerous groups and sponsored untold numbers of conferences and other events. Responsibilities extended in all directions from the supervision of Gallaudet University, the liberal arts institution for the deaf, to adult rehabilitation programs and university research grants in all areas of the country.

My good friend from campaign days, Bill Latham, owned several motels in Northern Virginia, and before my confirmation was official, he arranged for me to stay at the Quality Inn in Springfield, Virginia. The government paid for these stays, which Bill made sure were very reasonably priced, but once I had been sworn in as assistant secretary I needed a permanent housing arrangement. Around the first of April, I began looking at real estate and zeroed in on a condominium in the Watergate Complex. Sam Witt, a consultant who lived in Richmond, was selling a unit there, and it suited my needs about as well as anything would. Watergate South in Georgetown offered an excellent, safe location as well as a well-managed building with parking. We negotiated back and forth, and then Sam sold the condominium directly to me. After some alterations to accommodate my wheelchair, I set up housekeeping there, and Maggie joined me whenever she was free.

The day before my confirmation as assistant secretary, Congress reauthorized the Individuals with Disabilities Education (IDEA) Act, and one of my biggest priorities was to oversee the rewriting of IDEA rules and regulations, governing more than $11 billion in annual federal special education grants to states. These regulations would translate the law into real practice, but accomplishing that goal was a huge undertaking that dominated much of the early focus of my office. After the last reauthorization of IDEA in 1997, the corresponding regulations took more than two years to complete, but I set an ambitious one-year time frame for completion by December 2005. Drawing on a background of business management, structure and organization, I approached my new responsibilities with a business-like paradigm.

The new law dealt with rules for teacher qualifications, appropriate discipline of students in special education and the monitoring of special education programs. In connection with the rewrite, I inherited a swath of IDEA meetings and input sessions that were scheduled around the country. I began traveling to attend these gatherings almost as soon as the job began. It was a baptism by fire to be immersed immediately in these important decisions. An extremely well qualified woman from the office, Joan Mele-McCarthy, accompanied me on many of these business meetings, most of which were long distances from Washington. We had early trips to Los Angeles and Las Vegas, Minneapolis and New York. It was a real loss when Joan left the department for a promising career opportunity in Maryland.

Meanwhile, a second major thrust was the restructuring of the $2.7 billion Rehabilitation Services Administration, which provided vocational rehabilitation for disabled adults in the states. This restructuring was easier said than done, and it took at least two years to compile data and streamline the operation, all of which invoked considerable push back from regional offices. The person I worked with most closely was Andrew Pepin, a career federal employee who proved to be a wonderful colleague. He was extremely instrumental in enabling me to grasp the responsibilities at hand. We had over three hundred employees in new offices on Fourteenth Street at the Potomac Center Plaza, where the Office of Special Education and Rehabilitative Services had relocated about six months before my confirmation. Because of the recent move, there was much that needed attention and organization, but at least my office was a beautiful one, overlooking the Potomac River.

Reflections of Andrew Pepin, Administrative Executive
Office of Special Education and Rehabilitative Services

Working as closely as I did with John, day in and day out in the Office of Special Education and Rehabilitative Services, United States Department of Education, I came to know him well during our three years together. Throughout, I recognized many traits that distinguished him as a dedicated and effective assistant secretary.

One of the things that stood out in the conduct of his daily work was how he kept a written record of each day's activities. For all the years that I have worked under political appointees, John is the only one who meticulously documented his meetings, discussions, experiences and decisions. This practice spoke not only to his self-discipline, but how he saw his professional obligations, the importance of his work and his desire to account for his actions and leadership. More important, John saw recordkeeping, that ensured information was readily accessible, as essential to managing details.

Early on as I interacted more and more with John, I admired his focus and resolve. He knew how to set priorities and how to address them, and his ability to compartmentalize and structure his time around important daily activities gave those who worked with him confidence that he would make timely and deliberative decisions that would address their work and responsibilities. They felt valued, and John very seldom disappointed them or the organization as whole.

John was the consummate professional who always demonstrated untiring dedication to all aspects of his work and the people he managed. His reliability was unstoppable as was his resolve. His disability was never an impediment or focus. He carried out his responsibilities in a manner that was equal, fair, objective and with compassion, whether he was working on behalf of individuals with disabilities and on behalf of those without.

As assistant secretary, John worked within a dual system, in which he was a political appointee navigating a bureaucratic structure, managing federal career employees and imposing rules and regulations on both internal and external constituencies. John was always adept at threading the needle in this duel system, never having to compromise his ethics or principles. He believed that integrity and professional accountability went hand in hand and expected no less from his peers and coworkers.

When John first began working as assistant secretary, he knew nothing about the job or its responsibilities, but it took little time for him to become acclimated and knowledgeable. He was intent on becoming as educated as possible so that he could participate fully in concrete discus-

sions about our program challenges, demands and expectations. He wanted to learn from the people around him, and he always encouraged staff to speak their minds.

John had a keen and constructive ability to dissect a problem accurately and quickly. He had a remarkable grasp of business protocol and could analyze an issue and make prudent decisions that enabled the issue to move to the next steps. He exhibited a comprehensive and keen understanding of what it took to run an organization, and he enabled employees to succeed personally and professionally.

In summary and more important is to end with an observation that truly defines John's character. The relationship that evolved between the Hager and Bush families resulting from the marriage of John's son to the President's daughter was not only downplayed by John, it was never a topic that ever played out during John's appointment as Assistant Secretary.

John brought to the position qualities that made a lasting impact on me as a manager and more important as a person. I cannot speak highly enough of the opportunity that I was afforded in working with such an outstanding and remarkable individual.

Even while scrambling to organize the office — develop personnel, oversee operations and improve efficiency there — I continued to attend the IDEA input meetings that had been scheduled before my arrival. I also spoke at numerous national gatherings in the special education, disability and rehabilitation arena. It was rewarding when in the midst of this busy schedule, Nevada's Public Education Program (PEP) presented me with the "Hand in Hand" Award.

I found that it took about six months to grasp all the tasks at hand, to understand all the players and to begin having a true impact. There were several qualified personnel - Troy Justensen, Ed Anthony, Jennifer Sheehy, Patty Guard and Stephen Tingus - all key players. Intent on seizing the opportunity to accomplish some truly big goals, we worked together diligently in every part of the operation.

Oz Day, a fine and loyal friend whom I had known for some time from the disability community, insisted that I join the Metropolitan Club, which was located not far from the Watergate. I was unsure how much time would be available to enjoy the facility, but I took his suggestion and found it to be a great place to escape my responsibilities from time to time, especially with the club's special events.

Being a rather reluctant government employee, I made my way back home to Sulgrave Road for most weekends, and though I had resigned from many of my boards and offices in Richmond, I continued to stay in touch with these civic groups. Once my tenure with OSERS ended, I was heartened that most of these asked me to resume my prior roles of responsibility. While I was assistant secretary, I remained in touch with the University of Virginia's Center of Politics and my friend Larry Sabato, and when the Center held conferences in Washington, I found them to be a pleasant respite from the humdrum of federal government employment.

During the summer of 2005, Chief Justice Leroy Hassell of the Virginia Supreme Court called and then wrote, requesting me to serve on his Futures Commission. Much

Speaking on the road as assistant Secretary, 2008

to my surprise, the legal powers-to-be at the Department of Education approved. The Futures Commission was a very well run group headed by Chief Justice Hassell and Anne Marie Whittemore. It had a good cross section of distinguished Virginians, but mostly lawyers and Judges, so I was in a distinct minority and learned a lot. Our charge was to improve the justice system for the next twenty years, and over the course of numerous meetings during 2006, we made some excellent recommendations. The final report of the Commission on Virginia Courts in the 21st Century, "To Benefit All, To Exclude None," was in January 2007.

It seemed that an endless array of meetings, special events and gatherings in the disabilities community all hoped to have Assistant Secretary Hager in attendance. For instance, in July the Americans with Disabilities Act's anniversary was celebrated over two full days. Then late in the fall of 2005, Hurricane Katrina struck, and that precipitated many meetings to deal with various related priorities. I flew to Mississippi and Alabama and met with the governors, toured the affected areas, and visited some of our programs in those states. An intergovernmental task force formed to consider emergency preparedness for people with disabilities and that effort involved some creative leadership.

At this time, there was extensive focus on emergency preparedness, and I was selected as Education's representative due to my Virginia experience. There were two takeaways. First, after cutting through all the rhetoric, self-reliance and preparation are the foremost factors. Second, generalization does no good as all disability needs are different. Consequently, we approached the response by disability category, i.e. deaf, blind, mobility issues, etc. to build a program for each disability.

By early 2006, we had completed the input sessions of IDEA, and we began writing regulations and going to final draft in the Federal Register. The IDEA requirements aimed to ensure that all students received appropriate education, a goal we hoped to achieve through regulation of vital aspects of the student experience: early intervention, thorough reporting, neighborhood schools, highly qualified teachers and testing. In almost every aspect, it was cross-referenced with the "No Child Left Behind" program being pursued by other offices at the Department of Education.

I began working very closely with Margaret Spellings and other education leaders who had been brought in by President George W. Bush. The President's first inspiration to run for political office had sprung from his realization that eighth-graders in his native Texas were achieving dismal reading scores. He demonstrated a genuine interest in education and directed some lead individuals in the field to facilitate our work. The secretary and several of us assistant secretaries began making speeches all across the country as we sought to promote both "No Child Left Behind" and IDEA, neither perfect laws, but certainly a leap forward.

Certainly primary education is a supreme challenge which depends on many, variable factors. NCLB was designed to promote evaluation and testing, local control with accountability and enhanced results. It had its critics and took a long time to get through Congress. When President Obama took office, he highlighted perceived weaknesses of NCLB and initiated his own program, Race to the Top. Though his program was touted as the new gold standard for education, Race to the Top also had a tough time gaining Congressional approval. There seem to be no magic bullets today, and I am not sure Washington helps much. Certainly, when government spends huge sums of money, there should be definitive methods in place to track and evaluate the results

We developed an effective travel team composed of myself and two outstanding individuals — Jim Button, a seasoned employee who made our arrangements, wrote speeches and took care of details; and Anna Clay, a Carolina graduate and a terrific personal assistant. Jim, Anna and I met together with other staff members in a weekly scheduling meeting and outlined our plan of action. These were lively meetings, and in our travels the three of us crisscrossed the country to promote IDEA implementation and other OSERS priorities.

While IDEA remained the major focus, we worked on other, related projects as well. For instance, an extensive set of tool kits for special education was developed. These tool kits contained materials and guidelines that were helpful to individual educators and increased the effectiveness of implementation. It was my busy second year, 2006, that made my tenure a success as we endorsed and implemented two key concepts.

The first concept actually occurred to me during my initial year as assistant secretary, when I was asked to be the keynote speaker at the Virginia Department of Rehabilitative Services' annual conference in Williamsburg. An idea called "transition" was being highlighted, a term that refers to transitioning young people out of special education into further education or into jobs or other types of productive activities. Transition promoted a focus on the entire individual, not solely on his or her disability. At the time, many youths

ADA Anniversary in Washington, D.C.

were encouraged by their parents to collect Social Security disability payments, and with this funding available, the young people were not motivated to move into satisfying life situations. A variety of barriers limited their options and left no hope for a worthwhile future. It struck me that in discussing transition, the Department of Rehabilitative Services should break that pattern by taking a comprehensive approach to each individual. Rather than just looking at the youth's particular area of disability and inherent learning problems, we should consider all aspects of life: health, family, transportation possibilities, social needs, mental health, etc. To enable the young person to move forward constructively with his or her life, it might be necessary to provide a whole array of services. I took note of the transition approach, and a year and a half later, we were able to make transition one of OSERS' two major initiatives. We gradually gained and redirected federal funds and convinced many states to adopt support systems to buoy transitioning of young people. While we didn't conceive of the concept, we certainly ingrained it into actual practice, and the commitment to transition continues today as a major focus.

The second concept that I embraced was the recycling and reuse of assistive technology. Early on, we met with a friend from Salem, Virginia, Cabell Brand, whom I had known from the Virginia Health Care Foundation Board. Cabell had the concept that one could collect every sort of assistive technology – from the simplest types, like crutches or braces, to the most sophisticated, like speech recognition software and adapted computers. The products could be sanitized, sized if necessary, warehoused until needed and then given to individuals who would benefit from their use. He used the example of a child who outgrows his wheelchair but could pass it on to another child who needs the small one, and then the larger youngster would receive an appropriate size for his own use. I drove with Anna Clay, my personal assistant, to Salem to view firsthand Cabell Brand's organization, FREE. We were increasingly intrigued as FREE introduced us to a number of excited beneficiaries of this recycling-reuse concept. We took the ideas from FREE and held a national conference to highlight the possibilities. We were aware that others had tried variants of the concept around the country, and we visited several other operations, but the idea needed to be put into action. It was with funds from the National Institute on Disability and Rehabilitation Research that we were able to implement and promote the concept of assistive technology reuse.

In the past, there had been a reluctance to reuse devices because of the possibility of legal consequences, but we bypassed those concerns by giving away the items, thereby creating a great new solution to an old problem. As the program became established, we found that many of the recipients contributed to its sustainability by returning and supporting the program in a variety of ways. The reuse program concept became very popular and over the subsequent years spread like wildfire throughout the country, becoming a huge, decentralized operation which often works with local programs like Goodwill Industries. Today, the concept of reuse continues to flourish.

With OSERS' extensive budget growing to nearly $14 billion and with so many areas of responsibility, the level of diversity and sheer immensity of all that we were doing was staggering. Still I realized that the department's focus was not always prioritized or effective. Not one to suffer wasting money needlessly, I decided to run an efficiency test by selecting a single state and visiting every program that was funded by OSERS. We chose Oregon, which had probably twenty different programs under the OSERS grants umbrella – a diverse array of operations, many of which had never been visited by an assistant secretary.

We flew into Portland, Oregon, and spoke to the statewide transition conference in Salem. We went to the state capitol, the University of Oregon, Oregon State, and every other site where programs received our funding. It was an exhaustive but enlightening trip. On our last night, we somewhat reluctantly stopped and spoke at the Delphian School of Scientology at the top of a mountain in Sheridan, Oregon. Though they were not grantees, the director of Delphian had invited me to visit during a meeting we were attending in Washington, and the visit proved fascinating.

This experiment of viewing all the federally funded programs in a single state proved to be highly worthwhile. Since much of the money in our department was "pass through" money, meaning it was appropriated at the federal level but was intended for use by the states, we needed to see the programs to ensure that guidelines and rules were followed and goals were being achieved. Much of the balance of funding was through competitive grants. Most everyone we met on these trips was welcoming and appreciative of the interest and oversight. Later, we visited North Carolina, Florida, Connecticut and Pennsylvania with the same approach. Accountability was important, and we were paying attention. We were also learning how to tighten programs and grants to influence productive outcomes and wake up some people along the way.

Meanwhile on the home front, Maggie settled into a more moderate pace. Jack graduated with a Masters of Business Administration from the University of Virginia's Darden School in May 2006, and we spent that celebratory weekend in Charlottesville. He had accepted a job with United Technologies, for which he moved to Connecticut. Shortly, thereafter, Katharine Bigelow, whom he had started dating at Darden, moved to Connecticut as well, and they became engaged.

Henry continued working in Washington, where Jenna Bush was teaching school. But Henry was eager to attend graduate business school. He selected Darden, as Jack had done, so while Jack graduated in May, Henry entered Darden in September. Henry and Jenna became engaged in Maine in August of 2007.

The press made much of their engagement and what the *Washington Post* in October 2007 dubbed, "A Union of Families, Politics and Society." While we honored Henry and Jenna's desire for privacy and declined to be interviewed.

In the fall of 2006, Maggie and I participated in the week-long Old Masters Program on Purdue's campus. This was a distinguished group, receiving much recognition and being treated like royalty. It was great to be back in West Lafayette. In describing the background of my selection as an Old Master, I was cited for "outstanding contributions as an industry, government and community leader." Continuing the description, it was noted that I was "making a grand slam with a curve ball..." and that my position as assistant secretary of the Office of Special Education and Rehabilitative Services was "a great fit for a man who has refused to acknowledge disability as a barrier and has steadfastly and optimistically pursued success."

In November, our team at OSERS went to Houston, Dallas and Austin, Texas, for IDEA implementation and other initiatives. During that trip, we stopped to see my niece, Ginny Woods, and her husband, who had experienced a serious stroke the previous year. It was a good but sobering experience.

Every year during the approaching holidays, Harrison Tyler from Sherwood Forest organized what he called a disabled deer hunt, and though my hunting prowess seriously suffered once I was caught up in the Washington circus, I always attended his hunt — often inviting several friends to join. As a family, we tried to stay together during Christmas, but as the boys grew older that goal became increasingly challenging.

The year 2007 started full-bore. We joined the senior staff of the Department of Education for endless policy meetings on the implementation of "No Child Left Behind." Our team continued to travel, and I gave many speeches. One of my more interesting trips took us to Chicago, where Henry Betts, the Director of the Rehabilitation Institute and the doctor who had facilitated my entering Rusk Institute, was sponsoring a major conference. I was the keynote speaker. The afternoon before the conference, we were scheduled to visit Mayor Richard J. Daley, Jr. in his downtown office. The mayor had promoted several disability initiatives, and we were looking forward to the meeting, but as luck would have it, our plane was late. We were very frustrated that we were going miss our opportunity. When our plane finally landed in Chicago, Jim Button and I raced to a taxi and sped to Mayor Daley's office. Although we were about two hours late, Mayor Daley had waited for us, and we spent a long time together in deep conversations about

Chicago's disability programs. The next day I spoke at the conference, in which many of the mayor's staff participated. Upon leaving, Mayor Daley presented me with an elaborate, autographed book about Chicago.

We drove from the Windy City to West Lafayette, Indiana, returning again to Purdue where I was awarded an Outstanding Engineering Alumni Award in an exciting two-day celebration that featured Colin Powell as the keynote speaker. As usual, the university was very generous with its welcome and hospitality. During this visit, we toured a couple of OSERS research projects on campus. It was great to see what an outstanding place Purdue had become.

Jack and Katharine married on February 10, 2007, in New York City. Henry and Jenna came from Washington, and Maggie and I spent the long weekend in New York, enjoying the festivities, during which we hosted the rehearsal dinner at the Knickerbocker Club. The wedding ceremony was at All Souls Church before an expansive group of friends and family, and their reception was held at the University Club.

Every week was spent on the job, either in Washington or in OSERS-related travel. In March our group drove to Armonk, New York, and met with IBM executives in a cooperative effort between industry and government to develop technological assistance for disabilities. IBM's computer expertise represented true cutting-edge technology for the disability community. From there we continued on to New York City, and I spoke at a large event for disabled adults at an uptown theater.

In April, we were in Dover, Delaware, where we had been warmly welcomed at several stops. It was here that we heard the distressing reports of the Virginia Tech shooting, news that left us stunned as we drove back to Washington. It really hurt to hear about such a senseless act. I had had close ties with Virginia Tech, having been there repeatedly as Lieutenant Governor.

I ventured back to Richmond for the Capitol Gala at the newly refurbished Virginia State Capitol. The stunning project and its wonderful outcome came a little late for my personal use but is one in which all Virginians can take pride. I still love to visit the Capitol today and marvel at its magnificent restoration and extensive improvements.

As assistant secretary I served on several federal boards, including the Department of Transportation's United We Ride Commission, the Access Board, formerly called the Architectural and Transportation Barriers Compliance Board, the Labor Department's Task Force on the Aging of the American Work Force and Homeland Security's Interagency Coordinating Council — Emergency Preparedness for People with Disabilities. I was also a member of the Department of Health and Human Services' Federal Executive Steering Committee on Mental Health. Doesn't all this sound like Washington?

I was pleased with the accomplishments during my three years as assistant secretary but increasingly felt frustration at some of the bureaucracy and the seemingly senseless rules that constantly surrounded my work in D.C. I couldn't help feeling antsy while weathering the draining and somewhat confining parameters of my job.

When learning that Ed Gillespie, who had been chairman of the Republican Party of Virginia for about seven months, was leaving that post to start work in Washington as counselor to the President, I realized that the chairmanship of Republican Party of Virginia would again be vacant. Further, because of Ed's unexpected resignation, the new chairman would be selected in two weeks, not by convention, but by the State Central Committee. For whatever reason, I decided to throw my hat casually in the ring and commenced campaigning at night by phone. On Saturday, July 21, 2007, the Republican State Central Committee met, and much to my surprise I was elected chairman by a slim margin.

As a consequence of this new responsibility, my time in Washington would necessarily come to an end, though I remained in the office until the end of July. My travel team and I had scheduled a week-long business trip to Colorado, which I completed and found most interesting, as we covered several operations in that state. Still, it was definitely a trip with mixed emotions, since I knew it would be my last with the department. In subsequent months after my resignation, the other two members of my travel team also left the department. Sadly, Jim Button developed cancer and died about two years later. Anna Clay left for graduate school and did not return to OSERS.

I resigned effective, August 1, 2007. One report of my departure by Kara Arundel, entitled "Hager leaves OSERS" stated that in addition to focusing on regulations for IDEA, I oversaw issuance of regulations for modified assessments.

He urged schools and districts to comply with NCLB as a way to give students with disabilities greater access to the general curriculum. He was a proponent of inclusion of students with special needs and bettering transition practices. Hager also understood the barriers disabilities can create. He has used a wheelchair for more than 30 years since he contracted polio. "With his background in business, John Hager brought a focus on outcomes and results," said Madeline Will, vice president of public policy and director of the National Down Syndrome Society. "His interest in improving transition services and employment opportunities for people with disabilities is right on target for the 21st century," said Dan Blair, senior director for policy and advocacy with the Council for Exceptional Children.

There were several farewell parties, which Maggie attended with me. We left D.C. that Thursday and flew straight to Minneapolis, where we spent about a week with the summer Republican National Committee meeting. This gathering was the prelude to the National Convention in 2008, which also would be held in Minneapolis, and it provided our first opportunity to be up close with Mitt and Ann Romney.

Returning to Washington, I vacated my office but decided to retain the condominium in the Watergate. The depressed real estate market of 2008 offered little choice, and as chairman of the Republican Party of Virginia, I knew that I probably would have to spend a fair amount of time in Washington with the Republican National Committee. I also had been nominated for a position on the National Council on Disabilities, a post that would involve another Senate confirmation, and would require frequent stays in Washington. As it happened that fall, my nomination became caught up in Senate politics and was delayed. John Warner stepped in and tried to persuade the Democrats to approve my nomination, but to no avail. It seemed logical for me to be a valuable member of this

With Mitt Romney in Minneapolis

group, with which I already had ties, but politics prevailed and the nomination failed.

While assistant secretary, I had been selected to be a member of the national delegation to attend the Special Olympics in Shanghai, and despite my resignation, I was still able to be part of the national delegation. On September 29, 2007, the group flew to Shanghai for a week of official activities. The Special Olympics were treated as a warm-up for the Olympics the next year in Beijing, and everything was mirrored in the same way. The delegation consisted of several special people, and all of us were fascinated by the sights and sounds of Shanghai. Margaret Spellings, Michelle Kwan, Eunice Kennedy, Ernie Banks and others joined in the festivities, the official government visits and events with the athletes. It was thrilling to be a part of the opening ceremony — marching in with the other delegates, including Arnold Schwarzenegger, and the athletes.

I have so many memories of that week, my only trip to mainland China, and it was a real highlight to be a part of the group. This was a magic trip. We were escorted and treated royally at every step. We attended many of the events and marvelled at the performances of the American athletes. When we met with the Economic Minister at the palace, they removed one of the giant red chairs so I would have a place. Michelle Kwan and I hit it off, and – odd couple though we were – we seemed to go together to every event and be seated together during the festivities. She was lovely. We couldn't help but regret the end of our special visit as we began the long flights back to Chicago and Dulles.

Chapter 18

Good Times — Testy Politics

Back in Richmond full-time in August, I quickly focused on my activities with the Republican Party of Virginia. We were able to hire Cam Tyler, a recent Virginia Tech graduate as my assistant, and he was a great help. Charlie Judd continued as executive director and did an excellent job. There was a big bus tour and rally leading up to the November General Assembly elections, and we tried to help there and in other ways as much as possible. Results were mostly good though with no statewide elections in 2007, there was skepticism about how effective we were.

Maggie and I were invited to a black-tie dinner at the White House with the President of France, Nicolas Sarkozy, on election night. While that presented a bit of a dilemma for my attention, we attended this special affair and kept up with the results while trying to be worthy guests. I left early and attended the Fairfax County Republican "Victory Rally" which ended at a reasonable hour due to mixed results there.

After the election, a lot of planning and effort went into reorganizing the Republican Party operations and establishing financial stability. Everything was relatively calm and the State Central Committee meetings were uneventful. The Republican Advance at Crystal City was in early December, the first time in years that it had been held in Northern Virginia. It was successful in attendance and programing. We conducted a straw poll the presidential nomination, which seemed like a good idea. However, it was captured by outsiders and thrown to Ron Paul, which upset many of the weekend attendees.

Christmas was relaxed and quiet in Richmond. Henry and Jenna visited briefly on their way to Florida. Jack and Katharine stayed up North. We had no big parties and began to feel like two people growing older.

In early 2008, heavy involvement of the Republican Party of Virginia in activities related to the General Assembly session took center stage. We were promoting Party registration in the state, which was an initiative at the General Assembly which did not pass, as it hasn't despite many years of consideration. I spent three days in Washington at the Republican National Committee meeting. Most of our efforts in Virginia were directed at establishing the preliminary organization, coordinated with RNC, and a statewide preparation for the upcoming Presidential election. Finances were strong and everything was moving along.

Every fourth year, with 2008 being one of these, Colonial Williamsburg organizes a commemorative General Assembly session, a re-creation of the early years when Williamsburg was the state capital. During this commemoration, an entire weekend of social activities and events serves as a real get-together for many like me who had moved beyond the political offices in Richmond.

On February 8, 2008, Maggie and I were honored to host Richmond friends at an engagement party for Henry and Jenna in our home. In further preparation for Henry's wedding, Maggie and I flew in late February to Dallas and drove to Salado, Texas, a tourist destination with a frontier-town backdrop and the location that Jenna and Henry had chosen for all the events connected with their wedding except the ceremony and reception. There we finalized preparations for the rehersal dinner, which we would host.

In February, shortly after we returned from Texas, we drove to Albany, New York, where Katharine and Jack awaited the imminent arrival of our first grandchild. We were there a couple of days before Caroline Chase Hager was born, and we could celebrate her arrival with our son and daughter-in-law — a really new and exciting experience for all of us.

There was no slowing down that year with the resumption of my activities in civic groups from which I had resigned when working in Washington. I went back on the Sorenson Institute Board and soon thereafter became chairman again, a role that continued for eight years. I joined the Board of Virginia FREE, a business-related organization, and served that group as chairman of its nominating committee. I became vice president of Jamestown-Yorktown Foundation, Inc. board, which is the fundraising arm of the Jamestown-Yorktown Foundation. Over the years, I was a member of the latter board as trustee for three terms and chairman of the Committee on the Future. In 2013, Governor McDonnell appointed me again to the Foundation Board. Other memberships resumed and our lives took on a tone of normalcy.

In April, we attended the RNC's chairmen's meeting in New Mexico for a week. Although I had been elected chairman in 2007 by the State Central Committee, the State Convention holds an election for the position of chairman every four years in June, coinciding with the years of Presidential elections. This year there was another contender for the office, Jeff Frederick, who was capable, but who also was a right wing zealot. His bid to win the chairmanship from me would necessitate a huge contest for the position, so in April, I organized for the challenge and hired Ray Allen, who assigned Mike Brown to run my chairman's election campaign. Innumerable people supported me, and I realized that if they turned out for the convention and stayed, I should be able to hold onto the chairmanship. However, we also knew that the June conventions could be wildly unpredictable, and many potential delegates had become turned off by the process in previous years.

On Thursday, May 8, Maggie and I flew to Fort Worth and then drove to Salado, Texas, for Jenna and Henry's wedding weekend. We greeted family and friends who arrived for the wedding festivities. On Friday at midday, more friends arrived, and Maggie attended the bridesmaids' luncheon. That night, we sponsored the memorable rehearsal dinner at the Celebration Center.

The beautiful wedding at the ranch the following day will linger in many memories for a long time. Lots of friends and family made it even more special.

The next day, we gathered at breakfast and mingled with our guests as they flew out, one by one. Maggie and I stayed until Monday morning, which gave us time to catch our breath. Jenna and Henry cut their honeymoon plans short because the following weekend was graduation day at Darden School of Business. After returning to Richmond, we gathered again in Charlottesville to celebrate Henry's graduation. The newlyweds flew to Hawaii for their honeymoon and then moved to Baltimore, where Henry began working for Constellation Energy and Jenna went back to teaching.

Upon returning to Richmond, I resumed the chairman's race with a vengeance. I worked closely with the executive director of the Party, Charlie Judd. We prepared for the state convention, which was being held at the Greater Richmond Convention Center during the first week of June.

On Friday night of the convention I introduced Dick Cheney, who spoke at the gala dinner. The next morning, as the convention got underway, attendance looked good. However, the party was also nominating a candidate for the Senate, and the selection process dragged on for several acrimonious hours until Jim Gilmore finally defeated Delegate Bob Marshall by a narrow margin. Unfortunately, the contest had not only consumed a great deal of time, but also had created a great deal of animosity on all sides. Many delegates left after that decision had been determined, so the number who remained at the convention was a fraction of the morning's count. Worse still, many of those who left were my supporters while the bulk of Jeff Frederick's group stayed on hand. After having a virtual lock on the chairmanship and carrying a huge majority in the morning, I lost the election in the waning hours of the convention. Many staff from the Republican Party of Virginia walked out in protest, but the vote had been taken and that was that. There was some small vindication a little over a year later when the State Central Committee fired Jeff Frederick and threw him out of the office because of his poor performance and questionable shenanigans. The press was shocked about his election, yet maybe not so surprised due to the history of Republican conventions. There were a lot of sad supporters that day and a lot of vengeance in their eyes. It was what it was, and philosophically, I figured that at that point that I had really retired.

Looking back, I enjoyed a good year as chairman and had worked hard to set up the state's Victory operation for John McCain, who became the candidate for President at the National Convention later that summer. Frederick and his group dismantled the operation, and unbelievably in November, McCain lost to Obama in Virginia. The Party still has not recovered from the fallout from this period or from the split in the Party that resulted from this development and subsequent shenanigans. The battle goes on, sometimes ill-described as conservative vs. establishment. It is more than obvious that to remain a winning party, we Republicans must solve the rifts going forward, but the conflict seems to be inherent in the system and a by-product of the lack of full participation by the public. Both parties are coalitions of people, and when power and control are at stake, look out! This truth seems to hold from the most insignificant, local level all the way to the top national level. It will probably never change.

I have been blessed in my various campaigns to have lots of very dedicated and wonderful supporters. Henry Lane Hull described my service and philosophy about involvement in the *Rappahannock Record*, June 19, 2008:

If one were to poll across the Commonwealth asking the question, "Who is the most beloved living Virginian?" the answer most probably would be Lt. Gov. John Hager. He likely would come in first if one also asked, "What Virginian knows the largest number of fellow Virginians?" The reason for his popularity is his unique combination of gentlemanliness with utter dedication to being of service to others.

He has traveled to every corner of the Commonwealth, repeatedly, meeting with groups, both large and small, getting to know Virginians by their first names to such an extent that he is a walking Rolodex of names, faces and places. A saying has emerged that wherever two Republicans are gathered, John is present, and if a fourth person is there too, that would be his beloved wife Maggie, a complete lady if ever there was one.

Three decades ago, at the peak of his career, John came down with polio, a disease he contracted while changing his son's diaper. The ensuing paralysis ended his days on his feet, but in no way diminished his energy or enthusiasm for reaching out to other people. I have known John for almost 20 years and in all of our conversations the phrase which to me has been the most memorable is his constant refrain, "In my life, I always have tried to convert challenges to opportunities."

For all these years, John has sat in his wheelchair, which he always pushes himself, undaunted by challenges, unafraid of the future, ever looking for the coming of that conversion that he has effected so many times.

In our family my good wife and I have coined a verb, "to hagerize," which means to take a dire situation fraught with challenge and turn it into a bright spot for future development. To hagerize is to make success triumph over adversity, to see good win over evil, to bring order out of chaos, and to be contented with life's events all the time.

Al Smith, the former governor of New York, who was the unsuccessful Democratic candidate for President in 1928, was known universally in his time as "The Happy Warrior." In our era, that role belongs to John. He is the knight in a shining wheelchair, standing ever as the tallest person in the room, forging ahead with good cheer and leaving in his wake a reservoir of camaraderie and good will wherever he has made tracks.

When you face challenges, John's example can be the model for overcoming them, for making them into opportunities, and for enjoying life to the fullest each and every day. Verily, he is one of Virginia's greatest, and all of us are fortunate that his time is our time.

Chapter 19

Retirement (Sort of)

June of 2008 was a confused time. No one had expected me to lose the chairmanship, including me. I was pretty well disgusted and scared for the Republican Party and was ready to take a break after the convention. It was just at this unsettled period that I received a surprising and heartwarming award.

On his own, Henry had initiated my being named Father of the Year with the American Diabetes Association. I received the honor at their annual banquet, held with great celebration and with the family in attendance at the Jefferson Hotel. Coming during the particularly "down time" shortly after I lost the chairmanship, this special tribute was a definite morale booster.

Shortly afterwards, Massie Valentine, Jr., who was President of the Custis Hunting and Fishing Club, asked for my help in settling a dispute the club was having with a Mr. Pete Henderson over adjacent land rights and development. I became very involved in

Father of the Year Award with family

Custis at this time, and worked for years to resolve the problems. The issue would not be fully resolved until 2013.

The resumption of active involvement with several organizations kept the days busy enough, but life wasn't the same. I maintained some contact with my friends at OSERS in Washington, but after my resignation, these relationships faded rather quickly.

Maggie and I resolved that we would take more time "off," so we returned to Martha's Vineyard in July and extended our stay with a tour through New England. I made a decision that I would continue, at least to some extent, my involvement in politics and was invited to attend the Republican National Convention in Minneapolis. I flew in August from Boston to Minneapolis, only this time as a guest, and spent the week with the Virginia delegation at the convention, covered a lot of ground, enjoyed being a part of the gathering and managed to co-exist without any incident with the new chairman.

After Labor Day, we returned to Richmond and resumed our busy ways. Carol Price asked me to become involved as chairman with the National Council, a new advisory organization that was being formed for Stratford Hall, a magnificent place, home of the Lees and three signers of the Declaration of Independence. The idea of this separate group – the National Council – had its genesis in the original organization when a group of ladies saved Stratford in the 1930s, then became the Board of Directors and organized an advisory group. We selected about ten people to serve on the high-level group, with plans to meet three times a year, and while this was a new venture for me, it was one I enjoyed. I continue to chair the Council, through which I worked closely with Paul Reber, the executive director, until he was tragically killed on his bike in July 2015. Paul and I visited Mount Vernon and observed how that preservation organization functions, and in light of our findings, we revamped and restructured Stratford Hall's National Council. I am honored they selected me to lead the distinguished National Council as they work so hard to stay relevant and manage the huge operation with 3,000 acres, the famous Great House, the Potomac archeological sites, mill etc. I hope to be able to spend more time there and to make a real contribution. Each fall, we celebrate with the Lee Circle during an especially pleasant weekend.

Several members of the Juniper Club asked me if I would be willing to become involved there again, with the hope that I would spend some time "getting the lay of the land" in 2009 before stepping in as Captain of the Hunt the next year. In January, I drove to Florida for the Hunt, a two-week gathering of members at Juniper. I found that in the years since I had visited, the club had remained virtually unchanged and was a real throwback to the past, but it also provided an enjoyable break among friendly and welcoming fellow members. It was, however, a long drive to Florida.

Never giving up on politics, I attended the Republican National Committee meeting in Washington as a guest, and went again to the annual Washington gathering of the Conservative Political Action Conference (CPAC). Whenever staying overnight in Washington, we made use of our Watergate condominium, which we continued to own. Persistent depressed real estate values made this a less than opportune time to attempt a sale, but by this time, with only infrequent overnights in Washington, our condo had become something of an albatross, and we knew before too long something would have to be done.

By March, Maggie and I took a vacation out West. We flew to Tucson, Arizona, to see our friends, the Chilcotes, in Tubac, south of Tucson. We then spent time at the El Coronado Ranch on the border of Mexico, where we stayed with the Austins, friends of Maggie. They took us into Mexico, where we viewed their land restoration efforts. By rental car, Maggie and I also toured northern Arizona, highlighted by Sedona and the Grand Canyon. It was a great trip.

Shortly after our return from that vacation, we had the first indication that my sister was developing a health problem. Nancy suffered from a particularly unusual form of Parkinson's disease — Louie's Body Disease, a serious and incurable ailment. We drove to Durham to see her not long after we learned of the diagnosis. Nancy continued a long-term deterioration, which was heart-wrenching to witness.

This was a busy year for becoming involved with several new organizations and for my increased interest in leadership programs within the state. In addition to Virginia FREE, I joined the Boards of Virginia 21, an organization designed to involve college students in the state, the Thomas Jefferson Institute, a center-right, political think-tank that is headquartered in Northern Virginia, and Lead Virginia, a leadership development program for business. Recognizing that leadership is an acquired skill, one that can be learned, I devoted time and energy to working with these leadership-focused organizations and continued my commitments to Leadership Metro Richmond and the Sorenson Institute for Political Leadership.

In the fall of 2009, *Virginia Capitol Connections* published an article that I wrote entitled, "Leadership Programs Are Good for Virginia." I described some of the state's oldest, community or region-based programs such as Leadership Metro Richmond and similar ones around Virginia that work with emerging leaders to build connections, encourage community engagement and explore multiple perspectives. Lead Virginia, which was designed to meet the needs of business leaders, focuses on substantive issue-related content, rather than skill development. This organization aims to create a network of relationships with business leaders throughout the state and to enhance civic engagement by developing an understanding of key issues. Sorensen Institute's political leadership programs provide emerging political leaders with the training necessary to succeed in politics and community service. I detailed in the article the varied ways that these programs give substance to individuals who would answer Thomas Jefferson's call to "Come forward then and give us the aid of your talents and the weight of your character."

In July, we flew from Newark to Bermuda to celebrate with a group from Jamestown-Yorktown Foundation the four hundredth anniversary of the British settlement in Bermuda. This well-organized, week-long event was filled with memorable, special activities.

When we returned, I became involved in the upcoming election for governor of Virginia. I had known the Republican nominee, Bob McDonnell, for years and became a member of his Finance Committee. Like other Republicans in November 2009, we were elated when the Party won a clean sweep of the offices — governor, lieutenant governor and attorney general, quite a change from the previous year's losses. Afterwards in December at the Homestead, I attended the Republican Advance and enjoyed the buoyant atmosphere that everyone in attendance was feeling.

Maggie and I were invited to speak together at a meeting of the Women of the Church at First Presbyterian. The preparation for this presentation allowed us to reflect on our challenges and blessings.

In November, we resurrected our holiday parties and held two large ones, a neighborhood gathering and a belated seventieth birthday party for me. The year had been an unusual sort of year for us, but one that was full and challenging.

By 2010, I began to appreciate the reality of my retirement and the variety of opportunities we could enjoy. We maintained a different type of schedule, no longer striving to achieve professional goals but rather delving into many different interests.

In January, I returned to the Juniper Club in Florida to serve as Captain of the Hunt. The weather was cold during my time there, but attendance was good and I enjoyed the camaraderie. On one memorable day, I not only caught a big fish in the Juniper River, but I also managed to fall into the frigid water. The history of Juniper is captured in a book *Juniper, That's Me*, which has many stories of the club's 100-year history. The drive didn't get any shorter!

Maggie and I stayed in touch with colleagues in Washington and when invited, returned to attend various functions. We especially enjoyed several special events for the George W. Bush Center in D.C. before the new center in Dallas was completed. Since we had not yet sold our condominium at the Watergate, we took opportunities to be there as often as practical.

By this time, Jack and Katharine had moved to Old Greenwich, Connecticut, and on March 22, 2010, their second daughter, Eloise Thayer Hager, "Ellie," was born. Maggie and I visited shortly after her birth, a special family time. While we were in Greenwich, we drove to see the house "for all time" that we had bought in 1973. We knew that property values had soared in the years since we sold it, but Maggie and I were still fascinated at just how much escalation in real estate prices had occurred and how fancy the house and neighborhood had become.

In 2010, Virginia activities began to accelerate. As the Convention Center's representative, I became a member of a Coliseum Task Force formed by Richmond's Mayor Dwight Jones and his new Chief Administrative Officer, Bryon Marshall. After six months of diligent work with a consultant from California, we offered a significant proposal to construct a new facility to replace the city's aging Coliseum, but without adequate funding or a practical plan for execution of the plan, the proposed facility, sad to say, has yet to come to fruition. Someday soon it will happen.

Every five years, we have attended my Harvard Business School reunions, which are always interesting and well-organized occasions, and in June, Maggie and I participated in my special Fiftieth Reunion. Alumni from all over the country attended this milestone celebration, and the Business School seemed to outdo itself in making the gathering memorable. We spent three days, thoroughly enjoying the programs and visiting with former classmates.

The Fifty-fifth Reunion in 2015 would prove to be equally special. The individuals who return have been successful in their professional endeavors, have achieved so much and surprisingly in this age, have remained married to their original wives! I served on the planning committee and co-chaired the Memorial Service. Approximately one third of our classmates are deceased, and during the service, we tried to say something personal about each one of them. Maggie and I love to walk along the Charles River, and we particularly relished the program with the Boston Pops at Symphony Hall. Harvard does reunions right!

Shortly after returning from Harvard, we joined Governor Bob McDonnell's annual retreat at the Homestead Resort, and from there we left for Martha's Vineyard, where Jack, Katharine and their girls joined us for Fourth of July week. During this visit, I was elected as a director of the West Chop Club, where I continue to serve as chairman of Long Range Planning. A significant project to redo a major portion of the inn has come to fruition during this time.

West Chop activities include a Sunday service, where I took a turn talking about leadership, and "Windows on the World" presentations on Wednesday evenings, where I spoke about education.

The Polar Bear Club at the Country Club of Virginia has been a wonderful addition to my routine and a great club success. I can frequently be found swimming with other polar bears, and it is a pleasure to be able to extend the summer swimming season in a heated pool. This sport and exercise have meant a great deal and the fellow swimmers are a great bunch.

"Behind the scenes" describes my present involvement in politics. Numerous political activities take place annually, especially when the General Assembly convenes, and I participate in many of these events, maintaining my relationship with elected officials, state lawmakers and leaders within the local and state Republican Party. Politics has changed dramatically with the influences of technology, big dollars and polarization, but it still remains important for people to participate. Over time, many groups around the area invited me to speak, including the Chesterfield Chamber, CARMA in Williamsburg, Republican women's clubs and the State Fair organization, where I served as Safety Committee Chairman for several years. The Sorenson Institute also kept me busy speaking to classes in their programs.

After a year of resistance on my part, the board of Senior Navigator nominated me as a member. Senior Navigator is an offshoot of the Virginia Healthcare Foundation, which I headed several years back. This board, which almost immediately named me chairman due to the previous chairman's sudden illness, requires a great deal of time, but it is heartening to see the progress we have made in strengthening the operation and expanding offerings to the disabled community and veterans. It has been a pleasure to work with Adrienne Johnson and to help transform technology and outreach. It is a great story.

Another opportunity arose when Governor McDonnell appointed me to the board of the Virginia Museum of Fine Arts. It has been several years since my 1993 appointment and 1998 lieutenant governor membership, and becoming more and more involved has led me to co-chairman of Operations and an active Executive Committee member. The museum is doing great. It was uncertain if our new Democratic Governor McAuliffe would reappoint me, and when he did not, the decision dismayed the leadership at the museum.

My first years of "retirement" ended without any real feeling of retirement. I remained busy and engaged in interesting and worthwhile pursuits to such an extent that I never had a chance to ponder any free time.

Early in the new year 2011, I attended the very interesting Republican National Committee meeting in Washington, where the current chairman, Reince Priebus, was selected. We were able to rent our condominium at Watergate South in Washington to Ken Salzaar, Secretary of the Interior under President Obama. Three years later, Ken bought the Watergate condo, thus bringing to an end our involvement there and more than a few headaches that accompanied it.

My involvement with the Jamestown-Yorktown Foundation, Inc. cranked up, including leadership of a strategic planning effort. I also joined Kiwanis Club of Richmond and continue to participate in arranging some of the lunches they hold each week. Maggie joined the board of the Virginia Home, with which we had shared a close relationship for many years. Maggie's interests and expertise make her a perfect person to serve there.

In March, I returned briefly to Washington for Department of Education depositions in a lawsuit relating to the Rehabilitation Services Administration consolidation that stemmed from my term as assistant secretary. Whenever there is a suit against the federal government, the cases stay alive indefinitely in the Washington Circuit Court as the plaintiffs try to force settlement. Cases like this, for which I gave two days of depositions, continue even today, though they have little merit.

We began some extensive renovations at our home, which was almost thirty years old by this time. With the help of Ian Johnson, we designed and created a new garden in the backyard, and that has proved to be a pleasure. More than ever, we appreciate our great home.

Thanks to my active roles on boards and in politics, a pattern seemed to develop in which I spend significant time at the General Assembly and at major events. Adrienne Johnson and I worked together to achieve extra appropriations for Senior Navigator in 2012.

We went to Durham several times to see Nancy, who by this time was in the last stages of the dreadful Louie's Body Disease. Her illness made for such a hopeless situation, and the family watched its progression with sorrow. Henry accompanied me on my last visit before her death, the weekend prior to her passing on March 26, 2012. I delivered the eulogy at Nancy's funeral in Durham, which was a sad time for all of us. We all loved her and miss her very much.

In late April, Peter Broadbent, Davis Rennolds and I attended a number of political mass meetings in the Seventh District. We had decided to seek election as alternates

Greater Richmond Business Hall of Fame

to the Republican National Convention coming that summer in Tampa, and during May at the District Convention all three of us were elected as alternates.

Two major awards during May 2012, both of which were nearly a lifetime in the making, came as a real surprise. As a retired person, however, I was somewhat overwhelmed that I would be selected for recognition. The Junior Achievement of Central Virginia's Greater Richmond Business Hall of Fame named me as one of their three Laureates in a special ceremony at the Jefferson Hotel. As they described the qualifications, Laureates were selected with the following criteria in mind:

for their outstanding contributions to free enterprise and the promise of a better, stronger society... The individuals recognized have experienced a lifetime of business success and have established a legacy of leadership within their industries and community. Through their actions and accomplishments, they serve as role models for young people.

A second award, the Outstanding Virginian Award, was initiated in 1983 by the Virginia General Assembly. The recipient is announced in a ceremony at the House of Delegates and at the Senate during session in February — with the award presented in Northern Virginia at the 4-H Educational and Conference Center in Front Royal. The first recipient was Senator Harry F. Byrd, Jr., and subsequent honorees included governors, senators, congressmen, college presidents, business powerhouses and civic leaders — all of whom have pictures that hang in the conference room at the 4-H Center. It was humbling to take my place alongside such illustrious Virginians as the thirtieth recipient; several good friends and family members, including the Waldrops from Texas, attended the May ceremony, thus making it even more special. A year later I joined the committee that organizes the award.

During the presentation, several young people who were recipients of Outstanding 4-H Youth Achievement Awards asked me questions about my service and background. In response to their questions I told them that I consider an outstanding Virginian to be one who has a lasting influence on the generations that follow. I reiterated my philosophy:

Participation leads to inspiration. If you participate in activities, try to do the right thing and encourage things to get accomplished. It helps to inspire people and helps to bring others along in the process.

When asked about my service to those who are differently-abled, I recalled one of my proudest accomplishments was assisting young people in fulfilling their potential.

Young people with challenges of physical and mental disabilities must get off this idea that they are going to be on social security benefits and fade away... They can be independent and lead a better life...If you know where you want to go, you can get there, so you have to be focused on doing things every day, taking responsibility and applying hard work.

I gave the Memorial Day address at McGuire Veterans Hospital, which was just one of my many experiences involving veterans and the military. This focus became more prevalent when my good friend Paul Galanti was named Director of Veterans Affairs for Virginia. Many trips to events at the Virginia War Memorial convinced me to contribute all my military uniforms to that facility.

The Republican National Convention, which I had committed to attending as an alternate, was the highlight of the summer. Political friends, Alex Reber and Bill Thomas, joined me as we drove my car to Tampa and spent more than a week at the big gathering. Each day brought new activities and lots of excitement. We enjoyed all the sessions and met many old friends in the press building and elsewhere at the convention. It was a great time, and we thought Mitt Romney, our nominee, was unbeatable until the big disappointment in November. Bill has been a good companion at many political events.

Each year, the Commonwealth of Virginia and/or the Virginia Chamber co-sponsor conferences that cover topics like education, health, tourism and transportation. These are interesting to attend, and I reestablish my relationship with many friends and associates. An auxiliary role has become promoting the Convention Center, where most of the events take place.

During September, the Virginia Health Care Foundation held its twentieth anniversary event in Alexandria. There was a summit gathering that reunited many people who had worked on the foundation's efforts, and as part of the festivities, we attended a large dinner at Senator Mark Warner's home. The subsequent board meeting was a real throwback to earlier times.

My work at Senior Navigator stemmed from long involvement with safety net issues, and I redoubled my commitment there as we expanded our activities.

A new organization which I find very exciting is called Sportable – a group that was first organized by Kristen Lessig and serves to provide equipment for disabled youth athletes and to organize various sporting events for disabled young people. I was featured at their first annual fundraising event, which was a great success. My involvement with Sportable has continued because this positive group provides so much to a broad community. They enjoy enticing me to participate in various events around town, like the Ukrop's 10K every spring.

Maggie hosted a seventy-fifth birthday party for me in October 2012 – a big, blowout event that included family and many friends. It was different from our previous parties because I wasn't running for any office! We could relax and enjoy a glorious time with many good friends.

George Allen had received the Republican nomination to run for the U.S. Senate, and my help to this effort included service on his Finance Committee. I attended numerous events leading up to the election, including his debates with Tim Kaine. When George Allen lost, it was another blow for the Republican Party and mainstream Republicans. The situation only worsened with the Republicans' Presidential loss with many results that have proven to be disastrous.

The Thomas Jefferson Institute, for which I serve on the Board of Directors, began holding "Center Right" meetings on the third Thursday of each month. Those meetings have proven to be quite a success and keep us in close touch with General Assembly Republican leadership, key issues to be tackled, and good ideas for Virginia.

Christmas is always an exciting time, with Jenna and Henry joining Jack's family to be with us for the celebrations to the extent possible. We relish these occasions when the family can gather. Rare is the time now when we are all together, as our children's lives have become busier and busier. We all feel real relief when the annual Christmas picture is accomplished early in the year!

An extensive genealogy project was begun in earnest with Donna Schumate in January 2013 and completed in time to give *The Hager Family History* for Christmas 2014. Our research and picture search took almost two years, but the results are worth the effort, and we were pleased to share our findings with the family. We discovered previously unknown relatives and family connections, and we have traced the Hager family back to its German roots, as distant as my eighth great-grandparents in the early seventeenth century. We learned that my mother's family, the Rabbes, entered the United States as immigrants just three generations back. The basis on which the family rests is solid, thanks in part to those who came before us. Our ancestors displayed a Midwestern work ethic which focused on family, community, farming and progress. They were pioneers in their day and knew how to survive harsh times.

Maggie and I headed for New York to see our new granddaughter, Laura Margaret "Mila" Hager, who arrived ahead of schedule in April, 2013. Then two weeks later, we attended the dedication of the Bush Center and immersed ourselves in planned events there.

The exciting days in Dallas included a museum tour, a huge gathering on the mall at Southern Methodist University and the dedication ceremonies the next day. In the Bush Center we met many notable people and had a very special lunch with an array of celebrities and politicians. The distinguished company that gathered could have been a page of living history. It was a really fascinating opportunity to be back in the spotlight and to show well deserved appreciation for the Bushes, though touring the Center seemed to take a backseat to all the other activities. I hope to be able to return some day for a more leisurely visit. Obviously, the Bushes were swamped with obligations and attention to the many guests. We are fortunate to see much more of them at family events. When he learned that I was undertaking an autobiography, President Bush wrote these kind words:

I got to know John a while before his fine son, Henry, married my daughter Jenna. At first, I was struck by John's energy, optimism, and enthusiasm for life. When I heard his story, it made these characteristics even more meaningful. He is a fine example for all Americans, and I'm proud to call him friend.

Maggie and I attended Governor Bob McDonnell's Opportunity Virginia Retreat at the Homestead Resort, a bittersweet gathering since it was clear that it would be the last one of its type. The McDonnells had begun having legal problems in 2012, and they remain under intense scrutiny following the trial of July and August 2014. The situation was effectively satisfied in the courts but left many heads shaking.

The long-awaited closing of the land purchase at Custis Hunting and Fishing Club in King William County took place on July 24, the culmination of the many years of work. The final negotiations with Pete Henderson allowed Custis to buy approximately 150 acres adjoining the Mill Pond along with a 300-foot easement on all the property he owned that we were not purchasing. The deal was a great success, and most of Custis' membership supported the assessment and small membership expansion that was needed to finance the purchase. I had worked closely with William Walsh, a lawyer at HuntonWilliams, and his dedication to the project was extremely valuable. He worked *pro bono*, which was a great advantage to Custis Hunting and Fishing Club. Several of us put in untold hours to bring this about.

Reflections of Jim Alexander, President of Custis Hunting and Fishing Club, Senior Vice President, BB&T

In 2011, John Hager was in the midst of a long, drawn out process in which Custis Hunting and Fishing Club attempted to purchase land that bordered its 140 acres. Relying on his vast network of contacts, John immediately went into action and in May of 2011, set up a meeting with Kathleen Kilpatrick and the Department of Historic Resources to explore the designation of Custis as a historic site. The pond held significant historic importance and prominence because George Washington had surveyed the land in the mid-1700s and it had been owned by Martha Custis and Robert E. Lee, Jr.

Between 2011 and 2013, John led a number of meetings with ten different government agencies, including members of the Board of Supervisors of King William County, the county's delegate and senator in the Virginia General Assembly, with members of the Virginia Department of Agriculture in Tappahannock, with Virginia Department of Transportation. John has a soft-spoken yet direct manner of dealing with people. He commands respect. People know who he is, and rather like the old saying: "When John talks, people listen!"

In the fall of 2011, Hurricane Irene hit the area with some nine inches of rain, which produced massive muddy water and sludge flows through the pond. Within a month, a second storm dropped another nine inches of rain, further increasing the flow of mud. We could see that the water quality of the pond was in jeopardy, and we moved forward to protect the club.

With John's guidance in identifying agencies that could be influential in our efforts and with his broad network of contacts within these agencies, we ramped up our efforts with groups like the Department of Environmental Quality, Virginia Department of Agriculture and Consumer Services, the Three Rivers Soil and Conservation District, the Chesapeake Bay Foundation and Department of Conservation and Resources. Meeting after meeting took place as we sought to determine the extent and effect of runoff problems coming from Mr. Henderson's farm, and in May 2012, a complaint was filed against Pete Henderson with the Virginia Soil and Water Conservation Board. The complaint cited the erosion problems of Mr. Henderson's farm, and he was required to form a plan to address these problems.

His response included the planting of several thousand loblolly pines, putting stumps in gullies and ravines, and moderating the thinning of trees, which he was performing out of sight. Custis found his solutions inadequate and made an appeal, which went to the state of Virginia. Again, at every step of the way, John was able to make contact with different, influential people in state agencies.

Meanwhile, John had met and developed a relationship with two residents of King William County, David and Straughan Robinson, who proved valuable assets to our cause. The two were really only interested in Mr. Henderson's doing the right thing, and they reached out to John to tell him that they had a number of aerial photographs which showed a massive plume of muddy water running into the pond as well as development that had commenced on Mr. Henderson's land in areas that were out of the public eye.

While John and Massie Valentine, Jr. met often with Mr. Henderson, they could never reach the finish line with a resolution. He offered to sell us the land, and we countered with a lower price, which he rejected. In the meantime, Mr. Henderson had the land zoned for development. He created different plats for the acreage all around the pond, development that would affect the viewshed and would threaten with nutrient runoff the future water quality in the pond.

In April of 2013, John attended the King William County Ruritan Fish Fry, and he saw Pete Henderson at the event. Perhaps in response to the realization that we knew everything he was doing on his land that could affect Custis Mill Pond, Mr. Henderson approached John at the fish fry and said, "John, let's sit down and talk."

There, at the end of April, he and John had a conversation for about an hour, and by the end of June, we had a deal to buy a significant portion of the land. But to raise the million dollars needed for the purchase, the membership still had to be sold on the value of accepting assessments. As President, John took it upon himself to call members and explain why they should support the purchase of the 151 acres, and after extensive work through numerous steps, the sale was finalized.

To a great extent, John handled the negotiations with Pete Henderson, handled the state agencies, and then handled the shareholders of Custis Hunting and Fishing Club. There is no one else who could have accomplished what he did. Thanks to the purchase, the club now owns or has a setback easement on all the property surrounding the pond. In theory, the view from our cabin at the Custis Mill Pond will remain unchanged in years to come. Because of his political background, John realized the importance in being proactive in addressing people, but he also was just as interested in developing relationships, to become a spokesman for Custis among our neighbors in the county. More than anyone else, John recognized the importance of going to events like the fish fry or attending community gatherings and being seen as a good steward of the land we hold in the county.

I had met John, but I didn't know him well, and when I joined Custis Hunting and Fishing Club, I had an opportunity to work with him on these efforts to purchase the land from Mr. Henderson. He is truly one of the most interesting people I have ever been around. I also should be quick to mention that he is a very good fisherman. He is modest about his abilities, but he is adept at juggling his tackle box, fishing rods, packing a lunch and maneuvering through all it takes to fish. John does so much through his involvement in his family, the community, the club, individuals, and politics, yet he does all this in a quiet, unassuming manner. He is excellent at delegating responsibilities, and he trusts the judgment of people with whom he works. He also accomplishes so much more than most people could think possible. I honestly believe that he is the only person who could have gotten us to the finish line with Mr. Henderson, as he did for Custis Hunting and Fishing Club in June 2013.

When I assume the presidency of the club, and I can assure you that I will be relying heavily on John's guidance.

In September, I closed on the Watergate condo sale. Finalizing the sale was the last step of the long saga in D.C. for Maggie and me. I guess in some ways we miss having a home base in the capital, but other priorities have become more compelling.

Annual fall events include activities in Charlottesville, Yorktown, Stratford Hall and places all over Virginia. The Sorensen Institute began a new tradition with a fall gala in Northern Virginia to complement the annual spring gala in Richmond. We had successfully recruited all nine living Virginia governors to attend the spring gala, and it was

Sorensen Gala with Virginia's Governors

With Paul Ryan in Roanoke

especially meaningful to have a picture with that distinguished group. The Center for Politics also staged a memorable picture when it posed all eight of Virginia Presidents, depicted by re-enactors, at their annual conference at the Capitol.

The Federal Reserve Board asked me to speak at its monthly employees' gathering at their office here in Richmond. My topics were veterans and disabilities, an interesting duo of subjects.

A return to New York at Thanksgiving to be with Jenna, Henry and Mila was a fun weekend, but also a reminder of why I would not want to live in New York. There was some tough navigating through rain and traffic on the infamous I-95.

This time it was Jack and Katharine who called us home in a hurry for the arrival of our fourth, very special granddaughter, Ann Beatrice "Bea" Hager. We now have three grandchildren in Richmond – Chase, Ellie and Bea, so their birthdays and activities affect us and we enjoy being with them.

The first weekend in December is traditionally the Republican Party of Virginia's annual Advance, this year in Roanoke and featuring soon-to-be Speaker of the House, Paul Ryan.

Politically, 2014 began with a final breakfast with Bob McDonnell. There was a portrait unveiling for outgoing Lieutenant Governor Bill Bolling, and following past tradition, attendance, along with other former state office holders, at the state inauguration. With a Democratic slate, the way ahead promised to be different and somewhat challenging. Even the weather seemed to reflect the chilly state of Republican politics as

Shad Planking 2015

it was an unusually cold winter, something we are not used to.

Long being involved with the First Freedom organization, I have served as a judge in their annual student competition, in which high-schoolers write or video projects about religious freedom. The First Freedom Center was dedicated and is a small but worthwhile addition to downtown Richmond.

The Shad Planking holds a special place in my fond memories. I first attended in 1977, first spoke in 1999, and then in 2001 spoke when I was one of three candidates for governor. For the April 2015 gathering, I was again asked to address the gathering, an especially high honor. Robert Bain said that I represented the values of this group, and I was humbled to be selected over so many more famous and powerful individuals who presently hold political office.

There were several developments over the years with the original American Tobacco stock, which had become American brands. The international affiliate, Gallaher, was spun out with separate stock and an eventual takeover with a big payout. When American Tobacco was bought, American Brands became Fortune Brands. Fortune Brands spun out ACCO Brands and Beam Inc. stock. Beam now has been taken over, and Fortune Brands Home & Security remains. So some original holdings were productive. Todd Oney of Merrill Lynch picked up a certificate dating from June 1954 and marveled at it, even color-copying it as a keepsake. Henry confirmed my philosophy when he noted, "Dad, people who had no faith in the future and recommended a quick sale have been proven all wrong by your tactic of holding on."

There were a number of political events leading to the Seventh District Convention and the Tea Party's dominance over the establishment, which has not proven to be a good situation. Then in a shocking turn of events Eric Cantor, a good friend who served as Majority Leader in the House, lost his primary nomination. In talking to me Rudy Butler, a former supervisor from Goochland County, summed it up this way:

The people who swayed the primary nomination are the same people who defeated Hager for Governor. You would have won a primary, but they helped to defeat you, then to threaten Bill Bolling when he wanted to run for governor, and now to take out the Majority Leader, Eric Cantor. This cannot be a good thing for Virginia and it is disastrous for the Republican Party.

Similar activities and severe ramifications have rippled throughout the party in Virginia with uncertain outcomes.

One of my favorite mottos is, "We work for what we get, but we live for what we give."

Maggie and I both remain committed to civic and community involvement, and a variety of activities keeps us super involved. Preservation Virginia held its Hundredth Anniversary. Virginia Free went through a lengthy process to select a new executive director. As president of Custis Hunting and Fishing Club, I urged that we re-image and enhance the club through a series of difficult initiatives. The U.S. Global Leadership Coalition, a group involved with improving international relations, held an impressive luncheon at the Jefferson Hotel. I serve as a Virginia Advisory Board member for that national group. Richmond Regional Tourism and the Greater Richmond Convention Center continue to be very successful, and I feel a close working relationship with all involved and am proud of their achievements. We have a "Futures" study underway to maintain the level of superior performance achieved in recent years and promote external development. Former president of Virginia Commonwealth University, Gene Trani's "Future of Richmond" report cited the regional cooperation which resulted in the Convention Center.

In 2014, the State Board of Elections formed a General Registrar & Electoral Board (GREB) workgroup, which I co-chair with Jean Jenson, former State Election Chief. Our task is to revisit all aspects of the election system, make recommendations and then recruit patrons to move forth with legislation, all of which is important work for the future of the system. There is much that needs modernizing, and of course adequate funding would help. To promote the GREB effort, Maggie and I attended the Annual Homestead Retreat weekend of the Virginia Electoral Board Association in early 2015, an event which brought back fond memories. We have a great group, and this is an arena with many challenges to be addressed.

Fishing is also a passion and I had a wonderful Chesapeake Bay trip with John Barber and friends which produced for me one huge rockfish (see picture on next page).

Maggie and I both feel blessed to be leading our active and reasonably healthy lives. I will admit my traveling prowess isn't what it used to be, but I am probably not the only person who finds travel more tiresome, difficult and cumbersome than it was in days gone by. Maggie has been an awesome partner to endure, on my behalf, substantial inconveniences over many years whenever we travel, but we have never hesitated to venture forth.

One individual who has meant so much to us is Kim Hayes, a rare and talented lady who for several years has helped us almost weekly doing a multitude of projects in our home. She has a great job at Altria, met us through volunteering in the campaign and is now like a member of our family. We greatly appreciate her continuing assistance over a long period of time.

There has been so much to keep us busy and productive, at least in our minds. We love summer with the good weather, slower pace and fun activity. Work on our yard has been a dominant focus, an endeavor that seems to require constant reinvention. Contests with the deer also keep us entertained.

We are blessed with three granddaughters, Chase, Ellie and Bea in Richmond. They were joined a second cousin, Poppy Louise Hager, who along with sister Mila, are in New York City. Maggie is just the best grandmother.

Politics must be in my DNA because my involvement has continued, albeit at a more

Fishing with John Barber and Friends on the Chesapeake Bay

normal pace. In January of 2016, I became Virginia co-chairman of the Jeb Bush for President campaign. Subsequently after he dropped out, I joined the leadership team for Donald Trump. There were only limited opportunities to participate, but the Liberty Farm Rally was memorable. At a meeting with Kevin McCarthy, the new majority leader in the House, the Richmond Republican party honored me with a scholarship fund for a young Republican each year at Sorensen. The year ended with Trump's resounding win.

My version of giving back is to stay busy and not to be retired any more than I can help. Maggie and I enjoy many relationships with a variety of people and look forward to continuing the challenges of our many activities. My life mirrors my philosophy on being disabled: refuse to allow a disability to shape performance, and keep all mention of a personal disability out of conversation.

Life has had its share of real "ups and downs." I have learned from many people that a smooth path is the lot of nobody, and how you respond and forge a path is up to you. I recently read a description of Winston Churchill's life that struck a personal chord for me. It was drawn from the notable professor and author, Michael Ward's commencement address at Hillsdale College on May 9, 2015.

Winston Churchill's life is a particularly striking example of the law of undulation, this rolling English road, not only because his was a very long and very public life, but because its heights and depths were of extraordinary amplitude. A happy marriage with five children, but two predeceased him. A glittering early career, marred by the Dardanelles. Restoration to political prominence, but then the wilderness years. The triumph of his combat with Hitler, followed by summary expulsion from national office. And many other ups and downs besides.

But one of the things I admire about Churchill is that he didn't just let these things happen to him. His life may have been a rollercoaster, but he was more than a mere passenger. He knew that the wise man learns from his reverses; he doesn't simply defy them, but turns them to effect. Churchill responded to the low points in his life with the muscle of his will, yes, but also with the artistry of his soul.

With grandchildren Easter 2016

What an inspiration!

Despite the challenges of polio, I have always strived for self-reliance, but I do not consider my situation unique. At some point, everyone faces challenge, and it can only be overcome through hard work, tenacity and a resolute determination never to quit. I am also keenly aware that an individual cannot achieve much of anything without the assistance of others. So many individuals have supported me along the way, and for that, I feel extremely grateful.

While governments everywhere, political parties, the tobacco industry and numerous non-profits are undergoing much stress, I continue to feel that my participation in these and in so many other ventures has left a positive impact. I would not want to swap my experiences with anyone and yearn to contribute more. Maggie has been a stalwart partner, and Jack and Henry and their wives are exemplary. We count so many fine people as friends and truly value their friendship and support. How can someone be so blessed, particularly approaching eighty years old?

My worry is about the path ahead for so many. The American dream seems to have a cloud hanging over it, and I, for one, don't want to see that. We have the greatest nation with the greatest system of democracy the world has ever known, and it is the responsibility of all of us to defend and nurture it. We know Virginia is a special place, and we must keep it that way. The future is bright and we will carry on, but so much to do, so little time. God bless.

Hager family 2016